Noetic Sciences Collection

1980 - 1990

Ten Years of Consciousness Research

NOETIC SCIENCES COLLECTION

1980 - 1990

TEN YEARS OF CONSCIOUSNESS RESEARCH

EDITED BY BARBARA MCNEILL AND CAROL GUION

PUBLISHED BY THE INSTITUTE OF NOETIC SCIENCES

Design and Production Manager: Sharon Skolnick
Design and Production Assistants: Joanne Miller
                                   David Johnson

Published by
the Institute of Noetic Sciences
475 Gate Five Road, Suite 300
Sausalito, California 94965.

price: $12.00
$10.00 for members of the Institute of Noetic Sciences
order number PNC1R001

ISBN 0-9493951-02-X

Printed in the United States of America

Welcome to the world of noetic sciences, as represented in these articles, pictures and poems — members' favorites from the most recent ten years of Institute of Noetic Sciences publications. They are reprinted here almost exactly as they have appeared over the decade in our various publications.

Since the noetic sciences encompass knowledge gained rationally, experientially *and* intuitively, it seems appropriate that this collection contains food for thought as well as soul.

The Institute began in 1973 with a few hundred people interested in and supportive of consciousness research. Soon a *Noetic Sciences Newsletter* was started, followed by other publications including *Investigations, Special Reports* and occasional papers.

Today we have over 23,000 members, and publish the quarterly *Noetic Sciences Review*, which is what the *Newsletter* became, the quarterly *Noetic Sciences Bulletin*, catalogs of books and tapes, technical reports, a membership directory, and even books.

We surely can't wait another decade to print *Noetic Sciences Collection* Volume II.

— The Editors

Our appreciation to these artists
who have contributed
their work to our publications:

Facing Page 1: Margaret L. Jackson • Page 4: Victoria Rouse • Page 6: David L. Smith • Page 8: Elisabeth Targ • Page 28: David L. Smith • Page 31: Sidney Harris • Page 32: Ralph Merlino • Page 43: Sharon Skolnick • Page 55: David L. Smith • Page 58: Eric Heiner • Page 60: David L. Smith • Page 64: David L. Smith • Page 67: Ann McCoy, Jim Strong • Page 75: Carol Guion • Page 79: Carol Guion • Page 84: David L. Smith • Page 94: Calvin Yau Ching • Page 96: Calvin Yau Ching • Page 100: David Eisenberg • Page 102: Steele Photography • Page 110: Gordon Onslow Ford • Page 117: Sharon Skolnick • Page 120: A. Raja Hornstein • Page 123: A. Raja Hornstein • Page 129: Margaret L. Jackson

Acknowledgments

Reviewing materials for this collection evoked fond memories of the people whose vision and effort during the early years of the Institute's development established the foundation for the work we carry forward today.

First, of course, was astronaut Edgar Mitchell's vision of the need for an organization dedicated to the scientific study of human consciousness. This vision was supported in our early years and on a continuing basis by Institute Board members Paul Temple, Judith Skutch Whitson, Henry Rolfs and Dorothy Lyddon. It is tempting to embark on an entire history of the Institute, to remember everybody's hard work and generosity. Perhaps there will be a place for that in some future book, but for present purposes we focus on the publications represented in this book.

The Institute publications program began in 1976 when Diane Brown Temple and Brendan O'Regan started a *Noetic Sciences Newsletter* to reach beyond the small community supporting the Institute's work at the time. Fran Lindberg assisted with this early publication. The *Newsletter* readership formed the base for an Institute membership which has grown from a few hundred to 23,000.

The *Newsletter* developed into the quarterly *Noetic Sciences Review*, first published in winter 1986; a grant from Institute Board member Diane Temple helped this transition. Members' publications grew to include the quarterly *Noetic Sciences Bulletin*, *Investigations*, *Special Reports*, and occasional papers. The expansion in number, size, and frequency of our publications was possible largely as the result of computer equipment donated by Henry Dakin, also of the Institute Board.

We became Institute editors in 1983 and 1984 and were fortunate, then as now, for advice and support from Willis Harman, Institute President; Brendan O'Regan, Vice-President for Research; and Thomas J. Hurley III, Director of the Exceptional Abilities Program.

Thank you, too, to all on the Board of Directors, staff, and to the members who have contributed their writings, art, comments and support over the years.

— Barbara McNeill and Carol Guion, Editors

NOETIC SCIENCES COLLECTION

— THE CONTENTS

*The most beautiful thing
we can experience
is the mystery.*
—Albert Einstein

The year is 1980. Willis W. Harman has been President of the Institute of Noetic Sciences for two years, after careers as futurist, engineering professor and author. In this article he presents the case for using the noetic sciences as a fulcrum for the necessary shift in basic premises underlying our society. Throughout this book you will see how he has developed this theme over the decade, culminating with his article which ends this collection.

The noetic sciences, combining as they do all ways of knowing, emphasize intuitive knowledge — from which every stable society throughout history has drawn its basic values. "The single most powerful means of bringing about social change is through challenges to the legitimacy of institutions and institutional behaviors," he says. These institutions include the political, the corporate, the social, the scientific. And it is with this increased base of knowledge, broader range of exploration and heightened sense of the possible which the noetic sciences afford that the challenges can be issued, and the changes made.

Where is Our Positive Image of the Future? *by Willis W. Harman*

America began with an inspiring image of the future — a "new order of the ages" (the "Novus Ordo Seclorum" on the back of the dollar bill). Through most of two centuries a positive image of the future shaped our actions; at various times it highlighted Westward expansion, or economic expansion, or the hope of the Old World's downtrodden, or keeping the world safe for Democracy. Since the mid-1960's we have seen the image grow dim. No one who has observed the U.S. over the past decade has any doubt that a gloomy cynicism has set in.

America in the past few years has come to be, possibly for the first time in its history, without a clear positive goal. We look to a future that is economically uncertain, inflation-ridden, energy-starved; noisy, crowded, and polluted; plagued by threats from hazardous chemicals to nuclear holocaust; surfeited by technological gimmicks and disillusioned with the "technological fix"; nostalgic for a happier past.

Yet perhaps the present period, which may have appeared as a discouraging decline or a time of vexing dilemmas, is better viewed as the beginning of a profound transformation — a transformation which, could we but see its end, would provide the stirring image and sense of direction we presently lack.

Such transformations have happened before in history, but rarely. Lewis Mumford, writing in 1956 on *The Transformations of Man*, argued that there have been at most three or four such major transformations in the history of Western civilization, the last two being the end of the Roman Empire and the end of the Middle Ages. We may be, he said, approaching another such great transformation. If he is right, how wrenching and traumatic will the transition period turn out to be? That will depend to a great extent on how well we understand the approaching change and with what lack of fear we meet it.

Ours may be the first society in history to be able to prevision such a transformation and prepare for it. That is partly because of the tools for thought we have developed that can be turned to forecasting the future. It is also because of the general speedup of historical developments, what with a culture used to continual change and with worldwide instantaneous communication, such that the next transformation may fairly complete itself within the time-span of a single generation.

What kinds of signs would you look for to confirm a suspicion that a Great Transformation of industrial society were underway? Four, at least:

1. Signs that the ways and institutions of the old society were working less well than in the past, and appear to be still less well adapted to the future.
2. Signs that a widening group of people were perceiving the society to be headed toward an undesirable future, and that an alternative future image was beginning to emerge.
3. Evidence that signs preceding revolutionary change in the past are present today, and that a growing social force can be identified potentially capable of producing major institutional change.
4. Signs that the tacitly held basic premises of the culture might be changing. (Lewis Mumford claims, "Every transformation of man . . . has rested on . . . a new picture of the cosmos and the nature of man.")

Those signs are all present today.

Signs of breakdown

One of the signs that a society is approaching a critical time is when it contains within it basic contradictions that people would find too threatening if they noticed them — so they simply fail to see. As examples, consider the following:

- We are taught by society that fulfillment comes from the consumption of scarce resources. This assumption is woven through the structure of materialistic modern society; it permeates advertising; it underlies the standard economic indicators, the concept of economic growth, the desirability of obsolescence through "progress." The dominant institution in modern society is the economy, and the goals of the economy tend to be the goals of society. The economy is judged on the consumption of goods and services all of which use up scarce resources and exude polluting waste. Hedonistic consumption, once a vice, is now promoted; frugality, until recently a virtue, is now bad for the economy. Yet on a finite planet, "spaceship Earth," in the end we must become frugal. Eventually, the consumption ethic leads unwaveringly to increasing global competition and conflict.

- We are taught to think of employment as a byproduct of economic production — keep the production rising and people will have jobs. However, modern societies face limits to production; meanwhile pressures continue to increase labor productivity so the same production yields fewer jobs. Thus meaningful work becomes a scarce commodity. But in modern society employment in the mainstream economy is the individual's primary way of relating to society, of making a personal contribution and receiving affirmation in return. Satisfying social roles are essential to the well-being of all persons. What is the future of a society in which satisfying roles are so defined as to be an increasingly scarce commodity?

- Energy is so intimately related to jobs and productivity that we dare not consider seriously an energy policy that aims at a drastic cutback in energy use. Yet the costs of our foreign oil purchases, in economic and security terms, are undermining U.S. strength as a nation.

- It does not seem practicable, in conventional thinking, to ask the rich of the world to significantly decrease their material standard of living to redistribute to the world's poor. Yet in another sense they cannot afford not to. World distribution of food, income, and wealth is far more uneven than is the distribution in any single country, even those with the most notoriously unjust political orders. Economic forces and population pressures seem to conspire to cause the maldistribution to grow steadily worse. The rich "North" partakes of a feast that the world's limited resources cannot sustain, while the teeming populations of the impoverished "South" remain trapped by poverty, illiteracy, and high birth rates in a remorseless cycle of deprivation. The threat of ultimate global conflict over this disparity looms ever greater.

- We have been taught to believe that technology will solve social problems. Economic and technological development have indeed brought abundance, solved problems, and liberated humankind in numerous ways. Yet in recent years we have heard technology made the villain, accused of creating environmental and social problems, and even threatening democracy. Fundamentally, the very momentum of economic and technological growth leads toward the automatic making of far-reaching social decisions (for example, modern agricultural methods essentially eradicating the small family farm).

- If these contradictions were not enough to bring us to an Orwellian 1984, they are topped by our perpetuating the threat of nuclear holocaust and calling it "national security."

Towards an Alternative Future

The roots of these characteristics are centuries back. At the end of the Middle Ages there began, first in Western Europe and eventually in practically all of the world, the journey on the path which led to industrialization, modernization, economic development. Sociologists have used the term "secularization" to describe the predominant characteristic of this path — the shift of society's guiding values from the traditional religious base to impersonal, utilitarian values. The values that shape social choices were increasingly influenced by materialistic and economic factors. Transcendent spiritual values and goals became steadily less influential.

By the end of the 16th century this breaking out of the traditional mold had led to the beginnings of both capitalism and modern science. The new practical value emphasis generated effective and efficient new methods of production which brought the beginning of the Industrial Revolution two centuries later. Within another century the ethic of "controlling nature" through combining science with technology was firmly established. Knowledge that would generate new manipulative technologies was increasingly favored and supported over other kinds of knowledge (which were left to the humanities and religions with the tacit understanding that if science didn't deal with them they couldn't really be very important).

Knowledge about wholesome human values, ethics and behavior became neglected. Indeed, some of our eminent scientists assured us that freedom, dignity, love, integrity, creativity, and spirituality were "unscientific" concepts and it would be fruitless to seek fundamental knowledge of them. Economic rationality has come to substitute as a pseudo-ethic because we have become exceptionally confused about the eternal value issues. Thus profit passes as an adequate goal for the corporation, and GNP likewise for the nation.

Goods and services are increasingly produced by industrialized processes and offered and purchased in the mainstream economy. They are shaped more and more by the criteria of the economy. Our bodies are serviced by the "health care industry." We who are coming toward the end of our years will be taken care of by the "nursing homes industry." When our bodies are no longer serviceable they will be disposed of by the "funeral homes industry." Our education, travel, leisure, food preparation, social life, all tend to become "markets" to be satisfied with "products."

In the process, the per capita demands on physical resources (particularly energy) and impact on the environment have steadily increased, both because of rising spending levels and because of changes in the kinds of products bought (for example, moving from re-usable wooden boxes to aluminum and plastic containers; from natural fibers to synthetics).

Along with the impressive accomplishments in public health have come new threats to health as well — noxious and hazardous chemicals; artificial foods and unwholesome dietary characteristics; psychological stress from crowding, noise, and isolation from the natural environment; proliferation of nuclear weapons of mass destruction.

In response to the negative aspects of these characteristics of the long-term modernization trend, there have sprung up in the U.S. over the past 15 or 20 years a host of special new movements. (Similar movements with slightly different emphases have appeared in the other highly industrialized countries — Canada, Western Europe, Japan.) For convenience these can be grouped under four major themes:

- *Ecological Outlook* — concern for environmental protection, resource conservation, wilderness preservation, and fostering wholesome relationships between man (woman) and nature.

- *Appropriate Technology* — focusing on the relationships between people and technology, emphasizing use of small, decentralized technology that is under the control of the user; that does not cause undue insult to the environment; that is resource conserving; and that is compatible with a voluntarily simple lifestyle (favoring, for example, solar energy and conservation, and oppos-

ing dependence on gigantic coal-powered and nuclear-powered electric systems).

- *Person Liberation* — emphasizing development of self reliance and self-emancipation from prejudice and stereotypes relating to race and sex; from oppression by "patriarchal" social institutions; from the dehumanizing effects of the giant organizations of industrial society.

- *Spiritual Revitalization* — emphasizing the search for guiding meanings and values; renewed attention to the spiritual; release of full human potentiality; seeing health as holistic, involving mind, emotions, body, and spirit in organic unity.

Each of these movements — environmentalist, civil rights, anti-nuclear, feminist, holistic health, "conserver society," "appropriate technology," "human potential," and so on — seems understandable in its own terms. But if instead of viewing them one at a time one asks what the overall pattern means, it appears to be aimed at deflecting the various aspects of the long-term modernization trend, to bring about a "New Age" society that is qualitatively different from the post-World War II "late-industrial" society.

A widening group of people are associated with these movements or affected by them, and tending to perceive this society (and other advanced industrial societies) to be headed toward an undesirable future. An alternative future image of a "New Age" society is beginning to emerge, characterized by a synthesis of the four thrusts of the social movements mentioned earlier.

Signs of Transformation

Sociological studies of past periods of revolutionary change in various societies indicate that typically certain indicators show up sometime before the revolutionary change period, foreshadowing it. These indicators include alienation of persons from the institutions of society,

rising rate of mental illness, rising rate of violent crime, social disruption and use of police to put down dissension, tolerance of sexual hedonism, religious cultism, and economic inflation. All of these indicators are with us. (Barbara Tuchman's recent book *A Distant Mirror* describes the appearance of similar phenomena in a previous period of transformation, the 14th century in Western Europe.)

The single most powerful means of bringing about social change is through challenges to the legitimacy of institutions and institutional behaviors. We need only remind ourselves that in a few short years following World War II, much to the surprise of seasoned watchers of international affairs, score of colonies of the larger nations suddenly became independent countries. This remarkable liberation movement occurred with remarkably little bloodshed, primarily because legitimacy was withdrawn from the institution of political colonies.

Challenges to the legitimacy of the behaviors of large corporations and large nations, racist and sexist institutions, patriarchal customs, and the like have been frequently-used tools of the contemporary network of transformation-focused social movements. Thus not only do the signs of impending transformation seem to be present, but there is demonstrated public awareness of how to use legitimacy challenge as a tool for social change. Both of these facts make the transformational hypothesis more plausible.

Changing Premises

Finally, for an indication of how far-reaching the transformation may be, we need to look for signs of a profound change in the basic premises underlying industrial society. Most fundamental of all is the premise that what is real is measurable. From Galileo on, the conviction has grown that what can be quantified is important; what cannot is either unimportant or doesn't exist. In an industrializing society, knowledge that could be used to predict and control qualified as "scientific"; it became easy to forget there might be any other kind of knowledge. Yet every stable society that ever existed on the globe, ancient or modern, Eastern or Western, derived its basic value commitments from another kind of knowledge. That is the intuitive knowledge of deep inner experience from which sprang all the religious traditions of the world.

Western scientific-technological zeal tended to downgrade if not debunk this kind of knowledge. The growth of materialistic science eroded the transcendental base of Judeo-Christian values — or, more accurately, of the perennial wisdom of all the world's religious traditions. As a result we were left like a ship with ever more powerful engines, but no chart or compass. We acquired more and more "know-how," and seemed to know less and less about what is worth doing.

Both within the scientific community and in the broader culture can be found numerous indications of our becoming aware of this extraordinary and dangerous imbalance. Among the scientists we see new inquiries into unconscious processes, hypnosis, the psychosomatic origins of illness, biofeedback training, psychic phenomena, "levels" of consciousness. We are learning the extent to which we create or cure our own illness, the ways in which our minds are joined other than by ordinary visual or aural communication, the ability of the mind to "image" solutions to complex problems. In the culture at large the quest for individual spiritual meaning and for caring relationships has replaced both the old dogmatic religion and the nihilism of the mid-twentieth century. The shift in basic premises implied by this "new transcendentalism" is fully as great as the shift from the traditional religious beliefs of the Middle Ages to the materialsim of the industrial world.

Metamorphosis

If indeed the signs point to a coming profound transformation to some sort of trans-industrial "New Age," should we view the transition period with apprehension, even granting an attractive image of the long-term future? Perhaps there is a second case to be made for a positive image of the transition process. The analogy of metamorphosis, the process by which a caterpillar becomes a butterfly, is suggestive.

The metamorphosis of a larva to become an adult insect begins with the degeneration of much of the larval tissue. Simultaneously there is a proliferation of growth around special cells called "imaginal cells." These colonies of new cells in effect create parts of the new creature that will eventually emerge from the pupal shell. When they grow large enough, they merge to form the adult insect, and the remainder of the larval tissue in between disintegrates.

It may well be that the metamorphosis of industrial society has already begun, with thousands of "new age" organizations and experimental communities and voluntary associations playing the role of "imaginal cells," linked by a vaguely defined image of a sparkling new future.

Perhaps Lewis Mumford described it as well as anyone can, a quarter of a century ago:

> We stand on the brink of a new age: the age of an open world and of a self capable of playing its part in that larger sphere. An age of renewal, when work and leisure and learning and love will unite to produce a fresh form for every stage of life, and a higher trajectory for life as a whole.... In carrying man's self-transformation to this further stage, world culture may bring about a fresh release of spiritual energy that will unveil new potentialities, no more visible in the human self today than radium was in the physical world a century ago, though always present . . . For who can set bounds to man's emergence or to his power of surpassing his provisional achievements? So far we have found no limits to the imagination, nor yet to the sources on which it may draw. Every goal man reaches provides a new starting point, and the sum of all man's days is just a beginning. □

Victoria Rouse

It is now 1981, eight years after Edgar D. Mitchell, engineer, astronaut, author, founded the Institute of Noetic Sciences. The heightened experiences of being the sixth man to walk on Earth's moon and of traveling back home to the planet he now saw as both finite and aware inspired him to begin an organization which could make a profound difference in the way things are — to make things better for Earth and all her inhabitants.

IONS continues to attract attention and new support as the mainstream of world social consciousness turns in the direction we have helped establish over the past years. Dr. Harman's frequent papers at symposia and other major scientific gatherings are among the most erudite and challenging of any scholar in the field urging the scientific community to look beyond the limits of the methodologies we have been using.

It is increasingly clear that the vision of a noetic science upon which the Institute was founded is becoming a reality. The loyal support of our membership, the dedication of directors and staff, as well as the increasing awareness of broad segments of the population, have all combined to bring this vision into pragmatic focus.

Whereas in our formative years we timidly asked the question "Are there extended models of human capability which we should be using to understand what world society can become?", we can now confidently perceive that there are. And furthermore, we have a pretty good idea of what those models are like and how to go about achieving the potential they represent!

It has been apparent for many years that we standard-issue human beings, if left to our traditional thinking, would create the tools of our own destruction—and then proceed to use them. The pundits who advise that "Human nature will never change" gave us little hope that we, the citizens of Planet Earth, could ever re-organize our thinking and our institutions to avoid the seeds of disaster which we have sown throughout our history.

Message from Edgar D. Mitchell

Times are changing, however, and we can with assurance now state from our experience that humans are creative beings, more spirit and mind than body, limited in our capability to create a satisfying future only by the limitations we accept for ourselves. When William James suggested that we humans use only a tiny fraction of our potential, he challenged us to find out what we can be if we tap our unused internal resources. We believe that we can now, with some assurance of success, learn to tap those resources that we each individually possess and utilize them to change our limited view of what we are in order to assure a more sane and productive future both individually and collectively.

The Institute in its development continues to be in the vanguard of thinking in the area of consciousness studies, posing the challenging questions and suggesting possible answers, goading the traditional thinkers and assisting in organizing the most visionary. This we see as part of our task as we try to "think globally and act locally" to create a more satisfying future.

The support of our loyal members, both those of past years and those yet to be introduced, is sincerely welcomed as we go forward.

Edgar D. Mitchell

Psi Research in the Soviet Union

AN INSIDE VIEW

by Keith Harary and Russell Targ

Editor's note: Russell Targ is an experimental physicist with broad experience in lasers, microwaves, and plasma research. Co-author of Mind Reach: Scientists Look at Psychic Abilities *(Delacorte, 1977) and co-editor of* Mind at Large: IEE Symposia on the Nature of Extrasensory Perception *(Praeger, 1984), Targ was also the leader of the Stanford Research Institute team that has investigated "remote viewing" for much of the last decade, partially supported in its early stages by a grant from the Institute of Noetic Sciences.*

Keith Harary is a clinical and experimental psychologist who specializes in psi research, having worked at Duke University, Maimonides Medical Center, the American Society for Psychical Research, and SRI International. Targ and Harary, co-founders of

Delphi Associates, are most recently the authors of The Mind Race: Understanding and Using Psychic Abilities *(Villard, 1984).*

Journey to Moscow

In September, 1983, we received an invitation to visit the Soviet Union as guests of the U.S.S.R. Academy of Sciences. This gave us an opportunity to discuss our remote viewing work with Soviet scientists, and also to learn firsthand about the research that they are currently doing. We were accompanied by Elisabeth Targ (daughter of Russell Targ), a second-year medical student at Stanford who holds a translator's certificate in Russian.

Our host for the visit was Dr. Andre Berezin, a biophysicist working at a Moscow research hospital.

In Moscow, we had stimulating exchanges with physicists, psychologists, and medical researchers. The physicists were mainly interested in the details of our precognitive experiments. The medical researchers and psychologists, by comparison, were interested in the broader field of psi research and its relevance for their work.

At the First Medical Institute in Moscow we met Professor Andriankyn, Director of the Theoretical Department of the U.S.S.R Academy of Sciences and the official sponsor of our visit. Andriankyn's present concern at the First Medical Institute involves the non-drug treatment of mental patients. One focus of his work is the experimental use of low-frequency electric and magnetic fields.

At the same Institute, we also talked with Dr. Igor Smirnoff and his colleagues, who had just completed a computer-controlled experiment in what we might call "rat telepathy." This experiment, as it was described to us, featured two groups of caged rats housed a mile apart. Each group was conditioned to move to the left side of their cage when a red light was turned on, in order to avoid an unpleasant electric shock to their feet. Then individual rats were removed from each group.

Next, the researchers randomly signalled and shocked one rat—and discovered that his "brother" rat in the distant cage showed a significant change in his galvanic skin response, exactly as would be expected in response to shock! This experiment, which appears to be well controlled and seriously thought out, is similar to another carried out several years ago by another Soviet researcher. It, however, involved human subjects who were conditioned by electric shocks.

Some of the scientists who contributed to the above experiment are also involved in other research. Dr. Konstantin Gubarev, for example, is designing a computer program to analyze physiological data and to determine from it when a particular change in an individual's state of consciousness—such as dropping into a hypnotized condition—has occurred. (This would be quite an accomplishment; presently, it is not even clear to Western researchers that hypnosis is a discriminable state.) Gubarev's approach is to look at mathematical transformations of the basic physiological data, and to observe phase changes rather than amplitude changes in particular measures.

Another fruitful meeting took place with Dr. Yuri Gulyaev at the Institute of Radio Engineering and Electronics overlooking Gorky Park. (Gulyaev had visited SRI in 1978.) As we sat on comfortable red leather chairs in his spacious office sipping countless ceremonial glasses of Armenian cognac, Dr. Gulyaev described some of his most recent work.

In addition to performing his duties as Deputy Director of the Institute, Gulyaev is pursuing interests in psychotronics. With his colleague

Dr. Eduard Godik, he has been examining the electromagnetic and visible radiation emitted by the human body. In sensitive photon-counting experiments with a spectrometer that measures the wavelength of the emitted light, Gulyaev and Godik have found what may be physical evidence for the so-called auras that certain people claim to see surrounding the human body.

Gulyaev has also been able, to a limited extent, to continue his work on "eyeless sight" with Nina Kulagina. In one particularly interesting experiment, he mentally selected a book on the shelves of his office and asked Kulagina to name the letters beginning each paragraph on a given page. Only after her answer would Gulyaev then take down the book and open it. Kulagina could do this task with surprising ac-

curacy, Gulyaev reported, unless she was told to leave the room before the book was opened. She thereby lost her feedback and her responses fell to chance.

Gulyaev also presented us with a copy of I.M. Kogan's new book on applied information theory. In it, Professor Kogan argues that if psychic phenomena are to be explained at all, it will have to be through low-frequency electromagnetic principles. According to Gulyaev, the first person to propose that psi was carried by electromagnetic waves was James Clerk Maxwell, in the last century. His idea was described in a recent U.S.S.R. Academy of Sciences journal dealing with the measurement of bio-magnetic fields.

Psychic abilities are being developed and studied in government-sponsored research programs in both the United States and the Soviet Union. Yet despite decades of research that has produced steadily improving results, the prevailing opinion is still that psychic abilities and experiences either do not exist or are beyond our understanding.

The mass media have presented much distorted and misleading information in this area. Critics have attempted to make psychic functioning appear to be fraudulent, impossible, or ridiculous. Cultists and other undiscriminating enthusiasts have caused psychic functioning to become associated with irrationality and superstition. The governments of the U.S. and the U.S.S.R., meanwhile, have quietly spent millions of dollars in a long-term, careful, and successful effort to develop ever more proficient and potentially useful psychic abilities.

Much of our own research was in a U.S. government-supported program at SRI International (formerly Stanford Research Institute), where we investigated a perceptual ability called remote viewing.

The Mind Race

The principal finding from experiments in remote viewing is that most participants can and do

OVERVIEW

learn to describe buildings, geography, and activities at locations from which they are separated by both space and time, with surprising accuracy and detail. In some cases, participants have correctly described places which were thousands of miles away from them. In other cases, they have also correctly described events that would take place hours or days in the future. While some of the subjects were experienced psychics, remote viewing abilities have also been developed by previously inexperienced people whose psychic functioning appears to improve with practice.

The existence of this capability has by now been well established, and our understanding has reached the point where we can seriously consider transferring remote viewing technology from the research laboratory to real world applications. One such area of application, for businesses, is decision-making under uncertainty, especially in investment situations where prior information about future events often makes the difference between experiencing a loss or realizing a profit. Remote viewing may also potentially be used in conjunction with conventional methodologies to

provide specialized information for use in natural resource exploration.

Scientists in the U.S.S.R. have also been busily at work—the Soviet government has officially sponsored psi research since the early 1920s. Unfortunately, most reports on Soviet psi research have been accounts presented by journalists who have not had the scientific experience necessary to evaluate the purported developments in this field. Thus, such accounts have provided little accurate information about what progress the Soviets are actually making in their psi research programs, although they have played an important role in alerting us to the magnitude and direction of the Soviet efforts.

Is there an overall aim to Soviet psi research? Many laboratories appear to be conducting experiments whose main goals are interpersonal control and manipulation—for example, the modification of the feelings and behavior of remote humans and animals by psychic means. This focus represents a continuation of nineteenth century Soviet interest in developing a method for hypnotic control of behavior at a distance. However, there is also much interest in non-manipulative psychic healing among the Soviet people, and many Soviet scientists are struggling, as we are, to understand the human potential implications of psi research.

The authors, Keith Harary (left) and Russell Targ, at the Institute of Radio Engineering and Electronics in Moscow.

Elizabeth Targ

Remote Viewing in Yerevan

Toward the end of our stay in the Soviet Union we visited the city of Yerevan, in Soviet Armenia, where remote viewing experiments have been carried out in the Industrial Psychology Laboratory at the State University. This Soviet city, southeast of Istanbul and north of Baghdad, was warm and sunny in contrast to the snow we had left in Moscow. It was also much more relaxed, with people strolling around the city square's large and illuminated fountain in the evening to listen to music.

At the University in Yerevan we spoke with members of the Armenian Academy of Science. We then met, in a laboratory full of arcade-type video games used to study hand-eye coordination, with Professor Ruben Aguzumtsian, who had carried out a careful series of remote viewing trials using target sites chosen by an architect—an appropriate idea in this city of remarkable structures dating from almost the time of Christ.

The viewers and outbound experimenters for Aguzumtsian's remote viewing study were volunteers from a psychology class. For each trial an outbound experimenter, accompanied by two "guards" (or watchers, also from the class), would go to a distant location, open the envelope with the target information and then go to the appointed site. Meanwhile, back in the laboratory, an interviewer would encourage the viewer to describe his or her impressions about the site that was being visited.

Aguzumtsian decided to carry out this work after reading accounts of earlier SRI experiments in this area. His research not only confirmed the SRI findings, they also gave him the interesting experience of having a viewer describe a chosen target site before the target team had opened the envelope and traveled to the target! As in the SRI experiments, such precognition was an unexpected complication.

We hope soon to carry out a long-distance series of remote viewing trials in cooperation with Aguzumtsian's laboratory to see how we will fare when a ten-thousand mile baseline is used for remote viewing. In this research, of course, we will work with a viewer who has never been to Yerevan.

In our travels from Moscow to Leningrad to Yerevan, we met with many researchers who expressed the hope that open communication in this field could continue. They universally expressed the feeling that psi's importance lies in the development of human potential, not in its possible military or intelligence applications. Yet everyone we talked with also made oblique references to what we were not being shown, and certain laboratories were closed to us. We hope that in future cooperative meetings with Soviet scientists we can explore even further the details of their psychotronic research.

It is important that "The Mind Race" not be seen as a psychic competition between nations. It is, rather, a race for each of us to develop our own innate potential for extended awareness. Our most sincere hope is that we will each win our own mind race, thereby contributing to the betterment of life on this planet. ☐

From a review by William Whitson in the same Newsletter of The Mind Race: Understanding and Using Psychic Abilities *by Russell Targ and Keith Harary (Villard Books, 1984):*

After exploring every conceivable ritual that might prepare a person for "clear inner listening," these two scientists reach the astonishing conclusion that self-training to a high level of sensitivity requires attention to a mere handful of guidelines:

1. Your favorite psychic symbols (whether a feeling, an image, a color, a texture, a smell, or a combination of these) will be uniquely influenced by your own background, training and personality.
2. Crystal clear impressions of a distant place or thing (clairvoyance) are usually—although not always—examples of mental noise. The more spontaneous and surprising your impressions of a remote target, the more likely they contain psychic information.
3. Learning to use psi is mostly a matter of developing the ability to respond to gentle impressions, feelings, and images without embroidering or editing the initial responses. Become aware of certain internal experiences and look at them.
4. Psychic information is often nonvisual—perhaps an impression of an emotional response to remote places, objects, and events.
5. The form of that information will vary uniquely with your own emotional state, your favorite fantasies, your immediate circumstances.
6. Greater psychic clarity seems to accompany your acceptance of your own inherent ability and your willingness to "hear clearly."
7. Premature analysis clouds signals. Listen, feel, see by bits and pieces since slowly emerging shapes and forms are more likely to delineate the true "target."
8. You can discover an ideal environment for psychic clarity. More than likely, it is already a familiar combination of sounds, temperature, smells, and feelings. The "signal" is always there! Access depends upon subtle conditions within your own willingness to *be* rather than to *think*.

In 1985, the Institute published a special issue of its research bulletin
Investigations on multiple personality.

The selections which follow represent a portion of that report, which
was widely acclaimed by therapists working in the field.

Multiple Personality
*Mirrors of a New Model of Mind?**
By Thomas J. Hurley III and Brendan O'Regan

*"The mind is its own place, and in itself can make
a heaven of Hell, a hell of Heaven."*
John Milton (1608–1674)

The waking rational self is usually quite sure that we
are one mind in one body. The self that dreams knows
another world, but assumes it belongs in the realm of
imagination and fantasy. But can *waking* minds be
divided up in such a way that several streams of life
that are quite separate from one another can exist
concurrently in one human being? If so, then does the
old saying: "The left hand doesn't know what the
right hand is doing" become a kind of reality? Is there
more to tales like Dr. Jekyll and Mr. Hyde than we
ever thought? Well, in some senses, we experienced a
"first wave" resurgence of this idea in the 1970s when
the studies of split-brain patients hit both the science
journals and eventually the popular press with all the
force of a new myth in the culture. Yes, there were
clearly some important findings in the area, but they
all too rapidly became used as metaphors for all
manner of unrelated claims. We may now be about to
experience a "second wave" of data on the subject
with the recent resurgence of interest and research
into the phenomena of multiple personality.

One of the interesting aspects of controversies in
contemporary science and the study of the mind is the
way in which ideas move from center stage to the
periphery during one period, only later to be returned
to the center of attention. Sometimes this happens
because a phenomenon is simply too complex to be
addressed until the methods of science have evolved
to deal properly with it. On other occasions it occurs
because the strategies of its proponents are not soundly
formulated. Or it can occur because science-at-large
finds an idea simply too strange or preposterous to
deal with.

It seems that the scientific fate of the concept of
multiple personality has been a cross between the
latter two of these. Multiple personality was a topic of
great fascination at the end of the last century, and up
into the early 1900s attempts were being made to
explain it in terms of the proposed capacity of the
mind to dissociate. These ideas were proposed by the
First Dynamic School of Psychiatry, now an almost
forgotten school of thought from the turn of the century. But, one might ask: why was it forgotten and
why did the subject virtually fade from view? As Dr.
John Kihlstrom of the University of Wisconsin recently wrote (in Bowers and Meichenbaum):

> The eventual dominance of psychoanalysis in
> clinical psychology and scientific personology
> led investigators to be interested in different syn-
> dromes and phenomena, a different model of the
> mind, and the eventual replacement of dissocia-
> tion by repression as the hypothetical mechanism
> for rendering mental contents unconscious. At
> the same time, the behaviorist revolution in aca-
> demic psychology removed consciousness (not
> to mention the unconscious) from the vocabulary
> of science. At fault were the dissociation theorists
> themselves, who often made extravagant claims
> for the centrality of the phenomenon (of dissocia-
> tion) and whose investigations were often meth-
> odologically flawed.

Today, we seem to be witnessing a return to center
stage of a number of previously discarded concepts
that all seem to connect with each other in curious
ways. One might say that one part of the stage was set
by the split-brain data, which once again opened up
the concept of the divided mind. Then the rise of
cognitive science in the 1970s also helped to place a
concern with mental processes and consciousness

*Excerpted from *Investigations*, Volume 1, Number 3/4

back in the center of things. Also during the 1970s, the data on and respectability of hypnosis research grew and led to greater attention being placed on the concept of dissociation, which is at the core of hypnotic phenomena, once again.

In this issue of *Investigations* we will present an overview of the contemporary scene regarding the topic of multiple personality. There are several events that have occurred of late to cause a growing number of professionals to reevaluate their point of view on the topic. More frequent diagnosis of the phenomenon is but one aspect of this sudden increase in interest. Another aspect involves the growing body of research data showing that multiples display unusual degrees of variation in physiological, neurological, and immune system variables when they switch. Further, the amount of professional attention being devoted to the subject in recent years has grown enormously.

Social and Scientific Implications of Multiple Personality

The social implications of this sudden surge in interest are quite complex since it seems definitely connected to the recent awareness in the culture of the phenomena of child abuse and incest. The emergence in the media of more and more reports on the incidence of child abuse and incest in the US has reached a degree that almost daily provides yet another set of shocking headlines. Perhaps it is this latter phenomenon that alerted the therapeutic professions because now not one but two phenomena previously seen as rare seem to be seen in unheard-of numbers all over the US: child abuse and multiple personality.

As we now know, the two are intimately connected with one another. Virtually everyone who is diagnosed as being multiple has been severely physically and sexually abused—though not everyone who is abused becomes multiple. But, one might well ask, why are these phenomena being seen with such frequency today? There is clearly a darker side to our culture that we would rather not look at. Unfortunately, the dual phenomena of abuse and multiplicity leave us with no other choice. The almost daily onslaught of statistics from the courts and the media now leave little doubt that battered children and battered wives are all too common. What is at the root of all this obscene inhumanity? Is there some deeper process at work in the culture that we refuse to face? What aspects of the human psyche have run amok in this supposedly rational and civilized culture? People stretch for answers to these questions and the guesses run the gamut from alcoholism to possession and various sicknesses in between. As the story unfolds within these pages, these questions will occur to the reader again and again. There are no easy answers to any of these questions, but it may well be that a deeper understanding of what the phenomenon of dissociation is, how it works, and what can drive it can throw some light on these troubling questions. Perhaps then we won't have to remain at the mercy of the pathologies of dissociation involved not only in abuse and multiplicity, but also in other forms of extreme inhuman behavior, and can learn instead to tap into the productive and positive uses of this part of our minds.

On another level, the legal and criminal justice implications of the data are only beginning to emerge. It is only in recent years that the insanity plea has begun to include multiple personality in a limited number of cases. Two of the most controversial cases recently both involved male multiples, Billy Milligan and Kenneth Bianchi. In both cases there was extensive dispute regarding the genuineness of their multiplicity. In the Bianchi case, the eventual legal opinion was that Bianchi was a fake. However, a larger number of professionals familiar with aspects of the case feel that Bianchi was *both* a multiple *and* capable of faking, too. Several of those interviewed for this report suggested that multiples are more likely to end up, undiagnosed, in the criminal justice system. Female multiples, which make up the great majority of presently known cases, are much less likely to end up in the criminal system. These kinds of issues are only beginning to be appreciated and only time will tell the extent to which the legal and criminal justice aspects of the disorder will affect the system as a whole.

It would seem that the scientific implications of the phenomenon will be very much a factor of just how the subject is handled methodologically by scientists *and* how it is reported by both science journalists and the popular press. If handled in a way that emphasizes the sensational and paradigm-challenging aspects of the phenomenon, then the chances are that major opportunity for an advance in our understanding of the mind and the mind-body problem will be lost. If, on the other hand, the topic is approached with extreme rigor and caution, as well as respect for the subjects themselves, then the benefits could be enormous in terms of our whole understanding of not only how mind and body are in fact linked, but also in terms of psychosomatic medicine as a whole. The subsequent spill-over into issues involving education, therapy for all kinds of trauma, and the social and criminal realms could be significant. If this could happen then not only would we all benefit, but the pain and suffering endured by multiples would at least have been turned into something positive in the world, and help to prevent others from having to endure such a fate. Let us hope that this time around such a rich opportunity will not be lost!

—*Brendan O'Regan*

Inner Faces of Multiplicity
Contemporary Look at a Classic Mystery

Multiple personality disorder (MPD) is an extraordinary syndrome in which two or more integrated alter selves coexist simultaneously in a single body. It appears to have roots in severe child abuse, and is puzzling and painful both for the persons who suffer from it—who are called *multiples*—and for the therapists who treat it. Yet researchers and expert observers of the field now say that multiple personality may be the basis for a new understanding of the nature of the mind and its elusive relation to body and brain function.

In a multiple, different personalities who sometimes have no awareness of one another alternately control the physical body. The process by which control of the body passes from one personality to another is called *switching*, and when a multiple's personalities switch so do a variety of other features.

Alter personalities may differ in terms of voice, posture, physiognomy, handedness, and—if preliminary research studies are correct—numerous physiological features such as brain-wave patterns, immune status, and skin electrical responses. Behavior patterns, reported life history, and (subjectively perceived) sex and age also tend to vary. Different personalities have often mastered different physical abilities, interpersonal skills, and intellectual subject areas. Some may even command entirely different languages!

By studying such changes and the mechanisms responsible for them scientifically, researchers hope to illuminate a host of key topics in psychology, psychiatry, and related fields such as psychosomatic medicine and brain research. Studies of multiple personality are expected to shed new light on such questions as:

- What are the mechanisms of conscious awareness, and how can multiple streams of conscious activity occur in the mind at the same time?
- How do processes occurring outside of phenomenal awareness influence experience or behavior?
- How do mental and emotional factors influence pain perception, immune function, and other psychosomatic processes?
- What are the mechanisms of volition or "executive control" in human consciousness? What are the mechanisms of "downward causation" in patterns of brain activity?
- To what extent are personality traits or abilities such as intelligence, sensitivity, or creativity determined by genetic and environmental influences, and to what extent are they consciously or unconsciously "chosen"?

Cases of multiple personality have always fascinated lay audiences, from fictional accounts such as *The Strange Case of Dr. Jekyll and Mr. Hyde* to contemporary true stories such as *Sybil* or *The Minds of Billy Milligan*. They have also intrigued professional observers from the seventeenth century to the present. Until recently, however, psychiatrists considered multiple personality disorder to be extremely rare, and understood little of its scope or dynamics. Now, known cases and new knowledge about multiple personality disorder are growing at a rapid rate.

Based on clinical research encompassing hundreds of multiples, as well as on preliminary findings from controlled research, a broad picture of multiplicity is beginning to emerge.

Presence of Alter Personalities

When a multiple switches it is typically rapid, usually occurring in one to two seconds, although in some cases slightly more time is required. Switching may be a voluntary or involuntary event, initiated either through conscious willing, in response to an unconscious emotion or a situation that triggers "automatic" switching, or as a result of biochemical changes in the body.

Drs. Corbett Thigpen and Hervey Cleckley reported one of the first contemporary cases of multiple personality in 1954, in *The Three Faces of Eve*. They described their initial meeting with one of Eve's alters in a way that conveyed the eerie, trance-like quality that switching sometimes has:

> The brooding look in her eyes became almost a stare. Eve seemed momentarily dazed. Suddenly her posture began to change. Her body slowly stiffened until she sat rigidly erect. An alien, inexplicable expression came over her face. This was suddenly erased into utter blankness. The lines of her countenance seemed to shift in a barely visible, slow, rippling transformation. For a moment there was the impression of something arcane. Closing her eyes, she winced as she put her hands to her temples, pressed hard,

Multiple personality may shed new light on the nature of the mind and its elusive relation to body and brain function.

and twisted them as if to combat sudden pain. A slight shudder passed over her entire body.

Then the hands lightly dropped. She relaxed easily into an attitude of comfort the physician had never seen before in this patient. . . . In a bright unfamiliar voice that sparkled, the woman said, 'Hi, there, Doc!'

Actually to meet the alter personalities of a multiple for the first time is both fascinating and disturbing. If the disparity between one personality and the next is great—as when an adult is replaced by a child, or a female by a male personality—one's first question may well be, "Is this real?" or "Is (s)he acting?"

This question has been posed throughout the history of psychiatry, and in specific cases one cannot definitively answer "Yes" or "No" immediately. Diagnostic issues aside, however, it is interesting to note that what gradually impresses one meeting a true multiple is less the obvious differences between personalities and more the nonverbal, intangible dimensions of personality that are rich, subtle, and difficult to fake. These qualities of being tend to be subconscious and are usually perceived subconsciously; it is the discrepancy between them from one personality to another in a multiple that eventually shakes one's sense of what is real and what is not.

Still, the differences among alters can be impressive. In the notorious case of Billy Milligan—described by Daniel Keyes in *The Minds of Billy Milligan*—Milligan's twenty-four alter personalities included:

- *Arthur*, a 22-year-old Englishman who is rational, emotionless, and staunchly conservative. Arthur is expert in physics, chemistry, and medicine, and speaks with a British accent. He also reads and writes fluent Arabic. The first to discover the existence of all the others, he dominates in safe places and decides who will come out and hold the consciousness. Wears glasses.
- *Ragen Vadascovinich*, 23, the "keeper of hate." His name is derived from "rage again." Yugoslavian, he speaks English with a noticeable Slavic accent, and reads, writes, and speaks Serbo-Croatian. A weapons and munitions authority as well as a karate expert, he displays extraordinary strength, stemming from his ability to control his adrenaline flow. His charge is to be protector of the family, and of women and children in general. He dominates the consciousness in dangerous places. Ragen weighs 210 pounds, has enormous arms, black hair, and a long, drooping mustache. He sketches in black and

Actually to meet the alter personalities of a multiple for the first time is both fascinating and disturbing.

white because he is color-blind.
- *Adalana*, 19, the lesbian. Shy, lonely, and introverted, she writes poetry, cooks, and keeps house for the others. Adalana has long, stringy black hair, and since her brown eyes occasionally drift from side to side with nystagmus, she is said to have "dancing eyes."
- *Christene*, 3, the corner child, so-called because she was the one to stand in the corner in school. A bright little English girl, she can read and print, but has dyslexia. Likes to draw and color pictures of flowers and butterflies. Blond shoulder-length hair, blue eyes.
- *The Teacher*, 26. The sum of all twenty-four alter egos fused into one. Taught the others everything they've learned. Brilliant, sensitive, with a fine sense of humor. He says, "I am Billy all in one piece," and refers to the others as "the androids I made." The Teacher has almost total recall.

Milligan's alter personalities referred to being in control of the body as being "on the spot." One explained:

'It's a big white spotlight. Everybody stands around it, watching or sleeping in their beds. And whoever steps on the spot is out in the world . . . .Whoever is on the spot holds the consciousness.'

A multiple named Cassandra who was interviewed at the First International Conference on Multiple Personality/Dissociative States revealed a similar range of personalities. Several of her alters (she claims to have more than 180 personalities or fragments in all) spoke openly about their experiences and abilities.

- *Larry* is an adult male who sits on what Cassandra calls her Inner Council, whose purpose is to provide guidance and moral direction for the "family." As are several other members of the Council, Larry is an American Indian. Thoughtful and direct, he has a strong masculine face and manner and will not enter the body if Cassandra is wearing characteristic feminine attire. Larry is responsible for protecting the body from physical harm, a function he fulfills even when he is not in control of the body by virtue of being co-conscious.
- *Celese* is a 14-year-old member of Cassandra's family who has detailed knowledge of human anatomy and physiology, obtained through her

study of medical textbooks. Formerly a self-mutilating personality, Celese now serves as the body's healer. She claims to have healed third-degree burns, internal organ damage, and even brain damage using visualization, which she practices with exceptional refinement and precision. Celese is also an anesthetic personality, which means that she does not experience pain, and with men she is a delightful adolescent flirt.

- *Chris* is a 10-year-old boy with all the normal interests and ambitions of boys that age. He enthusiastically tells stories of playing ball and of going fishing, and looks forward to being able to drive when he grows up. Presently forbidden to do that, since he cannot see over the dashboard when sitting in the driver's seat, he nonetheless admits to once taking the car anyway. Purportedly he drove it by stationing four other alter personalities on its two front and two rear corners to direct him!

- *Stacy* is a shy little girl who plays incessantly with her hair, often hiding her face beneath it. She speaks in a high-pitched voice with a strangely archaic syntax and vocabulary, and controls the body only briefly. Stacy's name is derived from her function, which was to "stay" and "see" what happened when Cassandra was abused.

With more than 180 alter selves, by her reckoning, Cassandra is what psychiatrists call a "super-multiple." She would have astounded investigators of multiple personality prior to the present era, since most prior reports of multiple personality disorder involved cases of dual personality. Much more rarely, multiples with three, four, or possibly five alternate personalities were reported.

Cassandra is unusual even today, but her case is not unique. Dr. Richard Kluft of the University of Pennsylvania Medical School has found that the average number of alternate personalities in a multiple is eight to thirteen, though dual personalities are still "not too uncommon" in men and there are other "super-multiples" with more than a hundred alternates.

Dr. Frank Putnam of the National Institute of Mental Health reported similar findings at the 137th Annual Meeting of the American Psychiatric Association in Los Angeles. Putnam found an average number of thirteen personalities (or personality fragments) in one hundred multiples that he surveyed, and noted in addition that the greater the number of alternate personalities, the greater a multiple's self-destructiveness.

Putnam's survey also revealed that 75 percent of all multiples had child personalities under 12 years of age, 50 percent had alter personalities of the opposite sex, and over a third exhibited changes of handedness from one alter personality to another.

Inner Faces of Multiple Personality Disorder

Other common types of alter personalities found in multiples include *inner self helpers* and *persecutors*. First identified by Dr. Ralph Allison of Morro Bay, California, inner self helpers are exceptionally knowledgeable and helpful personalities who guide the multiple and sometimes aid the clinician in therapy. In his experience, said Allison in *Minds in Many Pieces*, inner self helpers often exist in a spiritual hierarchy with those highest in the hierarchy (those closest to God) being most reluctant to enter the body or communicate with the therapist.

Persecutors aim to dominate the multiple's inner family or even to destroy other alters. A product of the anger and hostility evoked by abuse, persecutors are nearly ubiquitous in multiples and are often responsible for sociopathic behavior that gets the multiple in trouble. They also embody strong masochistic tendencies, which psychiatrists say are common in multiples. Until they accept a cooperative role in the intrapsychic system (and like every other alter they personify important aspects of the whole personality), they are a source of misery and terror.

The fear that persecutors can elicit was described by Dr. Robert de Vito of Loyola University, who said in a paper prepared for the conference in Chicago:

If one could imagine the original personality 'on stage' with one or more alters 'in the wings' watching and/or talking to or about the original, one could begin to approximate the daily torment experienced by the original or host. When the original, host, or presenting personality becomes aware that an alter or group of alters want to torture, humiliate, or even 'murder' him or her, each waking moment is filled with dread. As a former patient of mine put it, 'It is as if I took out a contract on myself.'

Inner self helpers are exceptionally knowledgeable and helpful alter personalities who guide the multiple and sometimes aid the clinician in therapy.

The extent and strength of the dissociative barriers defining each personality vary tremendously. There may be personalities with continuous memory (given the name *memory-trace personalities* by Dr. Cornelia Wilbur of the University of Kentucky), personalities with continuous awareness, and yet others who are amnestic for all or some of those with whom they are sharing a body. In short, Dr. Eugene Bliss of the University of Utah has observed, clinicians may find all gradations of awareness and control among the personalities in a multiple.

Alternate personalities who are aware of the thoughts, feelings, or actions of other alters are said to be *co-conscious* (a term coined by one of the first US investigators of multiple personality, Dr. Morton Prince). Frequently, a primary personality will be amnestic for other alters, while one or more secondary personalities is co-conscious.

Co-presence is the ability of an alter to influence the experience or behavior of another personality. Psychiatrists such as Dr. Richard Kluft of the University of Pennsylvania (who coined the term) and de Vito think that co-presence may be a factor in producing many of the diverse symptoms that multiples exhibit. These encompass the full range of classical dissociative and conversion symptoms—blindness, paralysis, etc.—as well as unusual symptoms such as *dissociative void*, in which the body appears temporarily vacant of any personality. The latter, de Vito said, may reflect an internal struggle for executive control among alters.

Another unusual symptom sometimes observed in multiple personality disorder is *dissociative panic*. This occurs when no alter can maintain control of the body for more than a few minutes, so that a rapid cycling or switching of personalities results. An episode of dissociative panic was described in *The Minds of Billy Milligan* following the administration of the anti-psychotic drug Thorazine to Billy:

They threw him into a small bare room . . . and locked the door. When Ragen heard the door slam, he got up to break it down, but Arthur froze him. Samuel took the spot, dropping to his knees, wailing, 'Oy vey! God, why have you forsaken me?' Philip cursed and threw himself to the floor; David felt the pain. Lying on the mattress, Christene wept; Adalana felt her face wet in the pool of tears. Christopher sat up and

What happens to alters when they are not in the body is different for different multiples.

played with his shoes. Tommy started to check the door to see if he could unlock it, but Arthur yanked him off the spot. Allen started calling for his lawyer. April, filled with desire for revenge, saw the place burning. Kevin cursed. Steve mocked him. Lee laughed. Bobby fantasized that he could fly out the window. Jason threw a tantrum. Mark, Walter, Martin, and Timothy raved wildly in the locked room. Shawn made a buzzing sound. Arthur no longer controlled the undesirables.

An alter who is amnestic for other personalities experiences those periods when alters are in control of the body as "lost time," or blackouts. Such experiences are one of the most frequent symptoms of multiplicity, and they create tremendous bewilderment and confusion. Multiples may "wake up" in unfamiliar situations with no idea where they are, how they got there, or who the people around them are—even though those people may be well known to one of the alter personalities!

One of the consequences of such amnestic episodes is that multiples are frequently accused of lying, since an alter may deny remembering or being responsible for events or actions that occurred while another alter controlled the body. Some alters develop exceptional memories to compensate.

In *Sybil*, the story of Sybil Dorsett's pioneering treatment by Wilbur, Flora Rheta Schreiber described the pragmatic and emotional consequences of lost time. As a result of her amnestic experiences, Sybil remembered, she "found herself floating in and out of blackness":

Disguising the fact, she became ingenious in improvisation, peerless in pretense, as she feigned knowledge of what she did not know. Unfortunately, from herself she couldn't conceal the sensation that somehow she had lost something. Nor could she hide the feeling that increasingly she felt as if she belonged to no one and to no place. Somehow it seemed that the older she got, the worse things became. She began repudiating herself with unspoken self-derogating comments: 'I'm thin for a good reason: I'm not fit to occupy space.'

What happens to alters when they are not in the body is different for different multiples. Cassandra reports that her personalities frequently have out-of-body experiences in which they travel to a nonphysical domain that she calls the Third World. In other multiples, alter personalities report residing inside certain regions of the head or body. Some alters "sleep," while others are aware of their inner companions and can watch the activities of whoever is "in the body."

Some multiples have elaborate inner worlds in which they play and communicate with other alters. Some personalities may even live almost entirely within, and rarely or never enter the body. The experience of these and other mysterious alters with no known origin or function often have a surreal or numinous quality quite difficult to convey using ordinary language. A glimpse is provided by one of Milligan's alters who had no name:

'When I'm not asleep and not on the spot,' he said, 'it's like I'm lying face down on a sheet of glass that stretches out forever, and I can look down through it. Beyond that, in the farthest ground, it seems like stars of outer space, but then there's a circle, a beam of light. It's almost as if it's coming out of my eyes because it's always in front of me. Around it, some of my people are lying in coffins. The lids aren't on them because they're not dead yet. They're asleep, waiting for something. There are some empty coffins because not everyone has come there. David and the other young ones want a chance at life. The older ones have given up hope.... David named this place' he said, 'because he made it. David calls it the Dying Place.'

Exceptional Abilities

Some multiples learn to use their multiplicity in conscious and constructive ways. Cooperation among alters who coexist harmoniously may take many forms.

Alternation of personalities extends the time during which a multiple is able to function at peak capacity. A personality who is tired or has used alcohol or drugs, for instance, can yield the body to another personality who will be alert, sober, and able to continue functioning. A personality who is in pain can yield the body to an anesthetic personality who does not feel the pain, or to another personality who will remain in the body until he or she can no longer endure the pain and must switch.

Co-consciousness also facilitates cooperation among alter personalities. Using co-consciousness, Milligan's alter selves Arthur and Ragen would observe what was going on in the environment and decide who should be "on the spot." Cassandra's alter personality Celese, too, apparently uses co-conscious processing to continue with the task of visualization and healing even when she is not in the body.

"Parallel processing is not only possible with me, allowing a higher level of productivity than normal," Cassandra has written, "it is also inevitable."

Some multiples learn to use their multiplicity in constructive ways.

When the pressures of graduate school are beyond the limits of any one person, I call on the others to help me. When I am writing a paper on dichotic hearing, one of the others is composing the proposal for 'my' master's thesis. Someone else has prepared dinner for me and will later clean up the kitchen while I sleep....I can no more prevent the others from working than I can prevent the change of the seasons. Even as I write this, one of the others is probably thinking about something as obtuse as critical flicker frequency. We share the body so the time I am at the typewriter of necessity limits the others' use of the physical aspects of the body. It does not prevent any one of them from using the brain to plan, design, or compose....I think that this is mind wandering deluxe!

Multiples also exhibit other unusual abilities, according to clinicians who have worked with them. These include "perfect" memory (sometimes having a near-photographic quality as well as strong auditory, olfactory, and somatic components) and the ability to heal more rapidly than normal. Paranormal experiences are also reported to be common. Are these somehow related to a "passion to survive"?

Multiples also tend to be highly intelligent, perceptive, and sensitive. "I've never met a multiple with an IQ of less than 110," said Wilbur at the First International Conference on Multiple Personality, while Dr. David Caul noted that they are exquisitely sensitive to cues and signals. "They can smell a liar at a thousand paces in one-ten-thousandth of a second," he said. Are these traits, like their high hypnotizability, somehow related to the capacity for dissociation?

Such purported abilities pose questions and present opportunities for research.

—*Tom Hurley*

Etiology of Multiple Personality
From Abuse to Alter Personalities

Researchers have yet to fully understand the causes of multiple personality, but preliminary findings suggest that no single factor engenders the syndrome and no single intrapsychic pattern is common to all cases. Instead, according to Dr. Richard Kluft, "There appear to be both biological and environmental factors that interact with developmental and psychodynamic processes in each patient with multiple personality disorder. The uniqueness of this interaction in each individual case leads to the wide diversity of the condition's manifestations, structures, and treatment outcomes."

Kluft has developed a "four-factor theory" of the etiology of multiple personality disorder that reflects this conclusion. The four factors he deems necessary for the development of multiplicity are:

1. A biological capacity for dissociation.
2. A history of trauma or abuse.
3. Specific psychological structures or contents that can be used in the creation of alternate personalities.
4. A lack of adequate nurturing or opportunities to recover from abuse.

Kluft's model was well-received by his colleagues at the 137th Annual Meeting of the American Psychiatric Association in Los Angeles. It was published in a special issue of *Psychiatric Clinics of North America* (March 1984) devoted exclusively to multiple personality. Kluft hopes that the work he and others in the field have done to shape a broad picture of the etiology of multiple personality disorder will contribute to the formation of testable hypotheses about the syndrome.

Defense through Dissociation

In Kluft's view, the first and most important factor in the etiology of multiple personality disorder is *a biological capacity for dissociation*. Dissociation, according to him,

> is an unconscious defense mechanism which involves the segregating of mental or behavioral processes from the rest of one's psychic activity . . . and by analogy with hypnotizability, is probably not a capacity of all individuals. Instead, it is very highly developed and accessible in some, intermediately so in others, and minimal in yet others.

Psychologists say that dissociative mechanisms function in all of us, to some extent. The experience of dreams or spontaneous waking imagery, "the automatic" performance of "overlearned" behaviors,

and simple forms of state-dependent learning are all instances of dissociation. Subpersonalities may also represent dissociative processes at work, and hypnosis and trance are considered dissociative states par excellence.

By comparison with the norm, persons who develop multiple personality are *dissociation-prone*. Their response to the experience of extreme stress or abuse is to isolate the associated feelings and memories from conscious awareness, as memories are isolated from awareness in post-hypnotic amnesia (studies have found that nearly all multiples are highly hypnotizable). Dr. Eugene Bliss of the University of Utah explained how the same mechanism might apply to multiple personality:

> If hypnosis can allow the individual to forget experiences, feelings, or even native language, why should he or she not be able to forget himself or herself? There is a rapid switch and the individual forgets herself, or to describe it in a slightly different form, the individual goes into hypnosis, disappears, and then is hidden in hypnosis like a personality, while the (alter) personality emerges into the real world, no longer in hypnosis.

Dissociation is the core mechanism in other psychopathological syndromes besides multiple personality. Psychogenic fugue, psychogenic amnesia, and depersonalization disorder are among the *dissociative disorders* formally recognized by psychiatrists. Dissociation also plays a partial role in some kinds of phobia and anorexia nervosa. In fact, many people may use dissociation as a defense, said Dr. David Spiegel of Stanford University School of Medicine, but they don't dissociate *themselves*, as multiples do. Only in multiple personality disorder do dissociated processes and psychic contents form highly organized and autonomous personalities. This reflects the fact that there seems to be a critical period for the development of multiple personality in children, prior to the development of a mature ego.

Abuse and Alter Personalities

The second factor in the etiology of multiple personality disorder is some set of traumatic experiences that overwhelm the individual's capacity to cope with them by any means other than dissociation. A growing and terrible body of evidence now shows that this is usually *severe physical, sexual, or psychological abuse by a parent or significant other in the child's life.*

In a survey of a hundred multiples, Dr. Frank Putnam found that 97 percent of them had a childhood history of incest, torture, or other abuse. Psychiatrists now believe that as children, multiples created alternate personalities as a psychological response to such experiences.

Dr. Cornelia Wilbur of the University of Kentucky School of Medicine was the first contemporary psychiatrist to identify the role of abuse in the development of multiple personality disorder, in her pioneering psychoanalysis of Sybil Dorsett. Wilbur discovered that the severe and sustained abuse Sybil suffered at the hands of her mother had evoked intolerable feelings of rage, hatred, fear, and pain that Sybil learned to cope with by blocking them out of awareness entirely, through dissociation. The feelings and memories that Sybil isolated from awareness, however, were the nucleus around which her alter personalities later formed through inner elaboration and through reinforcement by repeated abuse.

> Normal at birth . . . Sybil had fought back until she was about two and a half, by which time the fight had been literally beaten out of her. She had sought rescue from without until, finally recognizing that this rescue would be denied, she resorted to finding rescue within. First there was the rescue of creating a pretend world, inhabited by a loving mother of fantasy, but . . . being a multiple personality was the ultimate rescue. By dividing into different selves, defenses against not only an intolerable but also a dangerous reality, Sybil had found a modus operandi for survival.

Wilbur discussed the nature and scope of the trauma that multiples suffer in a keynote address at the First International Conference on Multiple Personality/Dissociative States.

The *sexual* abuse of multiples has included rape, incest, sodomy, and fellatio, both heterosexual and homosexual, Wilbur said. Cases have been reported in which a child's caretaker(s) regularly invited other relatives or friends to participate in sexually exploiting him or her, and some multiples have been forced to witness the physical or sexual abuse of other children.

Therapists have also treated multiples who were *psychologically* abused by being compelled to participate in murder, or who were exposed to multiple murders. Cult activity involving ritual murder—reportedly still widespread in this country—was said to be the context, in some cases, for this diabolical kind of abuse.

Physical abuse of multiples has included burying, torture, and beatings. *Neglect* has included their be-

ing almost completely deprived of physical contact, or constantly having been fed inappropriate foods. If the latter practice is widespread, Wilbur noted, it suggests that nutrition may be an etiological factor in multiple personality disorder, or may figure in some of the unusual psychosomatic irregularities in multiples.

Multiples have also been given frequent enemas or massive doses of cathartics, because their caretakers believed they must be absolutely clean not only outside but *within* as well. Such *physiological* abuse has also included "home treatments" in which children were inappropriately given adult medication, which Wilbur said is common when a parent attempts to treat other abuses that have been inflicted on the child.

"Who ever heard of an abusive parent taking the child to the doctor?" she asked.

Survey results suggest that the number of a multiple's alternate personalities is related to the number of different types of abuse he or she suffered as a child (supermultiples have usually been severely abused well into adolescence, according to Kluft). Moreover, because of the multiple's history of abuse, at least one personality will almost invariably be an angry, hostile, and possibly violent alter.

The link between multiple personality disorder and child abuse creates special problems both for detecting multiple personality disorder in its early stages and for alleviating the conditions that foster it. Until recently, professionals tended to respond to reports of both child abuse and multiple personality with incredulity, disbelief, and misunderstanding. While such responses may be an understandable attempt on their part to maintain a sane and manageable perspective on reality in the face of the awful evidence presented by abused children, Wilbur said at the American Psychiatric Association meeting, they amount to a shared negative hallucination.

The problem of credibility may be particularly acute for child multiples. Since they are among the most severely abused individuals, they may also be experienced as the least credible. Incredulity and disbelief on the part of family and professional counselors, however, serve only to reinforce the child multiple's use of dissociation as the best available defense against trauma, or the "only way out."

"There should be a massive approach across the country toward the prevention of child abuse,"

In a survey of a hundred multiples, Dr. Frank Putnam found that 97 percent of them had a childhood history of incest, torture, or other abuse.

Psychiatrists now believe that as children, multiples created alternate personalities as a response to abuse.

Wilbur said. Research on multiple personality can help authorities and the public understand how important it is to control this terrible problem.

The Puzzle of Psychogenesis

Not all children who are abused become multiple personalities. What then are the other factors that place a child at risk for the development of multiple personality disorder? Researchers have a few clues, but their data is primarily descriptive—the mechanisms of *splitting* are poorly understood.

The third factor in Kluft's model of the etiology of multiple personality disorder thus refers simply to *all the psychological structures, ego contents, and other unique shaping influences that a multiple can enlist in the creation of alter personalities*. Taken together, these factors will determine the particular characteristics of each alter, many of the relationships among them, and the ways in which they develop.

Psychiatrists use the term "splitting" in several ways. Most generally, it simply refers to the creation of alter personalities. In psychoanalytic theories of multiple personality disorder, however, the term has a more specialized meaning. There, splitting refers to a specific defense mechanism that functions very early in life and results in a distortion of ego development. It involves the polarization of emotional identification so that the child fails to integrate experiences of "good" and "bad" in developing mental representations of the self and others. In the narcissistic or borderline personality disorders, splitting leads to uncertainty about identity, emotional instability, and problematic relationships.

Some features of multiple personality disorder support the psychoanalytic claim that ego splitting of this kind plays a role in its psychogenesis. At the American Psychiatric Association meeting, for instance, Putnam noted that many multiples split off *pairs* of personalities that seem to be emotional opposites. One personality might have a sweet, pollyannish disposition, he said, while her complement is a "bad" or "horrid" child.

Yet researchers also point out that other features of multiple personality disorder argue against a strict theoretical interpretation involving splitting. Not all personalities in a multiple reflect the contradictory psychic organization that would be expected, and individual alter personalities may grow and reach more mature stages of psychological development than borderline or narcissistic patients do. Moreover, in some cases a cohesive personality representing the whole self appears to exist in conjunction with all of the fragmentary alter personalities who represent split-off parts of the self. This hidden personality may have a normal, integrated self structure, and reflects a unity of personality that is totally lacking in the borderline or narcissistic disorders.

In a paper prepared for the First International Conference on Multiple Personality/Dissociative States, Dr. Richard Horevitz concluded that while some limited support for the presence of 'splitting' as a defense in individuals with multiple personalities exists . . . there is little evidence that the construct of 'splitting' explains the actual formation or maintenance of alter personalities with unique memories and histories, nor does it explain the 'switching' process between personalities.

Just what comprises the "window of vulnerability" for multiple personality disorder is thus still a puzzle for researchers. While they are amassing a growing body of clinical data regarding the creation of alter personalities and their subsequent intrapsychic organization, as yet no theory unifies their findings. "There are a lot of competing theories," said Kluft.

Clinical experience with multiples as well as survey results have shown that:

- Some alter personalities may begin as imaginary playmates and develop gradually, while others have no identifiable precursors.
- Some alters "live inside" for a while before coming out and assuming control of the body, while others emerge full-blown "on the spot" at just the moment they are needed.
- The initial "split" usually occurs before the age of five. Once the first personality has been dissociated, alters may form at any time thereafter.
- When an alter personality is formed, he or she may or may not deplete the parent personality of psychological resources.
- Alters can be clustered or related to one another in terms of emotional or psychological similarities among them.
- Splitting usually occurs along affective lines, and each alter tends to deal with a related set of conflicts and feelings.

At the American Psychiatric Association meeting, Wilbur said, "In the analysis of the various alternate personalities of a multiple personality, we find individuals who deal with rage and hatred, individuals who deal with hypocrisy and dishonesty in others, alternates who deal with envy and jealousy in themselves and in others, and individuals who encapsulate intense affect and conflict of all kinds."

Another way of putting this, according to Bliss, is that each alter is initially an invited guest, with specific functions for which he or she is responsible. In addition to alters who encapsulate emotions associated with trauma, there may be personalities who are responsible for developing valuable skills or abilities, others who express conflictual impulses and needs such as sexuality or aggression, and personalities who assume control of the body in specific behavioral roles or social situations.

Absence of Healing

The final factor involved in the etiology of multiple personality disorder is *a lack of restorative experiences following abuse and dissociation*. The incipient multiple never given a chance to heal adopts dissociation as a routine strategy for dealing with problems. Dissociative barriers are strengthened through reinforcement and elaboration, and alternate personalities assume an autonomous existence.

Studies by Doctors Bennett Braun and Charles Stern help to confirm the idea that multiples do not find the necessary succor or healing support in their environment. They have attempted to characterize the family of origin of the multiple, and the profile that emerges from their research is remarkably similar to that developed by other investigators studying families likely to include abused children.

The family of origin of the multiple:

• Espouses rigid religious or mystical beliefs.
• Presents a united front to the community, yet internally is riddled with conflict.
• Is isolated from the community and uncooperative regarding intervention or assistance.
• Includes at least one caretaker who exhibits severe pathology.
• Subjects the child to contradictory communications from significant others during childhood.
• Is polarized: one parent may be overadequate (the abuser), the other underadequate (the enabler).

Multiplicity is often seen in more than one generation of a family. While psychiatrists think this may reflect a genetic component of multiple personality disorder—perhaps linked to the psychobiological capacity for dissociation—it has also been found that the violent personalities of adult multiples attack their children.

It is this combination of genetic, psychodynamic, developmental, and environmental factors that perpetuates a tragic chain of abuse, dissociation, and multiplicity.

—*Tom Hurley*

Multiple Personality Disorder: Key Findings

• Victims of multiple personality disorder (MPD) are persons who perceive themselves, or who are perceived by others, as having two or more distinct and complex personalities. The person's behavior is determined by the personality that is dominant at a given time.

• Multiple personality disorder is not always incapacitating. Some MPD victims maintain responsible positions, complete graduate degrees and are successful spouses and parents prior to diagnosis and while in treatment.

• An MPD victim (a multiple) suffers from "lost time," amnesia or "black-out spells," which lead the victim to deny his/her behavior and to "forget" events and experiences. This may result in accusations of lying and manipulation and may cause severe confusion for the undiagnosed multiple.

• More than 75% of MPD victims report having personalities in their system who are under 12 years of age. Personalities of the opposite sex or with differing life styles are also common. Person-

alities within a multiple system often hold conflicting values and behave in ways that are incompatible with one another.

• 97% of MPD victims report a history of childhood trauma, most commonly a combination of emotional, physical and sexual abuse.

• Multiple personality disorder can be reduced or prevented by early diagnosis and treatment of traumatized children and by working to eliminate abusive environments.

• While usually not diagnosed until adulthood, 89% of MPD victims have been mis-diagnosed at least once. Common mis-diagnoses include: depression, borderline and sociopathic personality disorder, schizophrenia, epilepsy and manic depressive illness.

• When they first enter treatment, most MPD victims are not aware of the existence of other personalities.

• MPD victims require treatment techniques which specifically address the unique aspects of the disorder. Standard psychiatric interventions used in the treat-

ment of schizophrenia, depression and other disorders are ineffectual or harmful in the treatment of MPD.

• Appropriate treatment results in a significant improvement in the quality of life for the MPD victim. Improvements commonly include reduction or elimination of confusion, feelings of fear and panic, self-destructive thoughts and behavior, internal conflicts and stressful periods of indecision.

• Multiple personality disorder has been recognized by physicians since the seventeenth century. While often confused with the relatively new diagnosis of schizophrenia throughout most of the twentieth century. MPD is again being understood as a legitimate and discrete disorder.

• Multiple personality disorder is treatable.

From the National Foundation for the Prevention and Treatment of Multiple Personality

Multiplicity and the Mind-Body Problem
New Windows to Natural Plasticity

> *"Our vision of nature is undergoing a radical change toward the multiple, the temporal, and the complex."*
>
> *Ilya Prigogine*

Introduction

Classically speaking, we have always more or less assumed that we were one mind in one body. Therefore the mind-body problem, as it has been called since the time of Descartes, has been mostly about the problem of understanding the relationship between the diaphanous and the solid, or between the ephemeral though personally real world of the mind and the complex dynamics of the physical body. For some, it is the subjective side of reality that constitutes real evidence . . . the poetic veracity, so to speak, that ultimately determines what "feels" real. For others, this means little since it is the objective notion of change measured that says a real difference, an actual change has occurred. So for some people it is the weight of "subjective" evidence, in terms of people's *experience* of multiples that says the most. For others, what is more important is the growing body of evidence regarding the actual physiological changes, some of them extraordinary, that occur concurrently with a multiple's changes of personality.

Implicit in this approach is the notion that though there are obvious ranges in states of mind and in the dynamics of the body as a biological system, it is more or less assumed that certain kinds of variables remain relatively constant. They fluctuate but only within the limits of homeostasis. In recent years, this range has been somewhat expanded by what has been learned in biofeedback research, but even there the areas and range of control of variation have been small, even though important in their own right.

Some things, however, seem to be basic "givens" that we do not expect to change. Thus, for example, we assume that the person who is left-handed remains that way. There is a large literature on the subject of handedness, hemispheric specialization, and lately on the tendency of left-handed people to be more susceptible to autoimmune dysfunctions. This work basically proceeds on the premise that handedness is a trait that once established does not undergo sudden shifts. In another area, we assume that the person who is color-blind remains that way and we assume that the person who is allergic to poison oak cannot usually switch that sensitivity on and off. So even though we know there are areas of plasticity in the link between mind and body, we also assume a set of rules that limit this plasticity in fundamental ways. Of course, there are certain times when we focus more on plasticity than on the rules that hold structure in place—during childhood development and growth, for example, we naturally pay more attention to the capacity for change and plasticity. This, of course, is also the period during which multiplicity can become established.

However, the whole issue of mind-body plasticity seems about to undergo a major reformulation if what we are now beginning to learn from people with multiple personalities is developed fully in clinical and research terms. At the present time, the evidence is strong in anecdotal and case-history terms that persons with multiple personality disorder undergo dramatic shifts not just from one personality to another, but also from being left-handed to right-handed and from being allergic to nonallergic. There are also other indications of shifts in the status of the immune system that are unexpected in terms of their rapidity and extent. The fact that these people can make such switches "at will" (after therapy) opens up new avenues for the study of the mind-body problem that promise to tell us things about the connections we never knew and had no way of investigating until now.

Here we encounter "head on" the very complex problem of determining cause and effect. There seem to be basically three sets of possibilities to examine here:

1. Does a physiological or neurological switch "cause" the shift in their personality or mind of the multiple?
2. Does a shift in the mind come first and cause the physiological changes?
3. Do both co-vary with one another, linked in a complex dance of psychological and physiological styles?

What one usually finds among scientists regarding this question is that they consider one of these positions to be the obvious truth and the others either untenable or ridiculous. For the "mind = brain" group (physical monists) for whom the mind *is* the brain, and nothing else, the notion of a "mind-caused" switch is a tautology. This group tends to avoid discussions of volition and will, since they tend to place one in an uncomfortable "chicken-and-egg" position.

The "mind-over-matter" group (mental monists) see in multiplicity a clear vector of evidence pointing to the supremacy of mind defining what brains actually do. However, this group has its own problems, in that there clearly are limits and the brain-damaged don't recover by acts of will.

Finally, one is left with the co-variance group, who remain safely dualist and say that all we can do for now is to pursue the correlations between sets of evidence from the mental and the physical realms and hope that one day they can be unified.

All three approaches have something to offer if they remain rigorous—something that is methodologically hard to do given the complexity of the problems posed by multiple personality disorder. One of the great challenges will be to think through the actual methodological approaches that can actually distinguish between these three paradigms. Each one can tell us something and no doubt, as J.B.S. Haldane so aptly reminded us, the answer will be probably stranger than we are able to imagine.

Preliminary Evidence of Physiological Shifts in Multiples

We can categorize the types of psychophysiological changes now recorded in the literature on multiplicity into the following types:

Central Nervous System Changes

There appears to be a range of opinion regarding the kinds of changes in EEG noted in multiples switching personalties. On the one hand, Dr. Philip Coons in a 1982 study published in the *Archives of General Psychiatry* indicated that the "EEG differences among personalities in a person with multiple personalities involve intensity of concentration, mood changes, degree of muscle tension, and duration of recording, rather than some inherent difference between the brains of persons with multiple personality disorder and those of normal persons."

On the other hand, Dr. Frank Putnam of the National Institute of Mental Health (NIMH) has reported on a study of eleven multiples plus a control group of people simulating the disorder. When the multiples and the controls were compared, there was much greater variation in the EEGs of the multiples than in the EEGs of the control group, perhaps reflecting "neurophysiologic differences in perception across alternate personalities."

Other studies are underway by Dr. Daniel Weinberger at the National Institute of Mental Health to examine regional cerebral blood-flow in multiples. At the First International Conference on Multiple Personality/Dissociative States, Dr. Robert de Vito reported some preliminary results indicating changes in regional cerebral blood-flow in multiples as they switched personalities. He is speculating that "these different patterns reflect the different biochemical equilibrium states of the presenting personality . . . and that the clinical 'switch' from one to another may be the result of a 'biochemical switch process,' involving the complex phenomenon of memory."

Dr. Theodore Zahn of NIMH is studying habituation of the galvanic skin response to unconditioned stimuli across alternate personalities.

Allergic Responses

One of the easiest shifts to observe clinically involves changes in allergic sensitivity to various stimuli. There are cases on record of people being allergic to citrus in one personality and not allergic to it in another. Similarly, cases of allergy to animals—e.g., cats—have been observed to disappear when the subject shifted from one personality to another. These cases have been written up by Dr. Bennett Braun in the special issue of the *American Journal of Clinical Hypnosis* devoted to multiple personality.

Such shifts demonstrate that the systems involved in the allergic response are somehow capable of being triggered by changes in personality. However, it must be remembered that similar shifts have been documented in cases where the switching off of the allergy was achieved by a hypnotic induction technique. Here we are seeing the "cross-over" of data from

The whole issue of mind-body plasticity seems about to undergo a major reformulation if what we are now beginning to learn from people with multiple personalities is developed fully in clinical and research terms.

If a multiple can seemingly heal more quickly than others, what does this say about the possibility of evoking such a healing response in everyone?

the multiple personality disorder problem to the more general problem of understanding the mechanisms governing hypnosis.

Dermatologic Reactions
Closely related, and in some cases identical to, these allergic reactions are the known cases involving sensitivity of the skin. Braun reports on the case of a female multiple who was tortured by both her mother and brother. One form of this abuse involved putting out lighted cigarettes on her skin. When the personality that received burns took over during therapy sessions, the burn marks would reappear on her skin and last for six to ten hours. Braun also reports on a case where another female multiple had a personality-specific allergy to a particular kind of soap that her mother had used on her when abusing her as a child. The allergy only appeared when this one personality emerged. Again, such phenomena have been observed in the hypnosis literature.

Pain Control
In many cases throughout the literature on multiple personality disorder, there are reports of multiples with alternates that are either anesthetic and don't feel pain at all or cases where there are special personalities whose "job" is to "take the pain." Most, if not all, multiples were severely abused at one time or another, and it is not surprising that nature would have created a coping mechanism of some kind to deal with pain. However, the extent to which multiples seem to be able to use this mechanism appears to be exceptional though further studies will be necessary to determine if this ability is intrinsically different from what can be achieved under hypnotic conditions.

Healing
There is a rich lore in the literature on multiples indicating that they heal more quickly than other people. Given the rapid appearance and disappearance of symptoms such as rashes and allergies, it is perhaps not surprising that this could also extend to more generalized control of the healing process. The anecdotal evidence here comes from cases discussed separately by Putnam, Dr. Cornelia Wilbur, and Braun and includes cases where third-degree burns healed with extraordinary rapidity, and the sugges-

tion by Wilbur that multiples don't seem to age as rapidly as other people. Detailed research on these claims will be important for our better understanding of the healing process as a whole.

New Opportunities for Research

In each of the above categories, there exists in the medical literature a variety of reports at varying levels of detail on the extent of these changes. In some cases detailed study has been done and in other cases, clinical observations have indicated the shift as occurring. However, no detailed psychophysiologic research into the range of phenomena involved in multiple personality has been done to date.

The critic of the area will surely decide that these changes are within the "normal" range in the end, and that the more radical aspects of the conceptual implications of the phenomenon of multiple personality can therefore be "explained away." It may simply be easier to focus on "plasticity" when unusual changes are seen to occur. It may simply be easier to resurrect long-ignored data from the early history of hypnosis research and say: "Look, we have always known these kinds of things to be possible!" It is always interesting to see how the initially skeptical lean back to long-forgotten data when modern evidence builds a case for something they had decided to ignore.

A focus on plasticity and its role in the mind-body problem will certainly not be all bad, and could of itself provide a major impetus to research into what might be called mind-body training programs designed to enhance everyone's ability for self-control and peak performance. Already, results have been reported by Dr. Joan Borysenko of the Mind-Body Program at Beth Israel Hospital in Boston indicating that diabetics who do relaxation training can lower their need for insulin. Braun has reported on the case of a woman who is diabetic in one personality and not in another. Perhaps these two results connect with each other to reveal a psychosomatic link that could be exploited to help diabetics.

In such ways, detailed research on multiples' abilities may well allow programs such as Borysenko's Mind-Body Program to become even more powerful. If this alone happened, then the research into multiple personality would have yielded a highly important result. Add to that the deeper knowledge we may gain into the dynamics of psychosomatic illness and the value of the research increases even more. After all, if a multiple can seemingly heal more quickly than others, what does this say about the possibility of evoking such a healing response in everyone?

There is an intriguing trail of clues that suggest that certain kinds of dissociative states facilitate extraordinary healing. However, it may be possible to study these states in a more concentrated way with multiples since their various states are often so clearly defined and segmented from one another. One might speculate that on those occasions when healers do create change in a person, are they perhaps affecting the regions or processes of the psyche that multiples access?

Perhaps it will be possible to characterize the healing states that multiples use and train them in others. For example, the healing personality of Cassandra, named Celese, described during an interview how her own effectiveness was amplified by learning an anatomically accurate image of the area that she wished to affect. Coincidentally, recent research by Dr. Kenneth Pelletier at the University of California at San Francisco has begun to test whether or not biologically exact imagery is more effective than generalized relaxation or meditation.

Another hypothesis suggested by the healing behavior of multiples involves the question of what is called "parallel processing" and healing. In most studies of the use of imagery, for example, the imagery or visualization procedure is attempted by subjects for specific, limited periods of time. However, multiples claim that their healing personalty is *always* at work . . . just because they are not "out" in the body does not mean that their function is ceased. This suggests that experiments could be conducted using post-hypnotic suggestion to in effect *continue* the visualization process at a subconscious level to discover if this would increase the effectiveness of the process. The importance of this idea was indirectly underscored by Dr. John Kihlstrom writing in *The Unconscious Reconsidered* (a book edited by Dr. Kenneth Bowers and Dr. Donald Meichenbaum):

If attention can be divided, with one stream of complex, deliberate cognitive activity proceeding outside of awareness, this seems to cause some problems for the way we usually think about things. The empirical basis for (neo-dissociation) theory is sometimes problematic, but as in the case of subliminal perception, all that is needed is one solid finding to change the way we think about the mind. . . . If we do not take these phenomena seriously, and consider their implications for our understanding of the cognitive system, our evolving model of the mind may be led seriously astray.

This kind of experiment could be conducted initially to study the rate of wound healing in people with simple surface cuts, or in burn victims. Recent work reported at the American Society of Clinical Hypnosis Meeting in San Francisco suggested that burn victims can be greatly helped by hypnosis, so some practical outcomes may emerge quickly from this kind of work.

We may also expect our knowledge of how the mind-brain system actually operates in terms of parallel processing to be informed by the study of multiples. If it is true that most of us are using only 10 to 20 percent of our capacity, then it would seem that multiples, via their access to advanced parallel processing skills, may well be using much more than the rest of us. The possibility of tapping into these potentials in a healthy context could have enormous impact for our knowledge of and access to learning skills, to name but one application.

The healthy use of dissociative states is a field perhaps waiting to happen, and the careful study of multiples will greatly add to the store of our knowledge on how to do that. This suggestion is not intended to convey the image of multiples as guinea pigs; rather, as one multiple put it: "If something positive and useful can be learned from us, then at least all the pain and suffering we have been put through might lead to something good and worthwhile in the world." □

—Brendan O'Regan

References and Further Reading

Special Issues of Journals

Four professional journals have published special issues devoted exclusively to multiple personality. They are the most comprehensive and authoritative sources of information about multiple personality disorder, and contain extensive lists of additional references. They are:

American Journal of Clinical Hypnosis, 26(2), October 1983.

International Journal of Clinical and Experimental Hypnosis, 32(2), April 1984.

Psychiatric Annals, 14(1), January 1984.

Psychiatric Clinics of North America, 7(1), March 1984.

Also see *Brain/Mind Bulletin*, 8(16), special issue on multiple personality.

Review Articles

Bliss, Eugene L. "Multiple Personalities: A Report of 14 Cases with Implications for Schizophrenia and Hypnosis," *Archives of General Psychiatry*, 37, December 1980, 1388–1397.

Greaves, George B. "Multiple Personality 165 Years after Mary Reynolds," *Journal of Nervous and Mental Disease*, 168(10), October 1980, 577–596.

Kenny, Michael G. "Multiple Personality and Spirit Possession," *Psychiatry*, 44(4), November 1981, 337–358.

Schenk, Laura and David Bear. "Multiple Personality and Related Dissociative Phenomena in Patients with Temporal Lobe Epilepsy," *American Journal of Psychiatry*, 138(10), October 1981, 1311–1316.

Sutcliffe, J. P. and Jean Jones. "Personal Identity, Multiple Personality, and Hypnosis." *International Journal of Clinical and Experimental Hypnosis*, 10(4), 1962, 231–269.

Taylor, W. S. and M. F. Martin. "Multiple Personality," *Journal of Abnormal and Social Psychology*, 49(3), 1944, 281–290.

Books

Most books about multiple personality disorder in recent decades have been single case accounts without extensive theoretical content. More rarely, a contemporary author has attempted to place multiple personality disorder in a broader theoretical context. By contrast, classics in the field from around the turn of the century have a strong theoretical or conceptual bias. Today, that work is being revived through the study of dissociative processes.

Case Accounts

Allison, Ralph, *Minds in Many Places*. Rawson Wade, 1980.

Cleckley, Hervey and Corbett Thigpen, *The Three Faces of Eve*. McGraw-Hill, 1957.

Keyes, Daniel. *The Minds of Billy Milligan*. Bantam, 1981.

Schreiber, Flora Rheta. *Sybil*. Warner, 1974.

Theory

McKellar, Peter, *Mindsplit*. J. M. Dent, 1979.

Beahrs, John. *Unity or Multiplicity*. Brunner/Mazel, 1981.

Historical References

Ellenberger, Henri. *The Discovery of the Unconscious*. Basic Books, 1970.

Janet, Pierre. *The Mental Life of Hystericals*. University Publications of America, 1977 (orig. 1901).

Myers, FWH *Human Personality and Its Survival of Bodily Death*. Longmans, Green, 1907.

Prince, Morton. *Psychotherapy and Multiple Personality*. Harvard University Press, 1975.

Prince, Morton. *The Dissociation of a Personality*. Longmans, Green, 1906.

Sidis, Boris and Simon Goodhart. *Multiple Personality*. Appleton, 1905.

Taylor, Eugene. *William James on Exceptional Mental States*. Scribner's, 1983 (lectures delivered 1896).

Dissociative Processes

Bowers, Kenneth and Donald Meichenbaum, eds. *The Unconscious Reconsidered*. Wiley, 1984.

Hilgard, Ernest. *Divided Consciousness: Multiple Controls in Human Thought and Action*. Wiley, 1977.

Since his first visit to the West in the early 1970s, His Holiness' reputation as a scholar and man of peace has grown steadily. In recent years, a number of Western universities and institutions have conferred Peace Awards and honorary Doctorate degrees upon His Holiness in recognition of his distinguished writings in Buddhist philosophy and of his distinguished leadership in the service of freedom and peace. One such Doctorate was conferred by Seattle University, Washington. The following extract from the University's citation reflects a widely held view of His Holiness' stature: "In the realm of mind and spirit, you have distinguished yourself in the rigorous academic tradition of the Buddhist universities, earning the Doctor's degree with the highest honors at the age of 25. In the midst of governmental and diplomatic affairs you nonetheless found time to teach and record in writing your keen insights in philosophy and the meaning of the contemplative life in the modern world. Your books represent a significant contribution not only to the vast body of Buddhist literature, but to the ecumenical dialogue of the great religions of the world. Your own dedication to the contemplative life of the Buddhist monk has won the admiration and awe not only of Buddhists, but of Christian contemplatives as well, including the contemplative monk Thomas Merton, whose friendship and conversation with you were mutually cherished."

from the Conference on Inner Science brochure

Buddhist Inner Science: An Overview

His Holiness the Fourteenth Dalai Lama received wide welcome on his recent 44-day visit to the United States, during which time he was the featured guest and speaker at a Conference on Inner Science, co-sponsored by the Institute of Noetic Sciences.

One purpose of the conference was to examine ways in which Buddhist psychology might inform Western psychology with new understandings of the workings of the mind. Reporting on the event for The New York Times, *psychologist Daniel Goleman states, "Eastern psychology . . . may be on its way toward greater appreciation in the West in large part as the result of an influential group of researchers in the United States. Their in-*

terest, unlike the faddish involvements with Eastern thought of the 1960s and 1970s, is serious and scholarly." The meeting was sponsored by the Department of Religion of Amherst College and organized by the American Institute of Buddhist Studies headed by Dr. Robert A. Thurman, and Nena Thurman.

The following is a compilation of excerpts from the Conference Preamble. A number of Western psychologists responded to this material, including Dr. Jack Engler whose paper appears on pages 9 - 11 of this Newsletter.

The in-depth transcript of His Holiness' presentation is with the American Institute of Buddhist Studies in Amherst, Massachusetts, and a book from the conference is in preparation.

By His Holiness the Dalai Lama and Robert A. F. Thurman

The Treasury of Clear Science salutes the Buddha not as the founder of a religion but as the founder of an empirical scientific tradition. When day dawned on the Bodhi-tree, the Buddha achieved a perfect understanding of the nature and structure of reality, rather than a revelation from any god. By examining the causes of things mental as well as physical he maintained an experimental attitude: the attitude of science.

Thus Buddhist Inner Science is not a religious panacea to be adopted wholesale. It is a *scientific tradition* within the broader Buddhist communities that can be broadened, intensified, and implemented on an unprecedented scale in the modern culture. It does *not* depend on religious faith, or on any sort of "Eastern mentality". It is eminently rational, "Western", practical and effective. The Buddha himself began this way:

> Monks! Sages accept my words after careful testing
>
> As a goldsmith buys his gold only after examination
>
> By burning, cutting, and rubbing—
>
> And never just out of devotion to my person.

According to this tradition, the aim of science is enlightenment—the attainable state of understanding beyond all obscurity; the purpose of both science and enlightenment is to free living beings from suffering.

Since the Buddha, himself, discovered the Truth by examining the nature of inner and outer realities, he was more concerned with leading others to this understanding than with instilling beliefs in them. To teach a way to that understanding, he speaks of a Dharma or Truth, not a mere dogma but a doctrine of experiment and practice leading to reality itself. Although the Buddha's enlightenment is considered total, the complete solution of all problems and the perfect success in all scientific inquiries, it is not dogmatic or authoritarian; it insists that each person must become omniscient him/herself, and that he/she can only do so by investigating the world, learning about it, and cultivating the Higher Wisdom.

Thus Buddhism was free of the antipathy to empirical science found in anti-rational forms of theism. In Buddhism, faith and reason are not opposed, but are considered mutually reinforcing. In Buddhism, science or knowledge is not disembodied from will and emotion, from values and life. Thus the Dharma includes the higher education of mind through meditation—the religious, contemplative cultivation of positive states of mind—as well as higher education in ethics.

The Realm of Mind

Physics has provided the basis for the design of the fission and fusion bombs, biology—germ warfare, chemistry—nerve gas. And all of them have helped bring us to the brink of doom. But they still do not provide keys to ultimate power. If we do destroy ourselves, it will be the minds of human beings, the unhealthy emotions of individuals, the fear, the hate, the jealousy, and the greed of individuals that will trigger these horrors.

Obviously these emotions can only be controlled, reshaped and rechanneled by each individual, with techniques developed from a comprehensive, precise and effective Inner Science. For this reason, the Buddha focused on the language of "mind", and on its understanding and control. He rejected the fixed-identity "immortal soul" of his contemporary Vedic theists. But he also rejected the nihilism of the dogmatic materialists of his time who denied any sort of living, changing, energy-pattern of subjectivity.

The Buddha observed an individual continuity which he called the "conventional self", the "mind", "consciousness", or "soul". His introspection discovered a realm of subtle energy forces too fine to be dealt with reductionistically through materialistic language—a realm of mind, of living energy, of soul, of boundless life.

25 Centuries of Tradition

The Buddhist Inner Scientists formulated the *Clear Science Great Treatise* and its branches as a residue of centuries of therapeutic and transformative work with hundreds of thousands of entrants to the Community. Their clinics and laboratories were the monasteries that spread all over India in the five hundred years after Buddha, and began to spread all over Asia from around the third century BCE. The steady accumulation of research literature, training curricula and manuals for personal development continued as well as the evolution of monasteries into universities in the first half of the first millennium CE.

The latter half of the first millennium CE witnessed an exquisite flowering in India of the planet's highest and gentlest civilization of that time, but it eventually fell prey to less civilized invaders, and the Muslim conquests of the turn of the millennium appeared to be fatal. The monastic universities were wiped out along with Buddhism, village Brahminism being all that was allowed to remain.

After India fell, China, Korea, Japan and Southeast Asia all pre-

His Holiness the Dalai Lama with Robert Thurman and Thomas Hurley of the Institute staff

served something of the Clear Science traditions, but none of these lands received the full literature and practice. It was nearby yet inaccessible Tibet that preserved the great bulk of the traditions for a thousand years. Tibetan researchers, experimenters, scholars, philosophers and teachers developed theory even further, synthesized the vast Indian literature into practical manuals and preserved the living vitality of the tradition through their own unceasing study, inquiry, meditation and teaching. The present devastation of the Tibetan civilization has not terminated that vitality, and the meeting with modern "inner science" has already been stimulating within the tradition itself.

Western Second Renaissance

We offer what we have developed in Tibet to help you of the West to return the Inner Science to the centrality it should logically have. Our prayer for now is that you can re-discover Inner Science and experience a "Second Renaissance". The Eastern civilizations that flourished in the atmosphere of the Buddha Enlightenment can serve as the Greece of this new Renaissance. As the world knows, your outer sciences display an admirable determination to deal with each problem in a rigorous, rational and technically exacting manner. You can apply this same determination to a renewed study of the intangible: of the mind, even the religious territory of the spirit and soul. If you do so with fearless persistence, then there is absolutely no question in our mind that you can succeed in triumphing over the great danger of global holocaust.

You can use Inner Science to educate each individual to understand himself or herself, to control his or her negative emotions and distorted notions, and to cultivate his or her highest potentials of love and wisdom. And you can keep improving your Outer Sciences to better understand, control and beautify the environment for the greater benefit of all beings. There is an enormous amount of work to be done. Let us begin it here and now. ☐

The Clear Science Mind/Function Model

The unhappiness and suffering that we experience arise through our inability to control our own minds, and the happiness that we wish to achieve will only be achieved by learning to control our minds.

—His Holiness, the Fourteenth Dalai Lama, Opening Remarks

At the opening session, His Holiness elaborated on The Clear Science Mind/Function Model, explaining that its practice was not an intellectual exercise; rather it is an "attested fact" that a detailed analytic understanding of a particular mental process complemented by meditative practice gives control over the process and potential freedom from its influence.

Analytic understanding of the atomic components of blind rage, for example —what triggers it, how it directs itself, how it mobilizes mental, verbal, and physical energies—enables a habitually angry person to begin to control his or her temper, perhaps finally to become free of its domination.

The Buddha's teaching was that such analytic understanding, become higher wisdom, is the faculty that can remove the obstructions to liberation, to Nirvana. The analytic models of the mind are like finely ground lenses of the microscope or telescope of expert focused meditation, which enable the inner scientist to see the micro or macro dimensions of the inner universes.

The following outline of the Clear Science Mind/Function Model discussed in the Dalai Lama's very detailed presentation provides some sense of the rigor of this Buddhist practice.

A. Ubiquitous functions
  1. Sensation
  2. Recognition
  3. Intention
  4. Cohesion
  5. Attention
B. Determinative functions
  1. Interest
  2. Fixation
  3. Memory
  4. Concentration
  5. Intelligence
C. Virtuous functions
  1. Faith
  2. Conscience
  3. Sense of shame
  4. Non-attachment
  5. Non-hatred
  6. Non-delusion
  7. Diligence
  8. Fluency
  9. Vigilance
  10. Equanimity
  11. Non-violence
D. Root afflictions
  1. Lust
  2. Hate
  3. Pride
  4. Ignorance
  5. Doubt
  6. Prejudice
E. Twenty derivative afflictions
  1. Fury
  2. Vindictiveness
  3. Irresponsibility
  4. Resentment
  5. Jealousy
  6. Selfishness
  7. Pretension
  8. Hypocrisy
  9. Arrogance
  10. Cruelty
  11. Ruthlessness
  12. Shamelessness
  13. Lethargy
  14. Excitement
  15. Faithlessness
  16. Laziness
  17. Carelessness
  18. Forgetfulness
  19. Indiscretion
  20. Distraction
F. Variable functions
  1. Sleep
  2. Guilt
  3. Appreciation
  4. Examination

His Holiness also cautioned:

The Buddha's basic attitude toward conceptualization is that reality, which includes human life and experience, is always elusive to words and ideas, uncapturable by any description, and irreducible to any formula. Thus no construction corresponds to reality. It presents at best only a useful perspective.

So a particular model is only devised for a specific context, a practical purpose. This must be kept firmly in mind in surveying the variety of models within the Inner Science tradition. If you forget and think "This is what they think the mind really is!"; or even, "Ah, so they used to think there was such a thing as 'mind'!" then you will miss the point entirely. ☐

Placebos and Healing:

A New Look at the "Sugar Pill"

David L. Smith

by **Thomas J. Hurley III**

Editor's Note: This article is adapted from the current issue of the Institute's research bulletin Investigations, *which focuses on Placebo Effects. Each issue of* Investigations *features an in-depth look at a specific topic pertaining to mind/body interactions and consciousness research. Previous issues presented state-of-the-art overviews of Psychoneuroimmunology and Multiple Personality Research; forthcoming issues will examine Unconscious Processes and Positive Emotions Research. Single issues and bulk copies of* Investigations *are available through the Institute's Publications Service.*

Surprisingly enough, a process which has been the mainstay of medical practice throughout history has played almost no part in the impressive advance of scientific medicine in this century. How a person effects his or her own healing through a *placebo response* remains one of the mysteries of modern medicine.

The mystery of placebo effects is the mystery of the mind's role in health and healing. How can a mere sugar pill—the prototypical placebo—relieve severe pain? More generally, how can any treatment which has no characteristic physiological action relevant to the problem for which it is prescribed nonetheless effect both subjective and objective improvement in that problem?

That placebo effects occur is an open secret. Clues to their frequency, extent and magnitude are scattered throughout the medical literature. A 1955 study by Dr. Henry K. Beecher serves as a benchmark for scientific studies of the placebo.

Writing in the *Journal of the American Medical Association*, Beecher reported that an analysis of 15 studies, involving 1,082 patients, showed that placebos used in place of regular medication consistently produced improvement in a wide range of disorders. On the average, *35% of the patients to whom placebos were given experienced satisfactory relief from them*—despite the fact that the placebos should have had no objective effect on their condition.

The conditions which responded to placebos included wound pain, the pain of angina pectoris, headache, seasickness and nausea, the common cold, and anxiety and tension, according to Beecher. Subsequent reviews of placebo research have corroborated both that placebos affect a wide range of disorders and that approximately one-third of any group will strongly respond to them.

Nevertheless, among many physicians the prevalent attitude toward placebos is still one of disdain. "Apparently," Drs. Sherman Ross and L. W. Buckalew recently commented in *Placebos: Theory, Research and Mechanisms*, "some disciplines, or at least some of their practitioners, fear that recognition of placebo effects and the powerful influence a placebo can have detracts from their power, authority, and expertise, and ultimately serves as a source of embarrassment." Drs. Jon Levine and Newton Gordon of the University of California at San Francisco have further observed, "A physician who administers a placebo may be considered unethical, and the patient who responds to it may be regarded as a malingerer with no real disease."

Since psychological processes mediate placebo effects, it is sometimes believed that only complaints which are psychological in origin respond to placebos. Actually, placebos are just as effective at relieving "real" pain and at healing "real" disorders as they are at altering emotional states or cognitive processes. While in most cases the physical pathways mediating these changes remain almost wholly unknown, an increasing number of physicians and researchers see the placebo effect as additional evidence that physiological and psychological processes intricately and unavoidably interact in healing.

"The placebo is proof that there is no real separation between mind and body," Norman Cousins has written. "Illness is always an interaction between both."

The territory of placebo effects is still largely an unmapped one. Certain key features are well known, but major theoretical and methodological questions abound. Attempting to answer them, researchers are drawing an ever more fascinating picture of placebo phenomena.

Varieties of Placebo Experience

Like many physicians, most people think of the placebo as an inert substance such as a sugar pill with no recognized physiological mechanism of action or effect pertaining to the disorder for which it is prescribed. They also think that placebos work only because the patients for whom they are prescribed do not know they are receiving placebos. Yet some placebos are neither inert nor pills—and some placebos have worked even when patients knew they were getting placebos!

"The placebo is proof that there is no real separation between mind and body."

—*Norman Cousins*

In contrast to an inactive or inert placebo, an *active placebo* is one which *has* some characteristic physiological effect although not for the condition which it is given to treat. An excellent example of an active placebo treatment, according to Dr. Andrew Weil, is the prescription of antibiotics for virally induced sore throats. Despite the fact that antibiotics are ineffective against viruses (they do work against bacterial infections), many patients will experience rapid relief of their symptoms.

"How does an antibiotic cure a viral sore throat?" Weil asks in *Health and Healing*. "It can do so only by eliciting a placebo response, and the prevalence of such cures indicates the extent of real faith in the power of antibiotics on the part of both doctors and patients."

The pill-giving ritual elicits the expectant faith which triggers healing through the placebo effect. Other treatments may also function as placebos when they elicit the same faith. Successful placebo treatments have included injections of both active and inactive substances, surgery and biofeedback.

A particularly impressive example of a non-drug placebo treatment can be found in studies done during the late 1950s. At that time, a surgical procedure known as internal mammary ligation (which involved tying off certain arteries in the chest) was becoming increasingly popular as a treatment for the pain of angina pectoris, and enthusiastic researchers had published papers purporting to document its effectiveness. Yet additional controlled research showed that this surgical procedure *was no more effective for the relief of angina pain than was "sham surgery" in which an incision was made in the chest* (so that patients *believed* surgery had been done) *but in which no arteries were actually ligated*. In other words, the supposedly effective surgical procedure was no more effective than a placebo!

In these studies, as in most research involving placebos, patients who received placebo treatments were unaware of the fact. This element of *deception* in the use of placebos is one reason many physicians are reluctant to use them. They fear that if discovered the deception would undermine the trust on which the physician-patient relationship is founded. But as mentioned earlier, exploratory studies show that some patients respond therapeutically to placebos even when they know precisely what they are getting. In the most frequently cited case of this kind, Drs. Lee Park and Lino Covi administered placebos to fourteen psychiatric outpatients suffering from somatic symptoms and specifically told them that they were receiving sugar pills. Thirteen nevertheless reported relief, including objec-

Placebo: The Healer Within

A dramatic example of a placebo effect was reported by Dr. Bruno Klopfer in 1957. According to Klopfer, a man with severe cancer insisted that he be given an experimental drug called Krebiozen, then considered by its proponents to be a "miracle cure" for cancer. After a single dose of the drug, the man's cancerous masses "melted like snowballs on a hot stove" and he was able to resume normal activities. Later, however, the man read that studies had shown Krebiozen to be ineffective. His cancer began spreading again. Acting on a hunch, his doctor urged the patient not to believe the studies he had read. The doctor then treated the man with an "improved" Krebiozen. In fact, the doctor gave his patient only water. Nevertheless, the man's condition once more improved significantly! He continued to recover until he again read that the worthlessness of Krebiozen had been conclusively proven. Several days later, he died.

The placebo effect is a poorly understood process in which psychological processes such as belief and expectation trigger a healing response that can be as powerful as any conventional therapy—be it drugs, surgery or psychotherapy—for a wide range of medical and psychological problems. Placebos represent, in the words of Norman Cousins, "the doctor who resides within". The full extent and magnitude of placebo effects is still unknown, although clues to both their pervasive character and their power have existed in the medical literature for decades. Today, a new generation of investigators is emerging who could make significant strides toward breaking the code which has kept the secrets of the "doctor within" hidden for so long.

The range of medical problems, psychiatric disorders and psychological functions for which researchers have elicited placebo effects includes:

Medical problems

- Angina pectoris and essential hypertension.
- Cancer.
- Rheumatoid and degenerative arthritis.
- Peptic ulcers and nausea.
- Migraine headaches.
- Allergies and acne.
- Radiation sickness.
- Hayfever and cough.
- Multiple sclerosis.
- Diabetes.
- Organic brain disorders such as parkinsonism.
- Pain from a variety of sources

Psychiatric syndromes

- Depression.
- Anxiety.
- Schizophrenia.

Psychologically-sensitive functions

- Reaction time.
- Grip strength.
- Pulse rate.
- Blood pressure.
- Short-term rote memory.
- Mood changes.
- Self-perceptions of relaxation and activation.

tive symptom reduction, from the pills!

Other remarkable examples of placebo phenomena could be cited to illustrate additional features of this odd terrain. Placebos too have side effects, for example, as witnessed recently in a chemotherapy experiment in which 30.8% of those patients who received placebos (as a control group) lost their hair! Yet for all the intriguing data, placebo effects are still elusive and ill-understood. The psychological systems involved have only been described in the most general terms—suggestion, expectation and anxiety reduction are the processes most commonly implicated—and only in the case of placebo analgesia, in which the endorphins have been implicated, has a physiological mechanism for placebo effects been identified.

New Directions

Eventually, researchers hope to be able to trace a complete "placebo circuit", from the administration of therapy to the individual's conscious and unconscious thoughts and feelings to the physiological changes that occur in the impaired organ or system—and to do this for different cases of placebo healing. It is in the case of placebo analgesia that they have taken a step to fulfill this vision.

In 1978, Drs. Jon Levine, Newton Gordon and Howard Fields reported in the medical journal *Lancet* that placebos appeared to modulate pain relief through endorphins, the brain's own painkilling substances. Levine and his colleagues found that among dental patients suffering from post-operative pain caused by the extraction of an impacted tooth, those patients given a placebo experienced statistically significant reductions in pain compared to those given naloxone, a substance that blocks the action of endorphins. If those who responded to the placebo with pain relief later received naloxone, their pain increased to the levels experienced both by those who failed to respond to the placebo and by those who initially received naloxone. Since naloxone undid the analgesia derived from the placebo, Levine and his colleagues concluded that there is an endorphin-mediated component to placebo pain relief.

Subsequent studies have raised the possibility that both endorphin- and non-endorphin-mediated pathways are involved in placebo analgesia. Regardless, work in this area has been invaluable in rekindling interest in placebos and their effects. Several new developments now characterize the field.

1. *Researchers are seeking to identify and trace the physiological mechanisms of placebo action.* While the "endorphin connection" is the best established example of a placebo pathway, others must exist. The editors of the new volume *Placebos: Theory, Research and Mechanisms*, Drs. Leonard White, Bernard Tursky and Gary Schwartz, have noted, "There is no single placebo effect having a single mechanism and efficacy, but rather a multiplicity of effects, with differential efficacy and mechanisms." While these are still unknown, researchers can now begin to make some sophisticated guesses about their nature based on a growing understanding of how psychological processes such as stress and the positive emotions influence physiological processes and health.

2. *Researchers are refining their models of the mediating, or psychological, processes involved in placebo responding.* The psychological dimension of the placebo effect is easily recognized. Since placebos are usually substances which are administered because they are known to have no characteristic physiological effect on the disorder being treated, any change *must* result from the activity of psychological processes such as the patient's beliefs and expectations, which in turn mediate neuro- or psychophysiological processes. Cognitive expectancy theories and conditioning paradigms are among the new models contemporary researchers are using to understand how faith, expectation and such "intangibles" as hope and the will to live can elicit or enhance healing.

3. *More sophisticated research methodologies are being developed.* Growing awareness of the multitude of possible variables which can influence how placebos will affect those who receive them is leading to recognition of the need for multifactorial research designed to systematically identify and evaluate each of them.

4. *Interest in potential clinical uses of the placebo is growing.* Several proposals have been made for the constructive clinical use of placebos. They might serve as therapeutic agents in situations where an active agent is inadvisable or works too slowly, or in drug withdrawal or drug reduction

© 1979 by Sidney Harris.
From Chicken Soup and Other Medical Matters, *with permission*

"It was more of a *'triple*-blind' test. The patients didn't know which ones were getting the real drug, the doctors didn't know, and, I'm afraid nobody knew."

regimes. They can be used as substitutes for an active drug under a conditioning paradigm. Finally, according to Dr. Frederick Evans, placebos can also be used as diagnostic tools. In an interview, Evans noted that the patient who responds to a placebo "is likely to have, at some cognitive level, the resources to be able to influence, modulate, and control his or her pain" or other symptom. The question for the physician, therapist or nurse-practitioner then becomes how to further enlist the patient's self-healing capacities in the therapeutic process.

5. *New conceptual approaches are being applied to placebo phenomena.* White, Tursky and Schwartz propose the use of a *systems approach* to integrate the range of physiological, psychological, social and cultural variables that figure in placebo effects.

These and other developments clearly represent the beginning of a new phase in studies of the placebo—a phase in which placebo effects are recognized as valuable phenomena in their own right, and their theoretical and clinical significance is systematically explored. "It now seems that a series of new trends and developments in the biological and human sciences are making the climate more favorable for a re-consideration of the placebo

effect," said Brendan O'Regan of the Institute of Noetic Sciences in *Investigations*.

"Among them is the recent focus in the neurosciences on the degree to which the brain possesses capacities for change and self-repair—that is, its plasticity. As a result we know that the nervous system has previously unsuspected flexibilities in its repertoire of responses, and these may one day account for the effects seen in placebo research. In addition, the discovery of the now more than 50 different neuropeptides, including the endorphins, and other molecules mediating the brain's responses also seems to provide an additional avenue of explanation for placebo effects. Finally, the recent resurgence of interest in unconscious processes, and the increasing understanding of the mind's capacity for parallel processing of many kinds of stimuli—both conscious and preconscious—opens up lines of reasoning about placebo effects that were previously not known."

Fully capturing the substance and spirit of the "new look" in placebo research, he concludes, "Hopefully, this will mean that one more important facet of the mind/body system will fall into place and allow us to create treatment techniques that truly mobilize the whole human being's capacity for healing." □

Beyond Sports:

Imaging in Daily Life

**An Interview
with Marilyn King
by Barbara McNeill**

photo by Ralph Merlino

Editor's note: Visualization and imagery are familiar tools for Marilyn King, whose expertise developed over a twenty year athletic career, which included being on two Olympic teams as a Pentathlete. Long before sports psychology popularized these techniques, King and other athletes were using them daily to enhance their performance in competition. Their successful use demonstrates very concretely and dramatically the interaction between mind and body—for example the effect on performance of self image or of running "mental movies" of successfully completing an event.

A powerful example of the use of visualization comes from Marilyn's own experience preparing for the 1980 Olympic trials. Nine months before the trials, she suffered a severe back injury and was confined to bed. There she spent four months doing nothing but watching films of the best performers in the pentathlon events, and visualizing and feeling herself going through the same events. Despite her lack of physical preparation, she placed second at the Olympic trials. It was her psychological state, not her physical condition, she emphasizes, that made this victory possible.

Marilyn is Director of Beyond Sports, an organization seeking to extend the application of visualization, imagery and related skills from sports to a broader arena of individual and social issues. The Institute of Noetic Sciences recently awarded her a grant to help develop some of the ideas expressed in this interview, especially as they relate to education, empowerment of women and world peace.

INSTITUTE: How are you making the connections between what you learned in sports and some of your broader areas of concern?

KING: First, through sports I teach people the conscious use of their innate capacity to visualize. I help people understand and experience that the images they create are not random—that they do have real power. Visualization is like having a television set, with one difference. With visualization there's no on and off. The picture is always on. We are constantly creating images and these images affect our daily lives.

What we need, therefore, is to become aware and to learn to control the channels.

INS: As an athlete what has been your experience with visualization?

KING: In sports we use three kinds of visualization. There's visual imagery which means being able to project a visual image of yourself, kinetic imagery which means feeling or physically sensing as opposed to seeing (as a long jumper I could actually feel my body going through the motions), and auditory imagery. We usually use these three in combination. For example as you are standing on the long jump runway at the beginning of the event you *see* yourself accelerating, you *feel* the wind resistance, and you *hear* your footsteps as you accelerate.

We use these in three different areas. One is long-term goal orientation. A dramatic example of this is the case of Roger Bannister who, in the face of absolute "irrefutable" scientific evidence that the human being could not run faster than four minutes in the mile, had an image of being able to break the four minute mile. This proved to have been a *psychological*, not a physiological, block because within the same year that Roger Bannister broke the four minute mile, 52 other men broke the record too.

Second, we use imagery to envision, step by step, how we're going to accomplish that goal. That usually involves developing strategy with a coach and is a very specific science.

The third place we use imagery is in the competitive arena. We use the process of centering or concentration to eliminate outside distractions and focus inward. We also make "mental movies" prior to our performance in a particular event. Take, for example, the high jump. Currently the men's high jump record is 7 feet 10 inches. If we were to stand 60 feet back and look at the bar, or worse still walk up under it, most of us would be totally unable to imagine jumping over it. So one of the first things we as athletes have to learn to do is to imagine. I stand on the lift off, inhale, exhale, center and run a mental movie imagining myself as I take my first step, second step, accelerate through the curve, plant my foot, my body rises up over, my body arches backward, I visualize the successful completion of what it is that I am now about to attempt. Notice the level of detail in all this.

The possibilities for using imagery in sports are infinite. Basically they involve our ability to envision both a goal as well as the steps to achieving it.

INS: What has been your experience in sports with the role of belief systems?

KING: Before any significant accomplishments, there has to be something I call "the crack"—borrowing a term from Joseph Chilton Pearce.

> *I emphasize two things—internally motivated commitment to a goal, and the ability to image that goal in detail. When a person says "I* **wish** *I could become an Olympic athlete," that is actually a negative image, emphasizing what I am not. It's a step forward to affirm that "I* **want** *. . .", and it is still more powerful to imagine that "I* **will** *be an Olympian". But the most effective process is to affirm and imagine, as though it were really happening, "I* **am** *an Olympian". This profoundly integrates both the qualities of commitment and imagination.*
>
> *—Marilyn King*

Before I can make the commitment that I will be on the Olympic team, I have to have had some kind of crack in my own reality that allows me to think that maybe I could. There has to be a kind of consciousness shift—a window that opens up to allow me to see another possibility.

I'm interested in developing ways we can open these kinds of windows for people. I know of one technique that we use in track and field. My own coach Ed Parker taught me to use it with the high jump. In this event, particularly since the advent of the "Fosbry flop", you convert horizontal speed to vertical lift. Theoretically, the faster you can run, the more speed you have to convert. Now, jumpers usually warm up and train by jumping over very small ranges of height, varying the bar by six inches above the athlete's best jump. Ed Parker taught me to raise the bar as much as a full foot. Ordinarily athletes are absolutely positive, when they look at the bar that much higher, that they'll never clear it. I tell them to back up their approach by two or three feet and generate more speed which will convert into height.

Typically the athlete accelerates, plants a foot and "boom" . . . although they are incapable of controlling all that speed, they explode off the ground and find themselves higher in the air than they've ever been as a jumper. They are out of control but "woah"! They get it. They know they can jump much higher than previously imagined. When we lower the bar back down to the appropriate level they start to train with a very different image of their own potential and their own ability.

What we've done is to break through their worst limit—their belief about what they are capable of doing.

For me, the value of coaching doesn't lie in creating a stable of 7 foot 6 inch high jumpers, but in showing athletes that the first step to a stunning achievement is believing that you can do it. That's the power that sports has.

INS: How would you carry that principle beyond sports?

KING: For one thing, as educators we must help young people transfer that inspiration to reach beyond sports to other arenas. As long as kids cannot imagine, or are not allowed to imagine, being high achievers, doors slam shut on exciting possibilities. Dare them to mentally rehearse what it would be like if they really could . . . perfect their routine, finish high school and go on to college, travel to another country, get along with their parents, speak a foreign language, whatever. As long as a youngster can't imagine getting a passing grade in math, she won't even make the attempt. Were she able to use the critical lessons from sports, however—if she somehow breaks through and makes the mental movie, mentally sees herself pulling that impossible grade—she'll feel more positive about the steps to getting there: paying attention in class, doing her homework, asking for extra help.

With a visualization breakthrough under their belts, children are far more receptive to mastering the practical tools for realizing their new ambitions. They want to know about long and short range planning and goal setting—about how to decide on priorities. Once a kid grasps that potential is a state of mind, once a negative self-fulfilling prophecy begins to be replaced by a new script, a new film loop, watch out. Kids have tremendous energy. They want to learn how to work methodically, to achieve the goals they set for themselves.

INS: Where else do you see applications of these principles?

KING: Most people need to understand that once you dare to imagine something you begin to be flooded with ideas about how to realize that image. We know that visualization is what Charlie Garfield calls the "master skill" of high achievers and that it is an innate ability we all possess.

INS: So the lesson from sports is that visualization and imagery are key elements in significant accomplishment?

KING: Yes. But there's more. What any of us can actually accomplish depends on an energy source to fuel the effort. For example, people assume that it took a tremendous amount of will power and discipline for me to achieve what I did on the Olympic level. While that may be true, I was never in touch with either will power or discipline. What I did know every morning when I woke up was that there was nothing I wanted more on the face of this earth than to be an Olympian. You don't have to have will power to get out of bed to go do your favorite thing. You bound out of bed. The fuel for sustaining that kind of intensity, for feeling empowered and energized, is desire.

Most people know what it feels like to call on this resource. A few people spend whole lifetimes operating at maximum capacity. The critical difference is desire. I'm sure that you, for example, have at some points in your life functioned or performed at a level far above usual. I'll bet you find that those times of exceedingly high productivity were times when you were motivated by a feeling that came from deep inside you. An ordinary person who taps into desire will access inner strength and hidden resources that they never knew they had. Desire allows you

to focus on one specific goal and to pursue it at all costs.

INS: I'm inspired just listening to you. You are reminding me of times I'd forgotten.

KING: Yes, and if we look back and focus on those times, we can pull out what were the important ingredients in that performance of yours, that achievement of yours. You can call on those resources again and really fine tune them as tools you can use more readily.

Once you dare to imagine your goal, you are flooded with ideas about how to realize that image

Finally, daily commitment is an essential component. When you're talking about peak performance in any area—especially something like the Olympics of global peace—you have to make a 150% commitment to it. This is one of those things that people don't understand about commitment to goals at that level. During the process of my Olympic career, absolutely everything I did was in the service of my goal. If you saw me sitting in the laundromat, I was getting my clothes cleaned *now*, so that I could go work out *then*. The kind of food that I ate, how many hours I slept, when I took my vacation, whom I spent my time with—everything was in the service of my goal. When you set a goal like that, everything either contributes to or detracts from it. There is nothing in between.

INS: What are you doing to tie these principles to issues of global peace?

KING: One of the most recent things I've been working on is the concept of an International Peace Team of Athletes. I know that some people

say that sports and politics should be kept separate. But they are not aware that the first principle of the Olympic charter is to foster friendship and understanding through sports.

The Olympic experience can be a blueprint for what is necessary to achieve the ultimate success—peace on the planet. For one thing, athletes have a history of accomplishing the seemingly impossible. Most people cannot imagine being on the Olympic team or breaking a world record. But athletes can imagine the "unimaginable". World peace currently fits into that category. Also athletes know that if you have a dream you must do something every day in order to make that dream a reality. There are many other parallels between athletic success and global peace, having to do with fears and risks, teamwork, and personal satisfaction.

But the essence of the lessons from sports are, as I said earlier, desire, vision and commitment. The peace team is a vision of living in peace. As athletes who have represented this country around the world, we know that people are more alike than they are different. All people have the same basic needs and desires for security, love, and fulfillment. It's very encouraging to hear astronauts and musicians saying that we are all on the same team.

I haven't yet fully developed the implications of this plan, but I think it's a powerful idea. As athletes we do have a platform. Young and old people see athletes as heros and role models. The press is tuned in to athletes' lives. Finally, a network already exists for communicating our message.

Achieving peace on this planet is like winning the gold medal for the International Peace Team. It is a monumental task and any athlete can tell you what it takes. I hope to enlist my fellow athletes to carry the torch for world peace. When the world looks at a Mary Lou Retton they have a living visualization of what desire, vision and commitment can accomplish.

For more information about Marilyn King's work, write Beyond Sports, 484-149 Lake Park Avenue, Oakland, CA 94610. □

Altered States of Consciousness and the Possibility of Survival of Death

by Charles T. Tart, PhD

Selections from a Presentation for
The Symposium on Consciousness and Survival
co-sponsored by the Institute of Noetic Sciences
in cooperation with the Office of Smithsonian Symposia and Seminars
at Georgetown University, Washington, DC

Editors' note: *The presentation summarized here was one of nine from a panel of distinguished scholars and scientists, convened by the Institute of Noetic Sciences to address the question: does individual consciousness survive bodily death? This question raised related questions, equally provocative. What is the nature of mind? What is the nature of consciousness? Psychologist Dr. Charles Tart approaches these issues from the perspective of his work with altered states of consciousness (which include, for example, meditative states, hypnotic trance, dream states, states of sensory deprivation). Tart reviews the contributions of parapsychological research to the "survival question", and suggests directions for future investigation.*

The essence of the ideas I want to share is expressed in the following two sentences:

First, after some intital shock and confusion resulting from the process of dying, I will not be too surprised if I regain consciousness.

Second, I will be quite surprised if "I" regain consciousness.

To put it more precisely, I will not be too surprised if I regain some kind of consciousness after death, but that consciousness may be of a quite different sort than the ordinary state of consciousness I am accustomed to. Further, I doubt that "I", in the sense of my ordinary self, will be the self that regains some sort of consciousness.

By thinking about survival in terms of our ordinary, taken-for-granted "I" surviving, we have inadvertently confused the issue, so it is no wonder that we do not have a clear answer about the possibility of survival.

What we call "I" is actually quite changeable from minute to minute, rather than being as fixed as we like to think it is. Some of these forms of "I" occur often, so it is useful, especially if we are interested in personal growth, to speak of our many "I"s or subselves (Tart, in press). Many of these ordinary "I"s do not long "survive" (in the sense of maintaining their presence and integrity) the small changes of ordinary life, like strong emotions, hunger, sexual desire, fatigue, alcohol. If ordinary "I"s cannot survive these minor shocks, how could ordinary "I"s survive the vastly greater shock of death?

The question "Will I survive death?" cannot really be satisfactorily answered except as a subset of the larger question "Who and what am I?" This is the central question I will address as we explore the issue of survival of death.

The Nature of Ordinary Consciousness and of Altered States

Let us look briefly at the nature of ordinary consciousness (and the ordinary "I"s associated with it), and at the nature of altered states of consciousness, as background for examining the survival question.

Ordinary consciousness is a semi-arbitrary construction. In the course of growing up we have built up huge numbers of habits: ways of perceiving, of thinking, of feeling, of acting. The automated functioning of these habits in our ordinary environment constitute a system, the pattern we call our ordinary consciousness. Ordinary consciousness is stabilized, so it holds itself together in spite of varying circumstances. Forgetting the work that went into constructing this as children, and not realizing the cultural relativity and arbitrariness of much of it, we take it for granted as "ordinary" or "normal" consciousness.

We usually think of survival in terms of the survival of personality. Note though that personality, the set of characteristic behaviors and statements that distinguishes us from others, manifests through our state of consciousness. For our purposes here, "personality" and "state of consciousness" are largely synonymous. Every one of the psychological processes underlying ordinary consciousness can undergo drastic changes. To mention just a few: An ordinary face can be seen as that of an angel or devil. I don't mean *interpreted* here. I mean actually perceived. Your heart can be felt as a glowing mass of radiant energy instead of only a barely perceptible pulsation in your chest. Your memories can seem like those of someone else, or you may "remember" things that intellectually you know could not be known to you--yet they are "obviously" your memories. Totally new systems of thought can come into play for evaluating reality. What is most dear to you may change drastically. Space and time can function in whole new ways as in experiencing eternity.

Usually many of these sorts of changes occur simultaneously, and when they do we talk about experiencing an "altered state of consciousness". The change is too radical to see it as a variation of your ordinary state. It is qualitatively as well as quantitatively different.

The Dream State

To further our understanding of altered states, let us look at the most commonly occurring one, nighttime dreaming. Modern sleep research has shown that we all spend about 20% of our sleep time in a specific brain wave state associated with the mental activity of dreaming, whether we remember it or not.

In order to dream we must go to and remain asleep, i.e., we must induce an altered state of consciousness. Usually this means reducing exteroception (our processes for sensing the external world) and interoception (processes that give us information about internal body state) to very low levels. We turn out the lights and close our eyes, eliminating visual input, for example. We relax our bodies and don't move, eliminating interoceptive kinesthetic input. If we survive death in some form we will certainly not have the physical exteroceptors and interoceptors we had during life, so this customary input would be drastically reduced as in dreaming.

Further, we now know that there is a very active inhibition of what input does reach our receptors. If you deliberately stimulate a sleeper, but not intensely enough to wake him, and then awaken him and get a report, you find that most stimuli do not make it through into the dream world. The few that do are usually distorted so they fit in with the ongoing dream. Calling the dreamer's name, for example, could become another dream character asking him about the state of his health! If an after-death state is like a dream state, might similar distortions of our questions to the deceased occur?

Similarly our sense of identity, our emotions, and our evaluation processes can operate quite differently, as if the dream were of someone else with different emotional reactions and styles of timing. What is sensible by dream standards may be outrageous by waking state standards. The space/time sense is totally changed. If such alteration of the processing styles of emotion, evaluation, sense of identity and space/time sense occurs routinely in dreams while alive, why couldn't these and other alterations occur after death? Suppose the after-death state is more like a dream state than an ordinary conscious state? Would someone who knew your personality in its ordinary state recognize your personality in something closer to its dream state?

Let us look at another common characteristic of dreams: Dreams usually seem to just happen to us, rather than feeling like our active creations. Who is creating this world and these actions? Where does the scenery come from? How do various actors know when to come on stage? If the after-death state is like nighttime dreaming, will it be so passive? From the after-death side of things will we care about helping to prove our survival?

The subconscious is given the credit for the intelligent and active creation of dreams, since the dreamer declines credit. This is not a terribly good explanation, of course, but it is the best we have at this time--and a good reminder of how little we understand about our minds. If such a potent source of experience as dreams is controlled by mental processes we hardly understand at all, it reminds us of how careful we must be in extrapolating the characteristics of waking consciousness to the possible after-death state.

State Specific Knowledge and Altered States

One of the most important qualities of knowledge is that it is state-specific. *What you can know depends on the state of consciousness you are in.*

A simple analogy is using a net to troll through the ocean. If your net has a one inch mesh, it will not pick up anything that is smaller than an inch, thus excluding an enormous amount of life. If you understand this property of your net, your "data collection system", there is no problem. If you are too enamored of it, you are likely to think that ocean life is all bigger than one inch. You cannot study small life with your net.

Altered states of consciousness research has shown us that some kinds of human knowledge are state-specific. If you aren't in a certain state of consciousness, certain things cannot be known.

Some knowledge is only partially state-specific, in that it can be known in two or more states of consciousness. If you ask someone the street address of his home, for example, he will probably give you a correct answer in his ordinary state, in a dream state

(assuming you are some dream character asking the question), in a sexually aroused stated, in a depressed state, and in a state of intoxication. But there are things you can know in an altered state of consciousness that you cannot really remember in your ordinary state, much less tell others about in any adequate way. This seems to be the case with many of the great spiritual issues.

If we want to know all that a human can know, we must study some things in an appropriate altered state of consciousness. If we do not enter that state and work appropriately with it, we will never really know the answers. I think one of the tragedies of our times is that we have forgotten about the state-specificity of knowledge in regard to many vital spiritual questions. Thus we approach them only from an ordinary states perspective, and get answers that are distorted and pale reflections of reality. We have, as it were, traded direct knowledge of something like Unity of Life for abstract verbal statements and theories about unity. It doesn't satisfy, and it doesn't work very well.

Altered States and Survival

What does this have to do with survival of consciousness? Just this:

The direct experience of existing and experiencing in some form that seems partially or fully independent of the physical body is relatively common in various altered states of consciousness, and this kind of experience constitutes the most direct knowledge of survival an individual may have.

There is nothing wrong with indirect forms of evidence per se, of course, but by this wholesale rejection of direct altered state of consciousness experience, we force the survival issue to be solely one of indirect experience, of abstraction and deduction instead of direct experience. This also amounts to throwing away some of the most relevant evidence about survival, and may make it impossible to ever get a personally satisfactory answer.

Further, contemporary research in humanistic and transpersonal psychology has shown that the wholesale rejection of dream and other altered state of consciousness experience has strong and largely pathological consequences for our happiness and our full development as human beings.

There are many personal and cultural roots for the rejection of altered states of consciousness. The one we will focus on now is the dominance of materialism as a philosophy of life.

The materialist view of man, so widespread today, says that any discussion about human consciousness is essentially a discussion about computer circuits. Biocomputer circuits, to be specific, but nothing more than this. Consciousness is like an actively running program in the biocomputer; altered states are simply different programs. Various aspects of consciousness are merely subprograms of the larger program which is nothing but the totality of my biological, material self. The programs and subprograms may produce all sorts of outputs and experiences. Many of them are very useful to our pleasure and biological survival, but many of them are quite arbitrary or even nonsensical.

To put it simply, the materialistic equation is:

$$\text{Mind } \textit{equals} \text{ Brain}$$

and this is considered to be the complete story.

This completely materialist view, by invalidating vital aspects of human nature, creates a dismal outlook on life, an outlook that is usually not explicitly acknowledged because of its dismalness. When hope, love, and joy, when intellect and the materialist philosophy itself are reduced to their "ultimate reality" of nothing but electrochemical impulses in a biocomputer that originated by chance in a dead universe, what is left?

Because the practical and intellectual results of materialistic science are so powerful, we (including almost all scientists) are too impressed with the materialistic philosophy intermixed with it. We can consciously reject materialism because of the loss of vital spirit it leads to, but it is hard to effectively reject the cultural conditioning and emotional involvement that we as westerners almost invariably have in the "scientistic" outlook. Thus it is important for us to be able to rationally deal with the intellectual claim of comprehensiveness of materialism, not just take a position like "I don't like the way materialism feels, so even if I have to ignore my intellect I'm going to reject it."

The good news is that you don't have to be ignorant or unscientific in order to reasonably argue that the scientistic position is far from complete, and thus is not an all powerful set of reasons for rejecting the possible reality of the spiritual. Not that I'm arguing the opposite and encouraging you to believe everything that is labeled "spiritual": there is a lot of nonsense under that label that should be sorted out and rejected. But not everything.

Scientific Parapsychology as an Underminer of Materialism

The good news is based on the findings of scientific parapsychology, a collection of thousands of naturalistic observations and at least 700 laboratory experiments in the last six decades that, to my mind, conclusively demonstrate that there are aspects of the human mind that simply cannot be reduced to materialistic explanations. Thus the equation "Mind=Brain" is woefully incomplete, and should not be used to rule out spiritual realities or the possibility of survival on an a priori basis.

Briefly, parapsychological research has firmly demonstrated the existence of four major psychic abilities. "Psychic" means that while we observe information transfer or physical effects on the physical world, there are no reasonably conceivable physical means whereby the information transfer or physical effects can have come about. There may be other psychic abilities--I think there are--but they have not been investigated and established to the degree that these four have, so I focus on them as the foundations of parapsychology. The four are telepathy, clairvoyance, precognition, and psychokinesis.

Telepathy is the transmission of information from mind to mind, after we have ruled out ordinary physical means like talking to one another or sign language, and ruled out inference from physically known data. The laboratory studies that firmly established telepathy were mostly card guessing studies. A sender, isolated in his or her own room, looked at one card after another from a thoroughly shuffled pack of cards, trying to send his or her thoughts. A receiver isolated in another room wrote down his impressions of the cards. Perfect scores are extremely rare, but enough studies showed more hits than could be reasonably expected by chance to establish telepathy.

Clairvoyance is the direct extrasensory perception of information about the physical world, without the intervention of another mind which already knows the information by ordinary sensory means. The classical card test studies involved a percipient giving impressions of the order of a deck of randomized cards when no living human knew what the order of that deck was. Many studies showed enough hits to establish clairvoyance. The information transmission rate is about the same as in telepathy studies (5). Both telepathy and clairvoyance seem unaffected by physical factors like spatial distance or physical shielding.

Precognition is the prediction of the future when the future is determined in a random way, such that inference from present knowledge would not be helpful. The classic experimental design is to ask a percipient to predict the order of a target deck of cards, but the cards will be randomly shuffled at some date in the future. Precognition of this sort has been successful at intervals of up to a year. Curiously the average information transfer rate is much lower than in present-time telepathy or clairvoyance studies (5).

Collectively, telepathy, clairvoyance, and precognition are known as extrasensory perception (ESP), as they all involve information gathering.

Psychokinesis (PK) is the fourth well-established psychic phenomenon. It is popularly called mind over matter. The classic tests involved wishing which way machine thrown dice would turn up, although the target object is now usually an electronic random number generator. The frequency of PK appearance is about the same as precognition (3).

The importance of these psi phenomena, as the four are now collectively referred to, is that they are manifestations of mind that have resisted all attempts to reduce them to known physical forces, or straightforward extensions of known physical forces. I exempt some of the speculations on the frontiers of quantum physics to explain psi as "straightforward" extensions of physics, for they are controversial ideas in physics per se, involve such a radically different view of what is "physical" that they should not be lumped in with the old materialistic physics, and, quite important from a scientific view, have not shown any notable degree of success in understanding and controlling psi phenomena.

The psi phenomena are examples where we must say:

Mind *does not equal* Brain

Certainly some aspects of mind and consciousness are partially or wholly based in brain and nervous system functioning, but psi phenomena are not, and so openly demonstrate the need to investigate mind on its own terms. These psi phenomena do not "prove" survival, but insofar as mind has aspects which do not seem limited by space or time, such aspects of mind are the sort we might expect to survive bodily death.

Scientific Research on Survival

Modern parapsychological research has focused on the four aspects of psi mentioned above, but historically parapsychology, originally called psychical research, focused specifically on the question of survival of death.

Modern spiritualism was born near the end of the last century when mysterious rappings in the home of the Fox sisters were interpreted as PK-like effects of departed spirits who were trying to communicate with the living. In a short time Spiritualism was a world-wide religion. Its basic message was very appealing, and scientific in style. Spiritualism accepted the fact that much that was called religion, based on authority, was indeed just superstition. Scientists were right who said that experience, data, facts, were more important than belief or dogma. "Don't believe in survival," said the spiritualists, "test the idea of survival against the facts!"

Spiritualist mediums claimed that that is just what they were: mediums of communication, channels between the living and the deceased for exchanging messages. If you want to know if your Aunt Sara had survived death, don't believe or disbelieve the idea, sit down with a medium at a seance and ask to speak to Aunt Sara. When the spirit who claimed to be Aunt Sara is contacted and speaking through the medium, ask her questions about herself until you are convinced that it is indeed Aunt Sara speaking.

Many, many people carried out this experiment. Some were not convinced of survival. As the early psychical researchers noted, many of the ostensible spirits gave only the vaguest details of their earthly lives, or were just plain wrong in what they said.

Some seance communications from the ostensible spirits were of a very high quality, though, and convinced sitters of the reality of survival. Here is an example of the kind of high quality sitting that has been reported, this one from after the Second World War by the British investigator Rosalind Heywood:

"After the war I went to a Scottish medium to see if she could pick up something about a friend, a German diplomat who I feared had been killed either by the Nazis or the Russians. I simply didn't know what had happened to him. The medium very soon got onto him. She gave his Christian name, talked about things we had done together in Washington, and described correctly my opinion of his character. She said he was dead and that his death was so tragic he didn't want to talk about it. She gave a number of striking details about him and the evidence of personality was very strong." (1)

I believe any of us would be strongly impressed by this kind of evidence for the survival of death, and it has convinced a few parapsychologists.

Complexities of Survival Research

Survival research is now a very small part of parapsychology (itself a miniscule field--see Reference #2). Compared to the central role it once had, survival research has been almost abandoned for half a century. The reason is quite interesting.

When psychical researchers first began investigating mediums, the idea that living people had extraordinary psychic abilities was not generally accepted. If information from an ostensible surviving spirit was in accord with what the investigator knew about the deceased, he was inclined to accept it as evidence of survival: who but he and the deceased knew it? As researchers gradually established that ordinary people sometimes showed telepathy, clairvoyance, and precognition, however, the picture became more complicated. The validating information might have come from the deceased, but it might also come from the medium's unconscious telepathic reading of the investigator's (or some friend's of the deceased) mind, or from a clairvoyant pickup of information from surviving documents and records. If *pre*cognition existed, how about the possibility of *retro*cognition, where the medium's unconscious psychic abilities went back in time to get information about the deceased when he was still alive?

Added to these psychic complications were the facts arriving from the study of hypnosis and of abnormal mental states like those involved in multiple personality that showed that the subconscious part of a person's mind could do marvelous imitations of people. Further add in the fact that subconscious processes could distort a person's mental functioning to alter experience so it supported deeply held beliefs, and the grounds were established for a powerful alternative explanation of the best data for survival.

The Undead Deceased

To illustrate the complexities of survival research, let us continue the high-quality case we just looked at. I did not present the whole report on the case:

"If I had never heard any more, I would have thought it very impressive.

"But after the sitting, I set about trying to find out something about him. Finally the Swiss Foreign Office found him for me. He was not dead. He had escaped from Germany and had married an English girl. He wrote to me that he had never been so happy in his life. So there I think the medium was reading my expectations. She was quite wrong about the actual facts, but right according to what I had expected." (1)

Most parapsychologists abandoned survival research and focused on the psi abilities of the living because cases like this made it look just too difficult to decide between the survival hypothesis and the unconscious impersonation theory. The abandonment is probably premature, and a few parapsychologists are still actively working to devise better tests of survival that could distinguish these two explanations. Ian Stevenson, for example, a psychiatrist at the University of Viginia, has proposed that subconscious ESP on the medium's part might account for factual knowledge shown by an ostensible surviving spirit, but would not account for complex skills if they were shown. To responsively speak a foreign language you were sure was unknown to the medium, for example, rather than just mention isolated words or phrases from that language, would be very convincing. Unfortunately we do not have good cases of that type--yet. Perhaps we will.

As I stated earlier, however, what little survival research has been done was implicitly about the survival of ordinary consciousness. We have seen how ordinary consciousness and ordinary "I"s are just one manifestation of whatever our more basic nature is. Let us now look at possibilities of survival that include some of the realities of altered states of consciousness.

Models of Survival

• *Ordinary Consciousness, Equivalent Body Survival*

This model assumes that existence after death would be rather like permanent exile to a foreign land, but with consciousness and "external" reality much like they were before death.

• *Stable Altered State of Consciousness Survival*

This model would assume that there is a primary, "ordinary" (for the after-death) state of consciousness after death, with stable and comprehensible (at least from within) qualities. It would be an altered state of consciousness compared to pre-death embodied ordinary consciousness. . . .

• *Multiple, Stable Altered State of Consciousness Survival*

There may be several altered states of consciousness that the surviving person exists in from time to time. Communications from the same deceased person, but originating from different states, might seem contradictory or disjointed. . . . To gather evidence in favor of the possibility of survival, we have to make an assumption in this and the previous model, namely that at least some of the altered states of consciousness the deceased can communicate from bear a clear enough resemblance to the pre-death personality and state of consciousness so we can see the connection.

• *Unstable, Transiting States of Consciousness Survival*

I have theorized elsewhere (4) that the most comprehensive explanation for some of the altered states of consciousness phenomena we see, especially those induced by powerful psychedelic drugs in untrained individuals, is to recognize that we are not dealing with a single, stabilized altered state of consciousness but with continuous, unstable transitions from momentary configuration to momentary configuration. The colloquial term "tripping" illustrates the flavor of this. A person's condition, whether induced in life by a powerful destabilizing force like a drug or by the nature of the after-death state, is a lack of stability, a rapid shifting from one momentary configuration of conscious functioning to another. Such a condition would be rather like delirium. To both the person experiencing it and to outsiders, there would be moments of sense and lucidity, perhaps moments of even greater lucidity than normal, but overall it is confused rambling.

The Body as a Stabilizer of Consciousness

Given the importance of the body and brain as stabilizing mechanisms for both ordinary and altered states of consciousness, as we discussed above, the lack of a body and brain in an after-death state might well mean that it would be characterized by great instability. If we would investigate what happens to mental functioning in life when body awareness is greatly reduced or temporarily eliminated, we might have a better understanding of what an after-death state might be like.

Our discussion of dreaming earlier is quite relevant to this idea, for in dreaming we have almost no awareness of our actual physical bodies, only our mentally constructed dream bodies. Sensory deprivation studies also shed some light on this quesiton. Ketamine intoxication might also be an excellent analogue for studying the qualities of mind when no body is perceived in life. Used as an analgesic in surgery, it has also been used in much lower doses (about one tenth the surgical dose) as a psychedelic drug, with a major effect in some users of making the physical body effectively disappear from consciousness.

Interoceptive input from our physical bodies is not the only major source of stabilization of consciousness in physical life, of course, so it may be possible for stable states of consciousness to develop in an after-death state based on other kinds of stabilization processes.

More Appropriate Tests for Survival

We can summarize the implications for

The question "Will I survive death?" cannot really be satisfactorily answered except as a subset of the larger question "Who and what am I ?"

improving the quality of survival research now around the question of "Who might survive death?"

The ordinary personality, the ordinary "I", does not seem a likely candidate for more than temporary survival. It has little enough unity itself, being made of many "I"s itself, each of which often fails to "survive" the shocks of ordinary life for very long. The shock of dying might destroy many of these aspects of ordinary "I" either temporarily or permanently. Further, ordinary "I", ordinary consciousness, is heavily dependent on a number of body-based processes for its stabilization, processes like exteroceptive and interoceptive input. Without these processes consciousness can change drastically, as in ordinary dreaming. Unless something very analogous to an external world and body is provided in the after-death state, much of ordinary "I" would seem unlikely to survive.

If we want to ask "Does John Smith survive death?" we had better get to know the full range of possible manifestations of "John Smith" before he dies. Aside from knowing factual and personality details about the ordinary "John Smith", what is the drunken "John Smith" like? How about the "John Smith" when he has lost his body temporarily through sensory deprivation or ketamine administration? Or the "John Smith" after a profound meditative experience? Or the "John Smith" in a state of depression? Or the "entity" that may appear in some altered state of consciousness that tells us that "John Smith" is a small and not very important manifestation of something much greater? When we can identify all of these "John Smiths", we will be in a much better position to ascertain if any of them survive. □

References

1. R. Heywood quoted in W.G. Roll, "Will personality and consciousness survive the death of the body? An examination of parapsychological findings suggestive of survival." Doctoral dissertation, University of Utrecht, 1985 manuscript, pp. 178-179.
2. C.T. Tart, "A survey of expert opinion on potentially negative uses of psi: United States government interest in psi, and the level of research funding of the field." In W. G. Roll (ed.), *Research in Parapsychology, 1978*. Metuchen, N.J.: Scarecrow Press, 1979. pp. 54-55.
3. C.T. Tart, "Laboratory PK: Frequency of manifestation and resemblance to precognition." *Research in Parapsychology, 1982*. Metuchen, N.J.: Scarecrow Press, 1983. pp. 101-102.
4. C.T. Tart, *States of Consciousness*. El Cerrito, CA: Psychological Processes Inc., 1983. (Originally published New York: Dutton, 1975).
5. C.T. Tart, "Information transmission rates in forced-choice ESP experiments: Precognition does not work as well as present time ESP." *Journal of the American Society for Psychical Research, 77, 1984*. pp. 293-310.

Charles Tart is professor of psychology at the University of California at Davis. He is well-known for his writings on the systems approach to consciousness, state-specific sciences, converging operations methodology and for his experimental work in parapsychology.

Charles Tart's full presentation appears in the Institute-published book *Consciousness and Survival: An Interdisciplinary Inquiry into the Possibility of Life Beyond Biological Death,* edited by Bishop John S. Spong with an introduction by Senator Claiborne Pell.

You ask why I live
in these green mountains

I smile
can't answer

I am completely at peace

a peach blossom
sails past
on the current

there are worlds
beyond this one.

— Li Po

Healing, Remission and Miracle Cures

a lecture by
Brendan O'Regan
Vice-President for Research
Institute of Noetic Sciences

Sponsored by the Washington Committee of the Institute of Noetic Sciences

Friday, December 5, 1986 • American University, Washington, DC

I'd like to begin by reviewing a little of the history of the projects I'll be telling you about later in my talk. Those of you who are familiar with the Institute of Noetic Sciences know that we've sponsored a lot of work involving the mind/body relationship and its importance in health. During the 1970s, for example, we supported research of people like Carl and Stephanie Simonton, who were working with terminal cancer patients using psychotherapeutic techniques, meditational and guided imagery approaches and biofeedback to demonstrate that the mind/body relationship was indeed important and could affect the course of illness and disease. In 1975 people thought this kind of work was highly unusual. The general climate was one in which this kind of mind/body link wasn't well understood and many, many people expressed doubt that the link even existed in a way that had any significant effect on health. Some people were less polite and told us that we were crazy for supporting this kind of work.

But it's been interesting to see what has happened in the years since then. I remember a discussion with Carl and Stephanie back in 1976 when we were speculating where in the mind/body system psychological factors could have an impact. They said that their best *guess* was the immune system. There was no field then of psychoneuroimmunology, which has emerged in just the past five or six years. This field, as many of you know, is concerned with the links between the mind, the brain and the immune system and how they communicate with each other. It is through this system that psychological factors do indeed seem to have an impact on health and disease.

Although we didn't know this was the case back in the '70s when we supported these projects, we knew intuitively we were on the right track. There was enough anecdotal evidence to justify exploring this area. Today we are heavily immersed in this approach. And something else has happened as well. In the early 1980s we at Noetic Sciences realized that while we had been funding *practitioners* of alternative techniques in medicine who demonstrated effects, we weren't really looking into the *mechanisms* of these effects. We weren't getting at how the connection between mind and body is mediated, or "What are the mediating pathways?" as the question would be asked in scientific circles today.

So we started a program called the Inner Mechanisms of the Healing Response. One of the premises of the program is based on the observation that in medicine, or in science generally, progress occurs when it is recognized that certain seemingly disconnected things are acting together and forming a *system*. For example the circulatory system, the nervous system and the immune system were not recognized as systems until people gradually realized that they were indeed working in coordination as systems.

The Placebo Effect

We noticed that there were a lot of sporadic data "all over the map" about healing. Take, for example, the placebo effect in medicine. The placebo effect is one of those annoying things, from some points of view in medicine, that says that some people—approximately 35–40 percent—will get better when they take a "sugar pill" or an inert substance they are told is a drug that will help them. Some of their responses can be fairly modest, such as the relief of pain. Many people say, though, the pain is a subjective phenomenon or psychosomatic; so they're not terribly impressed by that result. Other examples are more dramatic. For example, in the 1950s it was common to perform a certain kind of surgery to relieve the pain of angina pectoris. At that time some experiments were performed which could not get by a Human Subjects Review Committee today, I assure you. In these experiments patients with that disease were cut open and then simply sewn back up again. The operation—a sham operation if you like—took place and the patients were then sewn back together. Those patients reported just as much relief from angina pectoris as the people who'd had the full surgery. So it turns out that surgery for angina pectoris produced a placebo effect.

There's another intriguing example from the *World Journal of Surgery*, which reported on the test of a new kind of chemotherapy in 1983. As is often the case in such tests, there was an experimental group that received the chemotherapy, and a control group that received a sugar pill or an inert substance. One of the effects of chemotherapy that we're all familiar with is hair loss—so people *expect* to lose their hair when given chemotherapy. In this study 30 percent of the *control* group—given placebos—lost their hair. That's a very physical effect! There's got to be some kind of mediating pathway for it. In fact, it's been named the "nocebo" effect, as opposed to the placebo effect which means "I shall please". This is not pleasing!

So those who think of placebos as having only modest, inconsequential and subjective effects should look at some of these data because there definitely are direct physical effects of placebos. In fact less kind people say that the history of medicine *is* the history of the placebo effect, at least until the discovery of drugs or antibiotics, because many of the substances that were administered before the 1930s have since been found to be pharmacologically inactive or ineffective.

But even recently within the realm of chemotherapy there are interesting effects. Dr. Bernard Siegel of Yale told me a story about a chemotherapeutic agent called cis-platinum. When cis-platinum came out, it was greeted with a great deal of enthusiasm. Doctors were getting 75 percent effectiveness from administering cis-platinum to their patients. But over time, doctors further removed from the initial enthusiasm would administer the chemotherapy in a sort of "ho-hum" routine way, and the effectiveness rate dropped down to about 25 or 30 percent.

Given these physical effects of placebos, one wonders what can be going on. There must be complex pathways between mind and body and indeed belief systems.

Multiple Personality

Then we at the Institute started investigating another phenomenon which had intrigued me for some time—multiple personality, which is exhibited by people who have been severely physically abused, even sexually, as children. Dr. Frank Putnam of the National Institutes of Health (NIH), one of the country's experts on that subject, has found that electroencephalograms (EEGs) of people who go from one personality to another will change as dramatically as though the electrodes had been taken off one person and placed on another. The difference in brain activity is that great. Most intriguing is that some of these people will be allergic to a drug in one personality and not allergic to it in another. Some cases have been reported of women who've had three menstrual periods each month because they had three different personalities, each one with its own cycle. A more peculiar situation that I have difficulty accepting—I've heard of four cases, but I've never witnessed one—is that of eye color changing between personalities.

What all of this implies is that there is an extraordinary plasticity in the relationship between mind and body. It's very interesting to examine this in multiples because it involves the same biology, the same genetics, the same physical being. Some, by the way, take the view that there is a connection between temporal lobe epilepsy and multiple personality; they say that completely different brain regions are being activated, so different sets of instructions are being sent out. But indeed, isn't that what we want to happen when we're trying to get someone to change illness in the direction of healing? Following this line of reasoning we decided to fund a study at NIH—it's ironic that Noetic Sciences gives money to NIH—to examine the immune systems of multiples while they change personalities. This study, which had not been done before, is now being conducted by Dr. Putnam in collaboration with Dr. Nicholas Hall at George Washington Medical School.

As all of this began to jell in my mind I thought, well, maybe there is something in addition to a nervous system and an immune system and an endocrine system—something like a healing system. Maybe it is a system that doesn't manifest unless challenged. Maybe it's a system that can lie dormant until confronted with stress, trauma, disease or illness of some kind. If that was so, then it would explain why it just isn't an obvious part of ourselves. As I was speculating along these lines, and about a year after I had written some notes about this, I found a statement from Norman Cousins in his book *Human Options.* He says:

> Over the years, medical science has identified the primary systems of the human body, the circulatory system, digestive system, endocrine system, autonomic nervous system, parasympathetic nervous system, and the immune system. But two other systems that are central to the proper functioning of a human being need to be emphasized. The healing system, and the belief system. The two work together. The healing system is the way the body mobilizes all its resources to combat disease. The belief system is often the activator of the healing system.

So I found I was not alone in thinking this way. We then asked ourselves, "How would we maximize the evidence of this healing system?" After all, this is not an accepted point of view; it's not taught in medical schools, I'm sure. We decided to look into a subject of which I'd heard rumors and anecdotal evidence for years—spontaneous remission.

Spontaneous Remission

Spontaneous remission is a phenomenon with a very curious history in medicine. The majority view is that spontaneous remission doesn't really happen—that it is, in fact, an artifact of misdiagnosis. According to this view the person never really had *that* disease, they had something else. This in itself is very interesting. If this turns out to be the case, then we should know the extent of it in medicine and attempt to get rid of it.

However, the dictionary definitions of "spontaneous" and "remission" are intriguing. The word "spontaneous" means "acting in accordance with, or resulting from feeling, temperament or disposition, or from a native internal proneness, readiness or tendency without compulsion, constraint or premeditation." Another meaning is "acting by its own impulse, energy, or natural law without external cause or influence." "Remission" means "the act of remitting, a natural releasing, resigning or relinquishing, surrendering. Forgiveness, pardon as of sins or crimes." There are some very interesting messages locked up in those words, so I thought we should look at the literature on remission to see what we might learn about the dynamics of the phenomenon.

It turns out, however, that there are no existing texts on the subject. Remission simply is not a subject a physician or a researcher can look up in the library, at least not yet. There are only *two* books on the topic, one by Everson and Cole on 176 cases of regression of cancer (but that book is out of print and one of the authors is dead); and the other by William Boyd on regression of cancer (also out of print and the author is deceased). There is only one document that you can get your hands on, which is a report on a conference that took place twelve years ago at Johns Hopkins University, available from the National Cancer Institute.

So a year ago we got busy on our computers and started going into the databases, and we have now assembled over 3000 articles from over 860 medical journals in over 20 different languages. By the way, one article can be about as many as several hundred cases. As far as I know this is the largest compilation of data on spontaneous remission in the world. We will be publishing our work on this early next year, and have already completed a draft of the first volume, which is entitled *Remission with No Allopathic Intervention.* Some very interesting pictures emerge from this.

First of all, we have found cases of remission from almost every kind of illness, not just cancer. We've selected about 800 of the most striking examples of spontaneous remission—out of 3000 articles—for inclusion in volume one of the spontaneous remission bibliography. We have many cases of remission with no medical intervention at all. These are the purest ones, the ones that give us the strongest evidence that there is an extraordinary self-repair system lying dormant within us. These make up about one-fifth of what we have collected. Then if you go to the cases where there's inadequate medical treatment, in other words something was done for the person, but they did not receive a treatment that would be expected to cure them in any way—for example, a biopsy is not considered curative—then you get about twice as many articles. It's fascinating to look at what you find. We've prepared an abstract for every one of these papers and have put all this information in an electronic database. We've also extracted some case histories. What you find in these histories is fascinating. I would like to give you some examples of the kinds of things we've found because when you hear actual cases you get a very good feel for what can happen.

Let me say that many of the people who write these medical journal reports do so with a great sense of apology, because they seem to be saying to their colleagues, "Well, we really did diagnose this correctly; we thought that the x-rays might have gotten misplaced so we took them again; and we definitely found that this person really had the disease." Then you get the same story all over again when they go through the remission. In effect, they are saying: "The disease really did disappear. We re-did the tests several times and to our amazement, the tumor was completely gone."

Here's a case from *The Journal of Thoracic and Cardiovascular Surgery*, 1954, a case of spontaneous regression of an untreated bronchiogenic carcinoma. If you'll bear with me through the technical detail in the following report, I think it will give you some sense of how thorough these reports are.

A fifty-nine year old white man was admitted to the George Washington University Hospital on May 19, 1947. The patient had been in good health until September of 1946 when he first noticed an increase in a chronic cough which he had had for years. In addition, he gave a history of malaise and increasing dyspepsia of two months' duration, and an 18-lb. weight loss over a period of six months. The patient suffered from chronic bronchitis of about 20 years' duration. He had smoked from two to three packages of cigarettes daily for many years. X-rays of the chest revealed an opacity in the right lung field at the level of the third and fourth intercostal spaces anteriorly. On July 20, a right thoracotomy was performed which revealed a carcinoma of the lung with involvement of the right helium and invasion of the mediastinum at the level of the inferior pulmonary artery. A biopsy of the mass was taken and since the lesion appeared inoperable, the chest was closed. Microscopic examination of the tissue revealed an epidermoid carcinoma.

During the post-operative period, x-rays of the chest revealed progressive clearing of the pulmonary lesion in the right lung. This became particularly apparent about six months after the exploratory thoracotomy. The incredible behavior of the pulmonary lesion naturally aroused suspicion that there had been a mistake made in the histologic diagnosis and perhaps a mislabelled specimen accounted for an erroneous diagnosis. Accordingly, new sections were made which again revealed epidermoid carcinoma.

The patient was readmitted to the hospital May 19, 1952, exactly five years after the original admission. A careful re-evaluation of his entire life history was undertaken to obtain any pertinent facts which could have influenced the behavior of the lung cancer. Nothing of significance could be found except that for four or five years he had been employed as a linotype operator with exposure to noxious fumes. This ultimately led him to change his occupation. [This is all you now hear about the patient as a person.]

Following the operation in 1947, he took two halibut liver oil capsules daily for a considerable period of time, four vegetable compound tablets daily, an occasional barbiturate for sleep and vitamin B-1 tablets. The vegetable compound tablets were analyzed and were found to contain asparagus, parsley, watercress and broccoli. The almost complete disappearance of the lesion in the right lung was constant, corresponding to x-rays of the past four years.

Notice that this patient *was* operated on and a biopsy was taken. However, no attempt was made to remove the tumor since it was regarded as inoperable. This is categorized as "no allopathic intervention" from a technical standpoint—though when one learns that biopsy procedures alone can appear to stimulate remissions, one wonders if this categorization will remain appropriate.

Emerging Patterns

I could quote many more of these cases but for brevity I'll tell you just a few of the patterns we've seen in the literature. One of the patterns is that you rarely hear anything of the patients as persons—what they believe, what they do, what they feel. It's just not included. That's understandable in the context of the time that these papers were written and the attitude in medicine then. But when you read enough of them, after a while you start to notice a mounting symphony of the absence of the person. I remember one paper by a Dr. Weinstock in New York about a woman who had cervical cancer that had metastasized throughout her body. She was considered beyond treatment and beyond help. As the paper continued it said, "And her much-hated husband suddenly died, whereupon she completely recovered." So you say to yourself—wait a minute, shouldn't we follow up these kinds of things? One is left wondering what might be behind that kind of statement.

Another pattern we noticed—quite independently of another research group that we later discovered had been following the same thing—is that many patients who go into remission had an infection at a certain point along the way. It might have been a bacterial infection, often some kind of skin infection, and it will be noted in the report that the infection caused a fever to which there was a reaction and then the fever subsided and slowly the tumor disappeared. We thought this was rather interesting. As we went back in time (you can go back electronically in the databases to 1966, but after that you're on your own in the old-fashioned way in the library) we finally got back to the twenties and the teens and we began to notice more reports of this kind of remission. We tracked these reports of remission following bacterial infections to a man named Dr. William Coley of New York. He noticed back in the 1890s that his patients who became infected with a bacterial skin infection called erysipelas would react with a fever and spend a few days fighting it off—as though the immune system were being activated to fight off the infection. Then in about 40 percent of the patients, the cancer would disappear. Coley turned this around and started *giving* people infections, infecting them directly with erysipelas in order to stimulate their immune systems; he did indeed achieve an interesting success rate.

But in 1935, when Coley died, chemotherapy and x-ray treatments for cancer began, and infection techniques seemed old-fashioned and no longer relevant. His daughter, Helen Coley Nauts, still alive at about 80 years old in New York City, told me recently that since she believed her father was doing something important, she had gone to a friend, Lloyd Old at Sloan-

Kettering, and said "What can I do to have this work taken seriously?" Old told her, "Gather a hundred cases, well-documented, fully detailed medical histories and bring them to me. I'll distribute them to my colleagues and we'll see." She came back with 1000 cases! Out of that came an organization in New York, Cancer Research Institute, founded by Coley's daughter to pursue this line of research. Just as a footnote, Old began to look into what it was erysipelas infection stimulated in animal systems, and this is how tumor necrosis factor was discovered; this was then cloned by Genentech and is now in clinical trial at Sloan-Kettering. So you have an interesting consequence of a very physical sort in the study of the kinds of systems involved in remission.

Our Remission Project has uncovered other interesting work in many other countries. We have about 250 papers in other languages, including Japanese, Swedish, German, Italian and Hebrew. In Sweden and Japan researchers have been removing plasma from people in remission, particularly with hematologic (blood) diseases, and have been injecting it into other people and, in some cases, are getting remission; this suggests there are blood-borne factors that I believe can one day be isolated from people in remission. This is yet another reason to gather data on these people.

Another quite different aspect of remission is the cases reported involving psychological and spiritual phenomena. Here is part of a report from a very interesting Australian physician, Ainslie Meares, who unfortunately died in September of this year. This case involves the regression of osteogenic sarcoma metastasis associated with intensive meditation.

The patient, aged 25, underwent a mid-thigh operation for osteogenic sarcoma 11 months before he first saw me, 2-1/2 years ago. [This report was written in 1978.] He had visible bony lumps of about two centimeters in diameter growing from the ribs, sternum and the crest of the ilium and was coughing up small quantities of blood in which he said he could feel small pieces of bone. There were gross opacities in the x-ray films of his lungs. The patient had been told by a specialist that he had only two or three weeks to live, but in virtue of his profession he was already well aware of the pathology and prognosis of his condition. Now, 2-1/2 years later, he has moved to another state to resume his former occupation. This young man has an extraordinary will to live and has sought help from all the alternatives to orthodox medicine which were available to him. These have included acupuncture, massage, several sessions with Philippine faith healers, laying-on of hands, and yoga at an Indian ashram. He had short sessions of radiation therapy and chemotherapy, but declined to continue. [This would be classified more as a case of inadequate treatment in technical terms.] He also persisted with the dietary and enema treatment described by Max Gerson, the German physician who gained some notoriety for this type of treatment in America in the 1940s. However in addition to all these measures to gain relief, the patient has consistently maintained a rigorous discipline of intensive meditation. He has, in fact, consistently meditated from one to three hours daily. Two other factors seem to be important. [Meares, by the way, is one researcher who describes more about the patient and not as much about the disease.]

He has had extraordinary help and support from his girlfriend who more recently became his wife. She's extremely sensitive to his feelings and needs and has spent hours in aiding his meditation and healing with massage and laying-on of hands. The other important factor would seem to be the patient's own state of mind. He has developed a degree of calm about him which I have rarely observed in anyone, even in Oriental mystics with whom I have had considerable experience. When asked to what he attributes the regression of metastases, he answers in some such terms as "I really think it is our life, the way we experience our life." In other words, it would seem that the patient has let the effects of the intense and prolonged meditation enter into his whole experience of life. His extraordinary low level of anxiety is obvious to the most casual observer. It is suggested that this has enhanced the activity of his immune system by reducing his level of cortisol.

So some clues come occasionally from people who are studying the mind/body relationship in relation to remission. But by far the largest number of cases do not involve this kind of information. You're simply told that people survived—period. In 1985 we went to the National Tumor Registry, which is operated by the National Cancer Institute. This Registry has eleven centers around the country, which keep track of all the incidents of tumors. If a patient goes to a hospital and cancer is diagnosed, the Tumor Registry is informed of the type of tumor, the patient's age, race, sex, and various other details. That's how the records on the incidence of cancer are built up. They don't track remission, however, and they don't even really track long-term survival anymore. But even so I went to the San Francisco Bay Area Tumor Registry, which covers the five Bay Area counties, and I said "Look, we're interested in remission." They said, "No, no, we don't have information on that here." And I said, "Well, how long do you keep track of patients? Do you keep track of them for five years, or ten years?" They said, "We keep track of them until they die." I said, "Oh? In that case, you could look for long-term survivors." They said, "Yes, we could." Their database had been computerized in 1973, and I was talking to them in 1985, so I said "Well, why don't we look in your records for people who were told between 1973 and 1975 that they had a terminal cancer, that it was not just cancer at a primary site, that it had metastasized throughout their body. Look in your records now in 1985 and see if any of them are still alive." They said, "Fine, we can do that very easily." They went into the database and came back with 100 names: 100 people still alive ten

years past a terminal diagnosis. We agreed that we'd better make sure these people were still alive; you know, this whole issue of just exactly when people are really dead is rather tricky because some people are still trying to collect social security, and there are strange things involving insurance claims. This is a kind of netherworld I hadn't penetrated before. They said "We will verify that they are all alive."

They were then successful in verifying that 89 of these individuals were still alive. These people all had different kinds of cancer. What startled me the most was that there were two cases of pancreatic cancer, which is normally very lethal. So we are now attempting to get the release of their names and permission to talk to them.

Talking to somebody in remission can be a very delicate process. We learned this when two women in remission came to visit us. (By the way, I can't verify this statistically, but we *seem* to hear of more women than men in remission.) One of these women came to talk to Caryle Hirshberg, my associate who has been doing our database search. She looked at Caryle somewhat suspiciously and said "You're not a doctor, are you? I don't want to talk to a doctor!" Caryle said, "No, I'm not. Really, honest." Then she said, "Well, I just don't want to be put down and turned away again, like I was so many times. I'm going to keep my state of mind intact, no matter what."

Unfortunately this has been what we've found frequently with the few people we've talked to—they've been turned away. I very much like what Yale surgeon Bernard Siegel, author of *Love, Medicine and Miracles*, says about this problem, "Talk to your patients. Never turn them away. Because even if you don't agree with what they're doing, they'll still come back and tell you about it." And the fact is that most people with remissions don't come back and tell anybody. At least, they don't tell their doctors. You will see cases in our files of people who were seen ten years later in the hospital for something else and the physician says, "My God, I thought you were dead! You were in here ten years ago for something. How come you're still alive?" So they sort of have to apologize, I guess.

You can see, it's a very complex business. But we thought we'd go a little further with this. I want to describe one other piece that has emerged as a curious pattern. I mentioned it earlier. We haven't analyzed this yet so I don't know what we'll do about it. One of the things that Caryle Hirshberg noticed was that when people who had kidney cancer had the kidney removed, the metastases from the kidney to the lung— the pulmonary metastases to the lung—would frequently disappear. This is not considered terribly surprising. You're removing the primary site of the cancer and so maybe it is not so strange that the area to which the cancer had spread would heal. But then we began to notice that when some patients simply had a biopsy of the kidney, their pulmonary metastases would disappear. In these cases there is no surgery to remove the cancer. Only the amount captured by a needle biopsy is removed. So there's some interesting relationship between the kidney and the lung and the simple act of biopsy. That's not a technically "clean" remission, but it says that biopsy can be part of the process of inducing remission somehow. When you intervene in one area, it sets up a process which can help in another. In a sense that is parallel to the infection cases.

Spiritual and Miraculous Healing

Going further, we then began to say, "We've heard for many years about claims of spiritual healing or miraculous healing. We see these claims televised every night. What about these cases? Are these remissions or something else?" I thought I should look into this in order to have a more complete perspective of the whole field. So I asked myself first, "Where will this have been documented in some way that I can make sense of?" Anecdotal claims are important because they tell us there is a territory to be investigated, but they are not evidence, really. Then I thought about Lourdes, in France, where an apparition of the Virgin Mary appeared in 1858.

Since then there have been approximately 6000 claims of miraculous healing. Mind you, there have been millions of people going there, so this is not a high percentage. Of those 6000, only 64 have made it through the procedures of the International Medical Commission to be officially declared miracles. The Commission was organized in a fairly sophisticated form in 1947, and they have records since about the 1860s, varying in quality during the early period.

Let me tell you a little bit about the Commission's procedure, so you'll realize that it is not easy to have a miracle, at least from their point of view. I am quoting here from a paper by St. John Dowling in the *Journal of the Royal Society of Medicine* of August 1984:

> At present there are 25 members of the Commission: thirteen French, two Italian, two Belgian, two English, two Irish, one each from Spain, Holland, Scotland and Germany. [Interestingly there are no members from the United States. I wonder about that.] Then they have a wide spread of specialties. Four each from general medicine and surgery, three from orthopedics, two each from general psychiatry and general practice, and one each from radiology, neuropsychiatry, dermatology, opthalmology, pediatrics, cardiology, oncology, neurology and biochemistry. Ten members hold chairs in their medical schools. All are practicing Catholics. Many are doctors who come regularly to Lourdes as pilgrimage medical officers, but some have little or no connection with the shrine.
>
> If, after the initial scrutiny and follow-up, the Medical Bureau thinks that there is good evidence of an inexplicable cure, the dossier is sent to the International Medical Commission which usually meets once a year in Paris. The preliminary investigation of the data is made, and if the members agree that the case is worth investigating, they appoint one or two of their members to act as rapporteur. The rapporteur then makes a thorough study of the case, usually seeing the patient himself [or herself], and presents the material in a detailed written dossier circulated to the members before the meeting at which they will make their decision.
>
> The report is then discussed critically, at length, under 18 headings, a vote being taken at each stage. In the first three stages, the Committee considers the diagnosis and has to satisfy itself that a correct diagnosis has been made and proven by the production of the results of full physical examination, laboratory investigations, x-ray studies and endoscopy and biopsy where applicable. Failure at this stage is commonly because of inadequate investigation or missing documents. At the next two stages, the Committee must be satisfied that the disease was organic and serious without any significant degree of psychological overlay [their words].
>
> Next it must make sure that the natural history of the disease precludes the possibility of spontaneous remission. [In other words, they throw out all cases where a remission could have occurred because, for them, remission is natural, not supernatural. *Their* rejects become part of *our* database. Hence the importance of talking to them.] The medical treatment given cannot have affected the cure. Cases ruled out here are those about which there cannot be any certainty that the treatment has not been effective. For example, a course of cytotoxic drugs would lead to the case being rejected even where the likelihood of success was small. [So they're operating with a fairly tough set of criteria.] Then the evidence that the patient has indeed been cured is scrutinized and the Committee must be satisfied that both objective and subjective symptoms have disappeared and that investigations are normal. The suddenness and completeness of the cure are considered together with any sequelae. Finally, the adequacy of the length of follow-up is considered. After this detailed study, the question, 'Does the cure of this person constitute a phenomenon which is contrary to the observations and expectations of medical knowledge and scientifically inexplicable?' is put. A simple majority carries the case one way or the other.

This then gives you some idea of the criteria being used at Lourdes. It suggests quite careful scrutiny of the claims. It is also worth noting that they discard a large number of cases that perhaps should be included if there were better objective means of documenting them. I am referring here to the cases with significant psychological overlay, as Dowling points out. If you look at the chart describing all the cures at Lourdes since 1858, you find interesting changes in the data over time. For example, at the beginning there are many references to tuberculosis of various kinds. These no longer appear today since we now can cure TB. A sceptic will of course cast doubt on the accuracy of the diagnoses of some of the earlier cures and maybe this is correct in some cases. I think it is fair to say that doctors back in the 1860s probably *did* know how to diagnose things like TB and that they could easily have been wrong in diagnosing various types of cancer, cysts of the liver and so on. But when you come up to the present time those kinds of objections should diminish to a marked degree—particularly in the cases since 1947 when more modern procedures were instituted.

I want to deal with one case in some detail so you get a feeling for what goes on in the more contemporary cases. First though, here is a little quote from a paper by James Hansen that appeared in *New Scientist* in 1982, entitled "Can Science Allow Miracles?"

> A miracle is when something that cannot happen does anyway. It is not a question of the manifestation of hitherto unknown natural laws, if there are such that multiply loaves and permit walking on water, but rather a temporary suspension of nature itself by some outside supernatural action. If this can happen, there is a problem. In science, exceptions do not prove the rule. Doing research at all means making at least a few basic assumptions: that nature is knowable, and that it is constant. Experiments can be done, and most important repeated. The genuine possibility of divine intervention as an unknown variable knocks the whole house of cards to pieces.

Let's see what you think of this particular house of cards with respect to the case I have chosen to go into in some detail. This is a man named Vittorio Michelli. I will now quote from the official report of the Medical Commission:

> He was admitted in 1962 to the Military Hospital of Verona in Italy suffering from a large mass in the buttock region limiting the normal range of movement of his left hip with leg and sciatic pain. After various unsuccessful therapeutic trials, radiological examination showed a structural alteration of the left iliac bone (osteolysis of the inferior half of the iliac bone and of the acetabular roof, amputation of the two rami of the ischium and gross osteoporosis of the femoral head) immediately suggestive of a malignant type of neoplastic lesion.
>
> At the end of May a biopsy was taken. The exposure of the tumor had to be made beneath the buttock muscles and the various sections revealed that the specimen under consideration was a fusiform cell carcinoma. The sick man was then immobilised in a frame from pelvis to feet and sent during the month of June to a Centre for radiotherapy. Four days later he was discharged—without having received any therapy at all—and readmitted to the Military Hospital at Trente.
>
> There during the next ten months there was no specific treatment, medical, surgical or radiotherapeutic, in spite of the fact that there was radiological evidence of persistent bony destruction; progressive loss of all active movement of the left lower limb; progressive deterioration. [In fact, the whole hip was being destroyed by the bone; it was being eaten away. He was literally falling apart—the leg was being separated, this mass was growing, and the actual bone of the pelvis was disintegrating.]

On the 24th of May, 1963 [this is now approximately a year after his original diagnosis] the patient left for Lourdes where he was bathed, in his plaster, several times.

One thing that happens at Lourdes is that people who go there are bathed in the spring. Some cynics say that the major miracle in Lourdes is that nobody has ever gotten sick from drinking the water in which these thousands of people have been bathed.

Upon bathing he had sudden sensations of heat moving through his body, which characterizes this kind of healing. We're not sure what it means, but you hear about it. When he arrived at Lourdes he couldn't eat and had lost vast amounts of weight. This information is all included in the report. After being bathed he felt an immediate return of his appetite and an amazing resurgence of energy. They took him back to the hospital, and frankly no one believed he felt better. Even people who let you go to Lourdes don't believe that it does anything, I guess! He started to gain weight and to be much more active. After about a month, his doctors finally consented to take his cast off and take another x-ray. They made an extensive report on what they found. In essence, they discovered that the tumor was getting smaller and smaller. It was regressing.

Then the tumor disappeared, and the bone began to regrow and completely reconstruct itself. Michelli was able to walk again two months after his return from Lourdes. I'll quote here from the report:

> A remarkable reconstruction of the iliac bone and cavity has taken place. The x-rays made in 1964 -5, -8 and -9 confirm categorically and without doubt that an unforeseen and even overwhelming bone reconstruction has taken place of a type unknown in the annals of world medicine. We ourselves, during a university and hospital career of over 45 years spent largely in the study of tumors and neoplasms of all kinds of bone structures and having ourselves treated hundreds of such cases, have never encountered a single spontaneous bone reconstruction of such a nature.

At the end of this report they say,

> Definitely a medical explanation of the cure of sarcoma from which Michelli suffered was sought and none could be found. He did not undergo specific treatment, did not suffer from any susceptible intercurrent infection that might have had any influence on the evolution of the cancer. [Notice here that they are aware that infections can stimulate remission.]
>
> A completely destroyed articulation was completely reconstructed without any surgical intervention. The lower limb which was useless became sound, the prognosis is indisputable, the patient is alive and in a flourishing state of health nine years after his return from Lourdes.

There are 64 of these cases if you want to go into some detail, but I thought I'd pick just one and tell you about it.

There was a very intriguing paper published in the *Journal of the Royal Society of Medicine* in August of 1984. The author, St. John Dowling, did a follow-up study of thirteen of the people who had been cured at Lourdes. Nobody ever seems to talk to these people, and in contrast, I think I should jump on a plane and go interview them all! Of the thirteen, he found that eleven were still alive and well and healed, showing no signs of their original illness. Of the other two, one was dead because of a tractor accident. The other one is interesting because it tells you something about this whole question of our knowledge about remission. This was a woman who was recognized as having been cured in 1954. She had something called Bud-Chiari syndrome and its apparent disappearance was recognized as a miracle in 1963, but she died in 1970 from complications of that syndrome. They now have to go back and re-evaluate that and say "Well, we didn't know that she could go into temporary remission." It is a case where a decision was made, but it was really a temporary remission, not a complete cure. There's always this very difficult territory of distinguishing between a remission and a cure. I've heard "remission" referred to in certain major hospitals as simply "time to recurrence". The physicians will often say that it's inevitable, that it will recur. Maybe it will, maybe it won't.

It is worth noting that this Commission has presumably the biggest database on remission outside of ours. Ours is now actually bigger than theirs, and as a result it turns out that we may be going to redefine how miracles are evaluated in the Catholic Church, to the extent that their definition of a miracle is dependent on the degree of their knowledge of remission. This, by the way, is not what I expected to do when I started the Remission Project.

At this point I thought to myself, here are these interesting healings occurring apparently as a result of an apparition that appeared in 1858. Is there anywhere *today* where an apparition might be appearing, and if there is, are there extraordinary healings associated with that? I discovered that there is indeed a site in Yugoslavia where an apparition of the Virgin Mary has been reported every day since June 24, 1981. It's in the little village of Medjugorje, about two-and-a-half hours north of Dubrovnik. I went there in May of 1986.

Now we read virtually nothing about this in the press here. There have been, to my knowledge, perhaps one or two articles. It's interesting that *The New York Times* wrote about it in November of last year and referred to it as "Yugoslavia's little economic miracle" because they could only deal with the fact of the increasing tourism to Medjugorje. To be honest, that is a significant factor here because two million people have gone to this little village since 1981 just to *be*

there. It's a major place of pilgrimage at this time.

I could talk to you for a long time about the apparition. Briefly, I learned there are six children, two boys and four girls, who see the apparition. It is not seen by everyone who is there. The purpose of the apparition, according to what it says to the children, is to bring peace to the world and to remind us of the need to become aware of God, *in our own way*. (These last four words are, by the way, making the Catholic hierarchy a little bit distracted because it doesn't suggest that everyone should become Catholic. Further there apparently was a bit of consternation in Medjugorje when a *Moslem* boy was healed.)

The children see this apparition every day around 6:30 to 6:45 pm. It doesn't matter where they are, but typically they gather together in a room to share the experience or to be there together. I interviewed two of them, one of the boys and one of the girls. Were they making this up? Are they credible? Did they seem to be presenting something that one could accept was an experience they were indeed having?

I won't go into a lot of detail now. However I became rapidly convinced that these were kids whose lives had been dramatically changed by the experience of the apparition in ways that made me feel that I would never want to exchange places with them. They have *no* privacy, for they are completely at the mercy of the millions of people going through there. They've been interrogated by the police, and the priest in charge has been put in jail and served 18 months of a jail sentence. The authorities don't quite know what to make of this and they put roadblocks around the village every weekend and try to track who's coming and going. So it's a very complicated story.

I talked to the priest who was the children's spiritual director, Father Slavko, a Franciscan monk with a PhD in psychology—which is not what you'd expect in a little village in the middle of nowhere, so to speak. He was intrigued that I was there to study healing because nobody, or very few, had come for that purpose. Most people come to pray and to hear what the apparition has to say about the danger the world is in, the need for world peace, and all of these basic issues. I said, "Yes, I'm interested in all that too, but I want to know if there's healing happening here." And the answer was yes—there are some 250-300 reports. He let me see the various files. I noted that some of them were very good reports, some of them were very poor. So you don't regard this as much beyond anecdotal evidence.

One of the better cases was a woman from Milan, Italy, who had been diagnosed and treated under every kind of circumstance that you could imagine for multiple sclerosis. She arrived in a wheelchair, was in the apparition room with the children one evening, and while they were having the apparition experience, felt this sudden movement through her body and stood up and said, "I can walk, I am healed!" And the priest said, "Kneel down and pray." He just was not interested in the healing. She has since been in good health and her case is being monitored in Italy.

There have been cases of people with remission from blindness, from cancers, from tumors, from all sorts of things, and they are now beginning to send cases to the Medical Bureau at Lourdes, which isn't quite sure what to do with them. It's very intriguing that this sort of thing is going on and the Franciscan is quite circumspect. He's saying that in his view, he can sometimes tell who will be healed. I asked "What do you mean? How you can tell?" He said, "It's very often the people who come and don't determinedly *want* healing who are affected. They come with an open mind and with the spirit of simply doing God's will. They may ask for healing but they have not come with this as the single-minded purpose of their trip."

This suggested an interesting psychological profile of those that would be healed and indeed, being in Medjugorje presents one with an intense experiential sense of the presence of simple faith and devotion. Interestingly, one gets the impression that one can easily tell the difference between the devout and the merely pious there. There is a sad, faraway look in the eyes of the devout that is unmistakable. It seems like a kind of yearning for something, the search for a memory, the need for an all-embracing experience of love of a kind not ever found. This alone suggests to the eye seeking clues that these people *are* in a very different place psychologically, emotionally and indeed psychophysiologically.

I was in the apparition room with the children when they were having the experience of an apparition. I did not see the Virgin, in case you're wondering. But there was a very strange set of sensations that accompanied it. It was as though there was this incredible wave of feeling throughout the room that hit one in the solar plexus—an incredible kind of sadness that made people cry. It was a very intense thing that quietly takes hold of you. I was not told about that in advance, and I was sort of taken aback by it. It's all the more intense and curious because there are so many people outside the room, clamoring to get in. I felt guilty being there because there were people outside who had incredible problems who wanted to be in there, and then I was taking up space. But when the apparition left the children, everyone outside began spontaneously singing the Ave Maria in all these different languages with no cues from those inside the room as far as I could tell. So it's a strange feeling, but you get a sense that something very, very intense is happening there. To me it is more complex than any religious system. It's a very deep experience. You come away feeling, well, if there are conditions of prayer and spirit and mind that can be conducive to healing, then surely this is a good place for them to be expected.

So we have now in fact begun to try to study some of these people. We have some cooperation from an im-munologist in Yugoslavia who may study some of them and do some tests. But it's difficult when you can't even write a letter there because of what the authorities might do. They have been known to confiscate equipment and forbid entry to people. It's a complicated story. I happened to be there, for example, when the cloud from Chernobyl blew over but we didn't even know it because we were cut off from the news. So I was startled when I later discovered that a researcher from Boston had gone there with some geiger counter equipment to measure radioactive levels, about two years ago. There were strange measurements on his geiger counter, way above the normal, when the apparition was appearing. One wonders just what that's about. He also measured the electrostatic field in the region where the apparition was appearing and noticed that it went up to about 70,000 volts per meter.

All kinds of studies have been made of the children, by the way. A team of French and a team of Italian doctors measured EEGs, and took electro-ocular scans. They've done everything to these poor kids while they were having an ecstatic experience of the Virgin. Somehow I didn't expect to react by feeling how ridiculous this seemed to be when one is actually there during such an event. An EEG is never going to capture an apparition, I don't think. But people were trying to do that.

There's a very interesting anecdote from another study that's going on. A doctoral student in Moscow, Idaho, put an ad in the paper asking if anybody in a 300-mile radius of that town had experienced a remission. She got 25 replies, and she started conducting interviews. Many who replied were farmers' wives. She asked one of them, "How did you feel when the doctor told you that you had this terminal illness and that you'd be dead in six months?" "That was *his* opinion," was the reply. The interviewer said, "Would you like to say more about that?" She said, "Well, you know we're told all these things by all these experts. We live on a farm, and all these federal people come in and they look at the soil and they tell us that nothing will grow and we should put these fertilizers in and we should do all this stuff. We don't do it and hell, things grow there anyway. So why would I listen to an expert?" I'm not saying to ignore your physician, but I'm saying that people of an independent mind and spirit seem to be people who have a better prognosis in these matters.

In summary I think that there is a lot we can learn by studying these kinds of things. We plan to gather people in remission; we hope to find out more about who they are, what they did and why they feel the way they feel.

Conclusion

I could go on with more and more of these stories, but time is limited. In conclusion let me mention some interesting clues coming now from the field of psychoneuroimmunology, that, as I said before, deals with the links between the brain, the mind and the immune system. We had thought that only those communications mediated in the mind/body system by the brain were important. But recently other systems have been discovered to be important, too. The major one is the recently discovered, and perhaps prematurely named—though I think it's not premature myself—neuropeptide system. When I was doing brain research twenty years ago, injecting radioactive isotopes into rat brains and doing all kinds of horrible things that I've since stopped doing, we knew that there were neurotransmitters. We knew that there were substances in the brain that were responsible for the transmission of information in the brain. There were about three or four of them known in 1967. Today there are some 50 or 60 neuropeptides that are known, and what's very interesting is that they're being discovered all over the body. They're not just in the brain, they're in the gut, in the kidneys, throughout the system. This is a different system from the nervous system, though it is also part of the nervous system. Some of these same neuropeptides are found in cells of the immune system. So the whole picture of distinction between brain and body is getting much more blurred than it has been. I'll quote from an interesting book that I would recommend your reading. It's called *The Psychobiology of Mind/Body Healing* by Ernest Rossi, just out from Norton Press. The last two paragraphs summarize where I think we may go with this in terms of the science of mind/body healing.

Thus the slower-acting but more pervasive, flexible and unconscious functioning of the neuropeptide activity of mind/body communication more adequately fits the facts of hypnotic experience than the faster acting, highly specific and consciously generated processes of the central and peripheral nervous systems. If we were to use a computer analogy, we could say that the peripheral nerves of the central nervous system are hardwired in a pre-set fixed pattern of stimulus and response, just as is the hardware of the computer. The neuropeptide system, however, is like the software of the computer that contains the flexible, easily changed patterns of information. The receptors and highly individualized responses of the neuropeptide system are easily changed as a function of life experience, memory and learning. Neuropeptides, then, are a previously unrecognized form of information transduction between mind and body that may be the basis of many hypnotherapeutic, psychosocial and placebo responses.

From a broader perspective, the neuropeptide system may also be the psychobiological basis of the folk, shamanistic and spiritual forms of healing that share many of the characteristics of hypnotic healing currently returning to vogue under the banner of wholistic medicine.

So there are some very interesting syntheses and fusions occurring. We at the Institute of Noetic Sciences are doing our best to spread seed grants around this country and maybe other countries to stimulate an integration of this kind of knowledge. We feel there is much to be learned from people in remission and people who have been healed in a spiritual way. They are, I think, our resource for the future.

Thank you.

Our efforts at the Institute of Noetic Sciences have always been in the direction of fostering a more integrated and holistic approach to science and nature. We must realize that remissions, for example, are the successful experiments of Nature from which we should strive to learn. They speak of the fact that there is a healing system within us that can, when triggered appropriately, recognize and eliminate cancer and many other diseases. The mind is certainly involved, albeit in a highly complex and varying way.

Brendan O'Regan is Vice-President for Research and has been the Director of Research for the Institute of Noetic Sciences since 1975. He received his BSc (Hons) Degree in Chemistry and Mathematics from the National University of Ireland and his MS Degree in Neurochemistry from Indiana University. He was Research Coordinator for R. Buckminster Fuller at Southern Illinois University for two years, and then became a science policy consultant to the Center for the Study of Social Policy at Stanford Research Institute. In addition he has been consultant to and/or associate producer of a number of documentary films on scientific research into human behavior for such clients as BBC, NBC and PBS.

David L. Smith

If one can flow with change now, then at the big moment of change called death,
one can let go naturally. It is very simple because the Truth is simple,
and change is the Truth, or true nature of this world.

Survival of Consciousness:
A Tibetan Buddhist Perspective

Editor's note: The accompanying article was adapted from a talk delivered by Tibetan Lama Sogyal Rinpoche at the Symposium on Consciousness and Survival, co-sponsored by the Institute of Noetic Sciences. Rinpoche was one of a panel of eleven scholars and scientists who were asked to apply insights from their research findings on mind/body relationships to the question: Does individual consciousness survive bodily death?

Not surprisingly, keynote presentations and ensuing discussions reflected a rich diversity of responses—ranging from the assertion that the question is meaningless to begin with, to Rinpoche's observation that in Buddhism survival is taken as given, the concern being rather with the quality of consciousness that survives after leaving the body.

What I would like to share with you is based on Tibetan Buddhist teachings, particularly *The Tibetan Book of the Dead*. This is knowledge of how to deal with death and dying. I hope it will help in preparing for our own deaths, helping dying persons, and also aiding people who are already dead, but who are not beyond reach of help. But at the same time I would like to say that to really equip oneself fully in this particular way requires a lifetime of dedication and training in the Buddhist point of view. One must have a certain understanding of one's own mind so that when a person is dying, the true nature of the mind is manifested in its fullest force. For one to prepare in this way for death or to help someone else who is dying, that person generally needs seven years or more of training in the understanding of the mind. Even so, I present briefly the fundamental attitude that is necessary in order to help the dying.

First, I would like to comment on the research and work that is being done in this country on death and dying. From my point of view there is something lacking, even in the marvelous work of Elisabeth Kubler-Ross and others like her. They rely only on the reports of people who have died and come back. I think it would be very helpful if there were more research into the wisdom of other cultures which are more deeply rooted and more ancient. The experiences of these people who have died clinically for a few minutes are only the first experiences that occur at death. These initial experiences cannot reveal the nature of the many other experiences that follow. So, one cannot jump to conclusions and assume that the entire death process is revealed in the few minutes these people have lived through.

The most crucial attitude toward death is acceptance. When death is not accepted, there is fear and panic. That is why Buddhist teachings stress the development of mindfulness and recognition of impermanence and death. *Everything that is seen, everything that appears in life is constantly changing or dying. If one can understand the aspect of change and flow with it, then there is less pain and suffering. On the other hand, if one tries to freeze this process by wanting things to be solid and to be always as they are now, when they break or separate there is tremendous pain, disappointment, and shock. The first thing one is taught in Buddhism is to see that the nature of life is change.*

The great Tibetan yogi Milarepa said that because he feared death and impermanence, he retreated into the mountains. There he meditated upon impermanence and death. Upon learning to accept them, he was able to come back into the world and start living again.

Death cannot be prepared for as if it were a moment that is somehow separate from the rest of life. Rather, it is prepared for from now onward by accepting the change that constantly occurs. If one can flow with change now, then at the big moment of change called death, one can let go naturally. It is very simple because the Truth is simple, and change *is* the Truth, or true nature of this world.

However, if the changing nature of life is not understood, then one pretends that everything will be all right and will remain the same. That cover-up thinking, which is done again and again, creates an insensitivity to change and even to death. This is one of the reasons that this generation has institutionalized death in hospitals. So many deaths are seen happening on television that one is no longer moved by it. It seems that

Until we reach a deeper perspective on the nature of death, and a new respect for its life-enhancing qualities, we will never be able either to properly care for the dying or personally understand and experience the meaning of life.

death only happens to other people. In fact, this is like the logic with which people hope to win lotteries! You think that you are the lucky one. But when death comes, you are unprepared. There is no way to know with certainty how or when death will occur. For this reason the holy places in Tibet contain prayers that say, "May my death be peaceful. May my death not be traumatic. May my death be clear to me so that it becomes an opportunity for liberation."

Luminosity of Inherent Mind

In order for death to be clear in that way, it must be understood that the mind has two levels. First, there is the inherent Mind, the awareness when our mind is truly clear—the deep Mind, which is like the sun, brilliant and shining. That is the Buddha-Mind. On that level our individual mind and the Buddha-Mind are one. Then, on the surface, there is the cloudy mind, the thinking mind, which is flickering, jumping, and confused. It is because this confused mind covers the sun of our original Buddha-Mind that we are stuck and not free. In order to recognize the inherent wisdom of the Buddha-Mind, the clouds of confusion and thinking must be removed. All the teachings are aimed at trying to remove the cloud of confusion that covers the sun of our inherent Buddha-Nature. Once these clouds are removed through spiritual practice, our true Mind can spontaneously manifest. The way of making this cloud disappear is by letting our grasping and confusion go.

Each of us has surely experienced a moment of life when we are able to let go a little bit, when we are calmer and in touch with a sense of a kind of spaciousness or tranquility. In that state the mind becomes clear, sharp, and direct. It is as though there is a crack in the cloudy sky, and the sun of our inherent Buddha-Mind comes out. In that moment there is a feeling of oneness and knowingness. There is also a vision of tremendous light.

That kind of mystical or spiritual experience comes very directly and vividly at the moment of death. Sometimes it comes so strongly that this light or sun of true Mind almost blinds us. We may faint or go unconscious at that moment, and as a result we withdraw. We don't let ourselves go and recognize the inherent Buddha-Nature of our own minds. We do not gain liberation.

You see, when you are dying, you are leaving your gross body and your world behind, but most importantly you have to leave behind your assumptions about the world that are in your head. But this letting go is not easy.

My teacher summed up this wisdom in one line: "At the moment of death, leave behind both your attachment and your aversion." The most important thing is to keep your mind pure without any grasping and to direct the mind into its inherent luminosity. This luminos-

At the moment of death, friends and relatives must release a dying person. When loved ones communicate deeply, there is a feeling of oneness—there is no separation. The dying person feels that he or she can go. A person can hold on and not die for many days if you do not give permission for them to go. This can be very traumatic. For the dying person the most important thing is to keep the mind clear and pure and not to think of those left behind.

In Sikkim in the early sixties, there was an old nun who had been practicing spirituality all her life. She became ill and could tell that she would die soon. She started packing her things up and simplifying her life. Then one morning my aunt, who is also a very great teacher, checked the old nun's pulse and saw the signs of the elements dissolving. She immediately called an old man in our family, who was also a great teacher.

It was about nine o'clock in the morning. He came into the room and told the nun, "I think it is time for you to go. You must see what your teachers have taught you to see. This is the time to put your visualizations into practice. Whichever wisdom of the Buddha you can relate to, unite your mind with that and don't think about us here behind. It is OK. I am going shopping; when I come back, perhaps I won't see you, so goodbye."

He did this with a smile and the nun also laughed. That kind of confident humor is important. Also, in that moment we cannot give the dying person new teaching. Whatever one believes in most is what should be affirmed. If a person believes in a particular form or image of God, that is the form that will comfort them after death.

ity or light is our experience of the emptiness of the Buddha Mind. When that luminosity appears, you can relate to that light directly with your inherent intelligence; then there is freedom. If that does not happen, you become lost in confusion. Then after the luminosity experience you wake up from the light and begin to relive the past experiences that were strongest in life. This return to the past creates rebirth, which is simply a continuation of our habits and tendencies. If you can cut away the force of these habits at the moment of seeing the luminosity and let go, you are free. But if you do not let go and rather dwell in your past, you will be reborn.

From the accounts of many Tibetans who have died and come back, we have learned how this process continues. After the experience of luminosity, if you fail to recognize it as your own true Mind, you faint or lose consciousness. Then when you wake up, you begin to feel like you are being blown everywhere. You cannot stay in one place. You are blown by the wind to all of the places you have been in life. It is said that you go to a place even if you only spit there once.

At this time your consciousness is so clear that you can read other people's minds. You become clairvoyant. This is a stage where the deceased's relatives as well as friends can help or harm a lot because the dead person can know their minds. If the relatives are fighting over the goods left behind, that can make the deceased one lose faith in them and turn vengeful. This can result in the dead remaining associated with the gross realm as a ghost. It is also possible that if a priest or someone else doing a service for the deceased is not sincere, then that person may lose faith in the teaching.

Helping the Dying

If you wish to be helpful to those who are dying or have recently died, the most important thing is to tell the truth. The person must be told that he or she is dying. If you don't tell them, there is much confusion. After dying, the person may not know that he or she has in fact died. Also, you must refrain from pleading for them not to go. This would make the person more and more attached. If you are a friend, you should be there in a strong and clear way. The person dying is feeling very insecure because their whole world is falling apart. The absence of strength in the face of another's death is a reflection of our own personal anxiety. To beg the dying person to stay in life is not in their best interest at all.

If you are there with the dying person, you can call all the power of all the Masters and the Buddhas and help the person. They should also ask the Buddhas to help them go freely and well. It is very simple. Buddhas are not biased. They come more easily to lamas than to ordinary people, but they come equally, like the way the sun shines equally on everybody. If you ask their help with confidence, their blessing will be there.

In *The Tibetan Book of the Dead*, one hears of many visions that come to a dying person. These visions are not accorded by different figures of Buddhas. Rather, they are the different energies in the mind that is leaving. In a sense, the true Mind is beginning to shine. As it does so, one is slightly awestruck by visions. Some of these rays are peaceful; some are powerful; some are quite wrathful. Because you are not used to these visions, you may react or recoil from them. But if you can realize that these visions are the display of energies of your own mind, then there is liberation and freedom.

Spiritual practice is a way to prepare for death. It is important if you have been practicing for awhile that you learn to "essentialize". In other words, you must know what your practice is so that in the moment of death you can do it very spontaneously. You can't just say, "Wait a minute; I have to do my practice". That does not work. It is a matter of whether you've got it or not. You must be involved in real meditation, that is, meditation that reveals the Buddha-Mind.

The best form of bereavement is also to do spiritual practice. Meditate and pray and try to reassure the dead person. Tell the dead to look into the nature of Mind. Tell him or her that all the experiences they may go through are only their own mental projections. They have more of an opportunity than us to recognize the true Nature because the mind is more receptive after death. So, if you tell the deceased these things, you will aid the release from this gross world. In fact, if you are really meditating when someone has died, you directly show the true Nature of Mind to that person. You don't have to say anything. If you know what your meditation is and can remain in that with great simplicity and strength, the deceased catches that clarity.

Therefore, if you are with someone who is dying, you must both let go. If you do this, it will be a tremendous learning process—for you as well because death is a powerful situation. It is really the moment of truth. It can change your way of life! If it is possible, the best thing you could do would be to go on a retreat after the death. Then really do as much practice as you can. Come face to face with the truth of impermanence. Even the greatest teaching of a Buddha's life is his death. This is one of the reasons many of the great teachers are ill at this time. They show us how suffering is a reality. In fact, in Buddhism facing the Truth is the most important thing.

Dying is itself the best way of living now. I'll give you an example. There was a great teacher who before he would go to bed every night would put away everything and leave nothing pending. He even put the cups upside down. Then the next day, if he had life, he was grateful and began again. That kind of preparation is not being futuristic; it is being very present. Even so, taking care of the present should also prepare us for death. Otherwise there is a problem being in the here and now. You can get stuck here if you forget about the inevitability of death. It is even worse to be stuck in the present than to be stuck in the past. So, you should be here now, but don't get stuck.

When clouds evaporate the clear sky is naturally there. After the fire, only the pure gold remains. So also, what survives after change is what is true. In this truth enlightenment takes place. This is the Buddhist sense of eternity, the space where even discontinuity is part of a fundamental continuity. Death itself is the open space of emptiness.

The Venerable Sogyal Rinpoche is an incarnate Lama, scholar and meditation master from Tibet. He studied comparative religion and philosophy at Cambridge University, and is now in Santa Cruz, California.

The presentations, including this one by Sogyal Rinpoche, of the 1985 Consciousness and Survival symposium sponsored by the Institute of Noetic Sciences are now a book, out this month. The cover photo, below, was given to us by Eric Heiner.

Consciousness and Survival: An Interdisciplinary Inquiry into the Possibility of Life Beyond Biological Death
Edited by John S. Spong, Bishop, Diocese of Newark with an introduction by Claiborne Pell

Being Peace
by Thich Nhat Hanh

From time to time, to remind ourselves to relax, to be peaceful, we may wish to set aside some time for a retreat, a day of mindfulness, when we can walk slowly, smile, drink tea with a friend, enjoy being together as if we are the happiest people on Earth. This is not a retreat, it is a treat. During walking meditation, during kitchen and garden work, during sitting meditation, all day long, we can practice smiling. At first you may find it difficult to smile, and we have to think about why. Smiling means that we are ourselves, that we have sovereignty over ourselves, that we are not drowned into forgetfulness. This kind of smile can be seen on the faces of Buddhas and Bodhisattvas.

I would like to offer one short poem you can recite from time to time, while breathing and smiling.

> Breathing in, I calm my body.
> Breathing out, I smile.
> Dwelling in the present moment
> I know this is a wonderful moment.

Even though life is hard, even though it is sometimes difficult to smile, we have to try. Recently, one friend asked me, "How can I force myself to smile when I am filled with sorrow? It isn't natural." I told her she must be able to smile to her sorrow, because we are more than our sorrow. A human being is like a television set with millions of channels. If we turn the Buddha on, we are the Buddha. If we turn sorrow on, we are sorrow. If we turn a smile on, we really are the smile. We cannot let just one channel dominate us.

It is really beautiful to begin the day by being a Buddha. Each time we feel ourselves about to leave our Buddha, we can sit and breathe until we return to our true self. There are three things I can recommend to you: arranging to have a breathing room in your home, a room for meditation; practicing breathing sitting, for a few minutes every morning at home with your children; and going out for a slow walking meditation with your children before going to sleep, just ten minutes is enough. These things are very important. They can change our civilization.

Life is both dreadful and wonderful. To practice meditation is to be in touch with both aspects. Please do not think we must be solemn in order to meditate. In fact, to meditate well, we have to smile a lot.

If in our daily life we can smile, if we can be peaceful and happy, not only we, but everyone will profit from it. This is the most basic kind of peace work.

Thich Nhat Hanh was born in central Vietnam in 1926, and he left home as a teenager to become a Zen monk. He founded the School for Youth for Social Service, Van Hanh Buddhist University, and the Tiep Hien Order. In 1966 he was invited by the Fellowship of Reconciliation to tour the United States to describe the enormous suffering of his people. Because of his fierce neutrality, he was unable to return home, and he was granted asylum in France, where he is head of a small community of meditators and activists. Nhat Hanh is the author of 66 books in Vietnamese, French and English.

This piece is excerpted from his Being Peace, *the third printing in 1988 by Parallax Press (PO Box 7355, Berkeley, California 94707), with permission.* Being Peace *is available through the Institute Book-Ordering Service for the member price of $7.20.*

David L. Smith

The accompanying article was adapted from a talk by Rachel Naomi Remen at the three-day conference "Helping Heal the Whole Person and the Whole World". Sponsored by the John E. Fetzer Foundation, the conference was attended by delegates from twenty-one countries and thirty-nine of the United States. Its purpose was to explore strategies for addressing the related problems of personal and global health. Dr. Remen was one of a panel on Strategies for Healing: The Spirit.

Spirit:
Resource for Healing

by Rachel Naomi Remen

I'd like to examine some of the implications of calling our field the *mind-body* health field. Such terms as mind-body research, mind-body health are spreading like a wave across the country. They're in every public media. I want to put out some thoughts about this. These thoughts are very personal. There's no need to agree with them. I just want to share them and perhaps they'll serve as a seed for further discussion.

The first thought I have is that I'm not at all certain the mind is the highest human function. Or perhaps the mind *is* the highest *human* function—but we transcend our humanness. Something in us participates in our humanness, but has its source and its connection far beyond it, and in that connection may lie the hope of healing.

When people, the public in general, talk about mind-body health they may be at risk of overlooking or forgetting this. They may be falling into what is a culture-wide tendency to deny spirit or even to omit it totally. The term *mind-body health* suggests to the public that our field is about gaining mental control of physical functions, that we are experts in fixing the body by using the mind. This makes sense to people, and they are interested, because the mind is a simpler, safer, cheaper, more efficient, more affordable way of fixing the body than, let's say, surgery. So the whole purpose of the field may be coming to be seen as the manipulation of the body to attain physical health. And I'm not at all sure that understanding how to manipulate the body to perfect function with the mind is a large enough purpose for our field.

Health is not an end. Health is a means. Health enables us to serve purpose in life, but it is not the purpose in life. Bernie

Health enables us to serve purpose in our life, but it is not the purpose in life. One can serve purpose with impaired health. One might even regain health through serving purpose.

Siegel pointed this out so beautifully in his talk yesterday in his case of John the landscaper—the man who wanted, in spite of his cancer, to make beauty in the world. *One can serve purpose with impaired health.* One might even regain health through serving purpose as John did.

I am also concerned that this is not just how the public sees us, but, in my less optimistic moments, I fear that the field may actually be deteriorating into a kind of mechanical or mechanistic enterprise. As if in pursuit of deeper and deeper understanding of how we live, how consciousness and the body interact, the mechanism by which emotion affects the T-cells, how the brain-waves change when we pray—that somehow in this pursuit something very important may slip through our fingers, and we might not even know it.

How we live is not as important to me as *why* we live. Why are we here in these bodies? What are we doing here like this? This mystery is more important to me than discovering how these bodies function.

I saw a cartoon in *The New Yorker* recently which shows two yogis sitting on a lip of a cave on top of a very high mountain, which I assume is a mountain in the Himalayas. Sitting there cross-legged, they obviously have been interrupted in their meditation by a 747 airplane which is flying by. One of them looks at the other and says, "Ah, they have the know-*how*, but do they have the know-*why*?"

So the real questions of health may not be questions of mechanism but questions of spirit. Healing is not a matter of mechanism; it is a work of spirit and we need to study those conditions that further that work. We need to remember that at the

Rachel Naomi Remen is Medical Director of the Commonweal Cancer Help Program and serves on the Scientific Advisory Board for the Inner Mechanisms of the Healing Response program of the Institute of Noetic Sciences. A physician in private practice in behavioral medicine and transpersonal counseling, she is adjunct faculty at Saybrook Institute, scientific advisory board member of the Institute for the Advancement of Health, and a member of the International Psycho-oncology Society. She is on the editorial advisory board of The Journal of Mind and Behavior *and is author of* The Human Patient *(Doubleday, 1980). © 1988 by Rachel Naomi Remen* very heart of spirit is mystery. And the problem with the mind is that the mind cannot tolerate mystery.

Now what are the practical implications of basing a healing system on an aspect of ourselves that can't tolerate mystery? We have a wonderful example of this in contemporary Western medicine. You know allopathic medicine is one of many medical systems developed by humankind in our pursuit of healing, and ours is the most mentally oriented, the most analytical of the healing systems. It is also the only healing system that does not allow the possibility of the mysterious or the miraculous. So what does it look like when the miraculous, the unexplainable does manifest itself? I think we can see it clearly if we consider those cases when people recover from an illness when all mental, medical, chemical means have been exhausted.

Brendan O'Regan has made a collection of these cases in his work as Vice-President for Research at the Institute of Noetic Sciences. These are well-documented cases known to medical science, and have been published in various medical journals throughout the world. They are usually presented as single cases and used as "fillers" between the "heavy stuff", the scientific studies. I've been reading them for years. Taken one by one they are puzzling, but no one pays them much attention. Brendan, however, has collected thousands of them. Thousands. That's another matter entirely.

I actually participated in one of these cases as an intern. We had a man with widespread metastasis of cancer to the bone; it was eight months since his last dose of chemotherapy and radiation and he was dying. He was admitted to our hospital at the Cornell Medical Center to ease his last days. In the two-week period while he was in the hospital, the 52 bone lesions disappeared and they never came back. So how did we react? Were we in awe? Certainly not. I remember my chief resident explaining to me that a mistake must have been made, this man didn't really have cancer. So his slides were sent for careful examination by a battery of independent expert pathologists and sure enough, these men confirmed that he did indeed have cancer. So he became the subject of Grand Rounds. And at this meeting of all the doc-

tors in the hospital it was concluded that for some inexplicable reason there was an eight-month delay in the action of this man's chemotherapy and radiation. I want to say to you, the mind is *limited*.

The mind denies that which it can't understand and we are a mentally identified culture. In valuing the mind as much as we do, we have a cultural tendency to deny mystery, to deny the spiritual. A form of denial, by the way, is delegating these matters. We tend to delegate the spiritual to others who are more interested in it, or who we feel are perhaps better equipped to deal with it. In reality, of course, the spiritual can't be delegated. We all participate in it. It is our very

The mind denies that which it cannot understand. In valuing the mind as much as we do, we have a tendency to deny mystery, to deny the spiritual.

nature, the core of our humanity. There is no situation that is not a spiritual situation, there is no decision that is not a spiritual decision, there is no feeling that is not a spiritual feeling. In fact, the very essence of life may be spiritual in nature. Life may advance some spiritual agenda that we all work towards together, without even knowing. There is a lot of mystery here. Perhaps all life is sacred.

In working with people who are dying and in reading a lot about near-death experiences, people seem to arrive at a sense of what life's purpose is—and it is not to be a doctor or to be well-known or even to make a social contribution. The purpose of life, as these people tell it, is simpler than this. The purpose of life is to grow in wisdom and to learn to love better. If life serves these purposes, then health serves these purposes and illness serves them as well, because illness is part of life.

When I think about mind I think about solutions, because the mind is a solution-giver. In a purely mental perspective, when something is broken *we* need to understand it so *we* can figure out better how to fix it. It's all up to us. It's very lonely, the mind. A spiritual perspective would lead us both to act and to trust the larger natural processes around us. We uncover a natural process moving to a natural resolution. "Broken" is only a stage in that natural process. Not everything that appears to be broken needs fixing, you know. And fixing, itself, is a very reductionistic approach to life and certainly to human beings.

Bernie Siegel said something very, very important about healing in his talk yesterday. He said, "We can grow strong at the broken places." I know that everyone of us understood what he meant, but we didn't understand it with our minds. The mind doesn't understand things like that. The mind fixes the broken places, studies the mechanisms of breaking in the hope of fixing. And yet we do become strong in the broken places. It's the most common thing for a clinician to see.

Let me give you an example. I had a man in my practice with osteogenic sarcoma of the leg, which was removed at the hip in order to save his life. He was 24 years old when I started working with him and he was a very angry man with a lot of bitterness, a deep sense of injustice and a very deep hatred for all the well people, because it seemed so unfair to him that he had suffered this terrible loss so early in life. After working with this man for a couple of years I saw a profound shift. He began "coming out of himself". He began visiting other people in the hospital who had suffered severe physical losses and he would tell me the most wonderful stories about these visits. Once he visited a young woman who was almost his own age. It was a hot day in Palo Alto and he was in running shorts so his artificial leg showed when he came into her hospital room. The woman was so depressed about the loss of both her breasts that she wouldn't even look at him, wouldn't pay any attention to him. The nurses had left her radio playing, probably in order to cheer her up. So, desperate to get her attention, he unstrapped his leg and began dancing around the room on one leg, snapping his fingers to the

continued on page 64

— On Defining Spirit —

What then is the spiritual? I find it difficult to define directly. It's much easier to say what it isn't than what it is.

For example—the spiritual is often confused with the moral, but it's not the moral. Morality is concerned with issues of right and wrong. Although often attributed to the "godhead", it actually has a social basis and reflects a social tradition or consensus. What is considered moral varies from culture to culture and from time to time within the same culture. Furthermore, morality often serves as the basis for judgment, for one group of people separating themselves from other groups, or one individual separating from others. Yet the spiritual is profoundly non-judgmental and non-separative. The spiritual does not vary from time to time because it is not within time. Spirit is unchanging.

The spiritual is also different from the ethical. Ethics is a set of values, a code for translating the moral into daily life. It defines the right way to relate to other people, to carry out business and to behave in general. If the moral is not the spiritual, then the ethical isn't either.

The spiritual is also not the psychic. The psychic is a capacity we all share, although it is better developed in some than in others. It is a way of perceiving—a sort of direct knowing of conditions in matter or in consciousness. We may use a psychic power to know the spiritual—but that which we know is not the means by which we know. As a way of perception, the psychic is closely related to our other senses. If psychic perception is spiritual—then seeing is spiritual and hearing is spiritual. A sense is simply a way of gaining information about the world around us. How I use what I see or hear, what it means to me, is what makes it a matter of spirit or not. I can use the psychic as I can use my other senses—to impress others, to accumulate personal power, to dominate or manipulate—in short to assert my separateness and my personal power. The spiritual however is not separative. A deep sense of the spiritual leads one to trust not one's own lonely power but the great flow or pattern manifested in all life, including our own. We become not manipulator but witness.

Oddly, the psychic is often used to "prove" the spiritual to the non-believer. Yet the spiritual is the one dimension of human experience which does not require proof—which lies beyond (and includes) the very mind which demands proof.

Lastly, the spiritual is not the religious. A religion is a dogma, a set of beliefs about the spiritual and a set of practices which arise out of those beliefs. There are many religions and they tend to be mutually exclusive. That is, every religion tends to think that it has "dibs" on the spiritual—that it's "The Way". Yet the spiritual is inclusive. It is the deepest sense of belonging and participation. We all participate in the spiritual at all times, whether we know it or not. There's no place to go to be separated from the spiritual, so perhaps one might say that the spiritual is that realm of human experience which religion attempts to connect us to through dogma and practice. Sometimes it succeeds and sometimes it fails. Religion is a bridge to the spiritual—but the spiritual lies beyond religion. Unfortunately in seeking the spiritual we may become attached to the bridge rather than crossing over it.

The most important thing in defining spirit is the recognition that spirit is an essential need of human nature. There is something in all of us that seeks the spiritual. This yearning varies in strength from person to person but it is always there in everyone. And so, healing becomes possible. Yet there is a culture-wide tendency to deny the spiritual—to delegate it at best, to ignore it at worst. In trying to point to it with a definition, I hope to initiate a kind of questioning of the role of spirit in health, in health care and in life.

—*Rachel Naomi Remen*

David L. Smith

continued from page 62
music. She looked at him in amazement, and then she burst out laughing and said, "Man, if you can dance, I can sing."

Now I want to tell you something that happened at the end of this man's therapy. At the end of therapy you do a review—people talk about what was significant to them and you share what was significant to you as a therapist working with someone. We were reviewing our two years of work together; I opened his file and there folded up were several drawings he had made early on. I wanted to return these to him, so I unfolded them and handed them to him. He looked through them and said, "Oh, look at this." And he showed me one of the earliest drawings. I had suggested to him that he draw a picture of his body. He had drawn a picture of a vase, and running through this vase was a deep black crack. This was his image of his body and he had taken a black crayon and had drawn the crack over and over and over. He was grinding his teeth with rage at the time. It was very, very painful because it seemed to me that this vase could never function as a vase again. It could never hold water.

Now, two years later, he came to this picture and looked at it and said, "Oh, this one isn't finished." And I said, extending the box of crayons, "Why don't you finish it?" He picked a yellow crayon and putting his finger on the crack he said, "You see, here—this is where the light comes through." And with the yellow crayon he drew light streaming through the crack in his body.

We can grow strong at the broken places. Now *that* is a process worthy of study.

I would like to share, too, some clinical hunches I have as a practicing physician. These hunches also derive from my own thirty-five-year history of chronic illness. I have Crohn's disease and have had major surgery seven times. I no longer have a colon, so I'm talking to you, really, from both sides of the fence. As a matter of fact I don't even have a fence.

Much illness may have its roots in unrecognized spiritual distress—issues of isolation, of anger, the feelings people have that they don't matter or that nobody matters to them. I think that depression is not so much an issue of nobody loving you. Depression is an issue of not being able to find a place to give your love, not being able to love enough. There is a general lack of meaning and purpose and significance that seems to underlie illness. What

we call stress might really be spiritual isolation. It might really be an insensitivity to and a lack of recognition of our spiritual needs. And so they are unmet because they are unrecognized—and we are spiritually isolated.

I was speaking about this with a friend of mine, Joan Borysenko, who in her innovative work teaches people deep relaxation and imagery—she encourages them to eat well, to exercise and to change their lifestyle. And she noted that occasionally she comes across somebody whose high blood pressure, for example, doesn't respond to any of these things. So she asks this person, "Is there anything that you have not forgiven yourself for?" And they respond and then they often do better. Non-forgiveness is a form of spiritual isolation. Spiritual isolation is bad for your health. Denying the spiritual is bad for your health.

What is spiritual isolation? Basically to me it seems that it is living with a closed heart. Some people have said to me "If my heart was open, I could forgive." But I think it's the other way around. Forgiveness is a choice. Forgive first—and then your heart *can* open. Another friend of mine, Dean Ornish, a cardiologist, once said to me that the most popular surgery in this country, coronary bypass surgery, is probably a metaphor. The problem with our culture is that we have bypassed the heart, especially in men. And we keep acting that out, over and over again, in the operating room.

It is very interesting how often the process of physical healing runs concurrent with the healing of the heart. A greater altruism, a greater compassion, seems to occur in different people as you work with them through severe illness.

I want to tell you a story of one of the people at Commonweal. Commonweal is a yoga-based retreat for people with cancer run by Michael Lerner in Bolinas, California. I am fortunate to participate there as the medical director. People who have cancer, and their families, come and spend a week with us. We do yoga, imagery, sandtray and poetry—and we live and walk in a beautiful natural setting next to the ocean. We have support groups and we meditate and we talk and we hug and we touch. One person who came is a survivor of Auschwitz. He is a chemist—brilliant, a very mental man. He is Polish, with a very deep Polish accent which endeared him to me immediately because it reminded me of people in my own family. Fifteen or twenty years previously he had had an episode of multiple sclerosis which had never returned, but now he has cancer. He wanted to see if he could use his mind to heal his cancer. At first he was taken aback by the Commonweal approach, because we do a lot of touching. He would say, "Vot is this luffy, vot is this huggy, huggy, huggy, vot is this huggy the strangers, vot is this?" And we continued to hug him anyway.

The fourth day of the retreat is usually a special time because by then the silence which has been generated by doing the yoga has become very deep inside people, and sometimes they can become in touch with their deepest intelligence. When this man began his yoga meditation on the fourth day he had a startling experience: He experienced himself inside a large field of shifting pinkish energy. When he talked about it later, he called it a "big rose", which was wonderful because his last name is Rose. He found himself inside the big rose and the very center of it seemed to be right here in his chest. As a matter of fact, it seemed to be his heart that was gen-erating this huge energy field around him. With this realization, he became very frightened because for him it was like having a "hemorrhage of energy". He had nothing in his previous experience to compare it to. When he told us about it later, he said how vulnerable it made him feel, because since his experience as a twelve-year-old boy in Auschwitz he had lived very cautiously with regard to his heart and loved only close people, only family. There is a lot of fear behind and beyond this way of loving. He had begun to feel that fear consciously and it was very uncomfortable for him.

The purpose of life is to grow in wisdom and to learn to love better. If life serves these purposes, then health serves these purposes and illness serves them as well, because illness is part of life.

We usually spend the last session tying up the loose ends. I knew how troubled he had been by this experience a few days before, so I turned to him and said, "How are you doing with the big Rose, Harry?" And he said, "Better." I said, "What happened that helped?" He said, "I took a valk and talked to God. It's better." "Harry," I said, "What did God say?" He said, "Ah, I say to God, 'God, vot is this, is it OK to luff the strangers?' And God said, 'Harry, vot is this "strangers"? You make strangers, I don't make strangers.' "

This is the man who has given a scholarship so somebody can come free to a retreat. When we asked him about it—if he wanted to review the applications—he said, "No, just give it to anybody." In a way what this represents is a movement towards essence. He had closed down a part of himself fifty years ago and in the process of working to heal his cancer this man had begun to heal himself as well. That is common, and it is very curious. It is as if the process of illness, limitation, suffering, the shocking isolation of a brutal disease, awakens in us the seeker, which is so much more than the scientist. We begin to sort values, what matters and what doesn't. We become open to looking at the meaning of life, not just the meaning of pain, of one's own pain, but even the meaning of life itself.

I'd like to close by reading a poem which was left to me in the will of one of my former patients, a sixteen-year-old girl whose death ended a seven-year battle with leukemia. Her mother brought me this poem in a sealed envelope. It had been left to me, so we opened it together. It said the following:

Cancer
I disappear,
devoured by pain.
I know
I am a speck,
a mote of dust dancing in a sun beam.
I know my little dance matters.
My life
serves life,
Itself.

A human being is not a mechanism, but an opportunity for the Infinite to manifest. The only thing *really* worthy of our study and attention is spirit. And at the heart of spirit is Mystery. Our need to be in control, our need for mastery, can stifle our sense of Mystery, can blind us to the Mystery around us. And if this happens to the mind-body health field we will all be the losers. □

This article was adapted from a talk presented June 25, 1988, in Kalamazoo, Michigan, at a conference sponsored by the John E. Fetzer Foundation. The conference, "Helping Heal the Whole Person and the Whole World", was designed to stimulate dialogue among innovators, researchers and decision-makers, to explore the related issues of personal and global well-being, and to mobilize plans of action.

The Foundation is producing a booklet and videotapes on conference highlights. For more information contact Tom Thinnes, Director of Public Affairs, John E. Fetzer Foundation, 9292 West KL Avenue, Kalamazoo, MI 49009; (616) 375-2000.

Audiocassette and videotapes are available from Sunrise Media, 96 Inverness Drive East, Englewood, CO 80112.

To live content with small means;
to seek elegance rather than luxury,
and refinement rather than fashion;
to be worthy, not respectable,
and wealthy, not rich;
to listen to stars and birds, babes and sages
with open heart;
to study hard;
to think quietly, act frankly, talk gently,
await occasions, hurry never;
in a word, to let the spiritual,
unbidden and unconscious,
grow up through the common—
this is my symphony.

—William Henry Channing

Sculpture by Ann McCoy *Photo by Jim Strong*

The "New Paradigm" and the Rule of Law

by Willis W. Harman

There is no real solution to our global dilemmas—environmental, ecological, economic, educational or of health and peace—short of extending the Rule of Law to the entire globe.

It may seem strange that one of the most important concepts in history is so little discussed. I refer to the idea of the Rule of Law.

The Rule of Law stands in contrast to the rule of arbitrary power as wielded by ancient monarchs or present-day dictators. In the Western democracies we may tend to take it for granted. Yet Geoffrey de Q. Walker, Australian author of a recently published book entitled *The Rule of Law,** argues that the Rule of Law is "under threat and its survival is in doubt." Its importance is most clearly seen if we recognize that there is no real solution to the dilemma posed by nuclear and other weapons of mass destruction, short of applying the Rule of Law to the globe. Although this was the basic idea behind the United

Nations, it has been consistently thwarted by the powerful nations, especially the US and the USSR.

Much has been said (in Institute publications and elsewhere) about implications of the emerging "consciousness paradigm" for health care, education, peace, care of the planet, and so on. Until the appearance of this book, not much has come forth about implications for the law. Walker's message is a positive one, and one of particular interest to members of the Institute of Noetic Sciences: The new paradigm is more supportive to the rule of law than is the old.

Not all our readers will be attracted to this book; a large portion of it is an erudite discussion for legal scholars.

However, the issue it deals with is one of the most critical faced by modern democracies, and one of the most important to be understood by any citizen of a democratic society.

Basically, the Rule of Law asserts the supremacy of law as opposed to that of arbitrary power. Beyond this, its definition is by no means a trivial thing. It is not, for instance, to be simply equated with "law and order" imposed by government. It does not presume that all laws imposed by governments are legitimate. It demands equality before the law of all persons and classes, including government and government officials. It requires the existence of an independent judiciary and legal profession. It requires of society an attitude and spirit of legality.

* *The Rule of Law,* by Geoffrey de Q. Walker, Melbourne University Press, 1988

The Rule of Law is
"the essential prerequisite
of our whole legal,
constitutional, and perhaps social,
order"
—Geoffrey de Q. Walker

•

The Rule of Law is
"synonymous with
the maintenance of civilized
existence"
—Jawaharal Nehru,
India's first prime minister

•

"It is essential
if man is not compelled
to have recourse
as a last resort, to rebellion
against tyranny
and oppression,
that human rights should be
protected by the Rule of Law"
—The United Nations
Universal Declaration
of Human Rights, 1948

•

"Whereas Canada
is founded upon principles
that recognize
the supremacy of God
and the Rule of Law . . . "
—Preamble to Canada's
Constitution Act of 1982.

If the rule of law is important to any country, it is all the more critical that it be applied to the world. For all the talk about peace and nuclear disarmament, the powerful countries of the world have not yet faced up to the truth that *it is no longer possible to achieve national security through military strength. Another way must be found to attain the state of national and global security we all desire. And that way will require that we apply to the world the same rule of law we cherish within our own national boundaries.*

Similarly, it is highly questionable whether there can be found adequate solutions to the other global dilemmas of our time—environmental, ecological, man-made climate change, chronic hunger and poverty—short of extending the rule of law to all of human society on a global basis.

Decline of the Rule of Law
The threat to the rule of law comes about partly from inadequate public appreciation of how easily it can be eroded by such attitudes as those at the heart of the recent Iran-Contra scandal. In his book Walker describes the deep roots of a crisis all of us are at least dimly aware of, that faced by constitutional democracy. He describes how the rule of law is being perverted by the undue intrusion of politics, by the activities of pressure groups, by discretionary powers given the courts, and numerous other aspects of the contemporary crisis in meaning and values. As he documents in detail (which we have no need to review here), "Our laws are losing their moral prestige and are forfeiting their controlling and binding power as factors in human conduct. The way is being opened for force and fraud to be the only controlling powers in human relationships."

Professor Walker then goes on to explore a topic of particular interest to members of the Institute of Noetic Sciences—namely, how the current reassessment of the place of consciousness

in the scientific worldview reinforces the rule of law concept.

The Systemic Crisis of Western Society
As the twentieth century draws to a close, the evidence is being taken seriously more than ever before that Western culture is approaching a historic crisis more fundamental than any it has faced for the last 2000 years. Walker chooses the sociologist Pitirim Sorokin's four-volume work written between the two world wars, *Social and Cultural Dynamics*, as the study which best organizes the evidence for this crisis.

Sorokin's method was to study the content and form of a wide range of cultural and social indicators for as far back in history as there are any records. He studied the system of truth (science, philosophy, and religion), the fine arts, ethics, law, the family, government, economic organization, liberty, international relations, and a variety of other institutions and activities. He viewed also what might be regarded as pathological symptoms such as crime, war, revolution, suicide, mental disease, diminished creativity, and charted their incidence and intensity at various periods of history. From a grand synthesis of all of these threads, Sorokin developed the theory that the history of culture and society is based on the cyclical rise and fall of two basic value systems that he called the "ideational" and the "sensate". The ideational value system sees true reality as lying beyond the material world perceptible to the physical senses—that is, in the spiritual realm, known only through inner experience. This value system espouses legal and ethical standards that are rooted in that profound inner experience; law is a reflection of the "natural law" discoverable through personal revelation and mystical insight. Ideational values were dominant in Western society between about the fifth and tenth centuries, and comparable periods can be found in

Walker contends that the factors contributing to the breakdown of the rule of law are not happenstance or isolated. They are part of a general pattern of the breakdown of the old order of Western industrial "sensate" society, and the transition to a new set of value emphases and underlying assumptions—a "new paradigm".

other cultures such as the Hindu, the Hellenic, and the Buddhist.

The sensate culture rests on the positivistic belief that only that which can be perceived with the physical senses (namely matter and energy in their various forms) has any reality. Thus all laws and ethical values are relative and are based only on empirical, utilitarian considerations. In the West sensate values have been in the ascendant since about the time of the French Revolution. Parallels can be found in the late Egyptian civilization and in the last centuries of Hellenic civilization preceding AD 500.

On occasion societies have for a time achieved a balance between these two tendencies, which Sorokin called "integral" culture. This is characterized by a harmonious blending of spiritual and sensory values, and in many respects represents the finest flowering of any culture. In the West, the years approximately 1500 to 1800 are such a period; this is the age that gave us Bach and Shakespeare, Newton, Leibnitz and Descartes, Rembrandt, Michelangelo and a pantheon of other great figures who built up the cultural capital on which we are still drawing.

It is characteristic of the transition from one of these phases to the next that there is a wave of social dislocation reflected in all the variables mentioned above. From Sorokin's analysis there is ample indication that the sensate period of Western culture is coming to an end.

The breakdown of sensate cultures has, in the past, presented a grim spectacle. The mental and moral order of sensate values and meanings collapses and chaos ensues. The distinctions between true and false, right and wrong, beautiful and ugly, positive and negative disappear. No generally accepted socio-cultural norms remain and there is an increase and sharpening of antagonisms and conflicts.

Sorokin did not see this projection as a pessimistic one. As he saw it, the possibility existed of a new transcendental worldview emerging that could be the foundation of a new integral value system. Indeed, there are many indications over the past quarter century that something of that sort may be exactly what is happening.

Thus it is Walker's contention that the factors contributing to the breakdown of the rule of law are not happenstance or isolated; they are part of a general pattern of the breakdown of the old order of Western industrial "sensate" society, and the transition to a new set of value emphases and underlying assumptions—a "new paradigm" in the contemporary argot.

The Rule of Law in the New Paradigm
We need not review the "new paradigm" for members of the Institute; aspects of it are dealt with in every issue of the *Review* and it is articulated in several of the books listed in the "Global Mind Change" section of the Institute catalog. All of us are familiar with the premise that the old Newto-

nian-Cartesian view of the universe as a machine, of man as separate from his environment and his fellow human beings, of object as distinct from subject, is giving way. One proposed replacement is a new holistic or "systems" perspective that sees the essence of all phenomena as interrelatedness. The new paradigm replaces the metaphor of the machine with that of the living organism, and insists that when we are considering the likely effects of an action we must look at its impact on each part of the system, rather than treating the parts as separate, isolatable components.

"The new paradigm," says Walker, "is broadly acceptable to people with a wide range of antecedent outlooks, both in industrialized societies and in the Third World; it is compatible with traditional belief systems around the world; and being tolerant and non-authoritarian, it does not threaten anyone—it does not require that any individuals or groups be arbitrarily coerced, expropriated, or liquidated.... It is not even opposed to big business, as such—it simply asks that corporations and the market system be animated by a new spirit—a spirit that would fill the void left by the demise of the old Christian morality with the new ethics of ecology and self-realization.... Businesses that fail to adapt to these new values will pay the price automatically. Quite apart from any legislation, they will progressively be deserted by their customers and will find it harder to recruit good employees."

The seventeenth-century scientific revolution gave to our law, and our concepts of the rule of law, many of the characteristics that we take for granted today. Positivistic philosophies that denied any basis for a presumed moral order, which were so influential in science, infected the law as well. One result of the doctrine of legal positivism was to diminish the role of the public and their attitudes in the formation of the law. It emphasizes law as an instrument which legislators can use to modify a world that is essentially separate from themselves. It led to a formalistic view of the rule of law that left it as a purely subordinate notion that could be overridden at any time by the legislature.

Just as the "scientific" paradigm influenced the law of today, so emergence of the new paradigm will further alter both the perceived role of law and the nature of law. It involves a direct break with the long-established materialist and behaviorist doctrine that dominated science for so long. The emerging science of consciousness will change concepts of free choice and motivation, and of the value bases underlying the law. Holistic ways of perceiving will reduce the tendencies of governments and legislatures to portray themselves as separate from, and superior to, the people.

The current legal context, with its adversarial emphasis, tends to cast issues in either-or form; an outlook in which pairs of opposites look more like the two sides of the Tao may lead to the possibility of other outcomes than win and lose.

New ways of making ethical decisions are also likely. The acceptance of Freudian theories led to the widespread recognition, in law and penology as elsewhere, of the reality of subconscious motivation. The new image builds upon that by making use of the focus in the new psychotherapies on "*supraconscious choice*". In transpersonal psychology one seeks to align conscious choice with the highest discernible supraconscous choice—be it labeled "intuition", "higher Self", or whatever. Walker reports that "techniques for training individuals in making supraconscious choices are already being used quite extensively in the prison systems of both Australia and the United States, resulting in "sharp, long-term, and unprecedented drops in recidivism".

Just as the "scientific" paradigm influenced the law of today, so emergence of the new paradigm will further alter both the perceived role of law and the nature of law.

"As the advocates of the holographic worldview see it, the new paradigm will give direct access to the energy from which the tangible universe emerges, a force which has traditionally been described as an energy of love." This process "implies a method of deriving ethical and legal guidelines that is radically different from the purely empirical and usually elitist approach of the last two centuries. . . . Through a process of planning from the bottom up, the people will change institutions, structures and laws. Leadership for change will become a community-wide social and individual learning and healing task." It seems that "the new scientific-philosophical paradigm, with its often-remarked congruence with Eastern mysticism, has helped to increase our fascination, not with the contents of the mind, but with whatever awareness may lie above it."

Summary
Professor Walker summarizes his argument in the following way: "Not only is the rule of law perfectly compatible with what we know of the new worldview, but it is the prerequisite for any successful transformation. Experiments with new-age values and lifestyles are taking place only in countries where the rule of law prevails, and to the extent that it does. It provides the security and freedom of action that these new ventures require. At the same time, it helps to reduce friction between various groups following different paths, including those who believe that the old values, or some variant of them, are still the best solution. Without the rule of law to provide a framework for experimentation and for the containing of rivalries, the transition may come to be seen as too painful, threatening or disruptive, and may be prevented from taking place at all.

"Such is the crisis of the rule of law. On the one hand it is threatened with extinction. On the other hand it has the opportunity, if it can survive, of playing a more brilliant and momentous role than ever before."

Willis Harman is President of the Institute of Noetic Sciences.

We must make a clear distinction
between the two kinds of strong "I":

There is a strong feeling of "I"
which causes one to forget other people,
to consider oneself superior,
and to exploit, bully, cheat.

That kind of egoistic mind is very negative.
So it is difficult for this egoistic attitude and the altruistic
to come together.

The other strong feeling of "I"—
I can do, I must do—
this is very necessary.
I must subdue my anger.
I must reduce my attachment.
I must develop altruism.
I must forgive my enemies.
That kind of egoism is positive.
Without that I can't act with conviction.

—Tenzin Gyatso, the XIVth Dalai Lama of Tibet
**From a meeting with Institute of Noetic Sciences' tour group
on their second trip to Dharamsala, August, 1989.**

Conscious Living, Conscious Dying

with Stephen Levine and Jeffrey Mishlove

LEVINE: Healing is not limited to the physical body. For example, I've seen people who died with their heart open, leaving more healing behind than someone who lived but continued judgment and aggression in the family. The family was unhealed, though the person's body was healed.

In fact, I've seen parallel situations, with two people with similar diagnoses, where one fought the illness. It was them against the illness, and contention filled the room. Just when they most needed mercy, it was least available to them.

MISHLOVE: From themselves.

LEVINE: From themselves. And they pushed everybody away, and whether they lived or died, they created schism in the family, judgment, guilt, feelings of unworthiness in those who loved them most, because nobody could help.

And I've seen other people in the same situation—same pain in their body, same pain in their mind—say, "I don't have a moment to lose. I can't stand to live a moment longer with my heart closed. Too much pain for me, too much pain. The world doesn't need another closed heart."

Maybe the sign of real healing is, what are the people bedside left with when someone dies? Are they left with their hearts full and a sense of connectedness to that person, or are they left frightened of death, scared of that person, thinking about how things didn't work out, wondering how they could have helped more.

MISHLOVE: Is there a sense—I've heard this reported by some doctors—that the kind of people who do experience a physical recovery from a serious disease are ornery kinds of people, who are fighting for their lives?

LEVINE: Aggression can be a very strong part. But when people can fight their illness, it becomes "me" against "my illness". It becomes separation and anxiety. Our sense is that when you touch that which is in pain with mercy and awareness, there's healing. Where there's awareness there's healing.

To heal is to become whole, right? To come back to some balance.

Yet one doctor who helps people heal through modern methods says that those who heal are his superstars. And then another doctor I know says that patients who heal are the exceptional patients. Well, what does that make everybody else—a second-stringer, a loser? That very conceptual framework where you are a good person if you heal makes you a bad person if you die. Who needs to die with a sense of failure? It's very dangerous, those ideas. They're very well intended, because I know those fellows, and they're good fellows, and they sincerely want to help, and they've helped many.

But many have been injured by the idea that, for instance, you're responsible for your illness. You're not responsible *for* your illness; you're not responsible *for* your cancer; you're responsible *to* your cancer. Because if you're responsible for your cancer, then how are you ever going to heal? If my conditioning caused it, do I have to get rid of all of my conditioning to be well? I know people who have meditated for fifty years and are not done with their conditioning, and when their time is short, energy is low, it just strains them, and maybe causes schisms within.

When we see that we are responsible *to* our illness, then when pain arises we can send mercy, we can send kindness. You and I, we're conditioned. We walk across a room, we stub our toe. What do we do with the pain in our toe? We're conditioned to send hatred into it. We're conditioned to try to exorcise it.

MISHLOVE: Like, "How stupid I was to do that."

LEVINE: Yes, and we cut the pain off. In fact, even many meditative techniques for working with pain are to take your awareness, your attention, and put it elsewhere. Just when that throbbing toe is most calling out for mercy, for kindness, for embrace, for softness, it's least available. In some ways it's amazing that anybody heals, considering our conditioning to send hatred into our pain, which is the antithesis of healing.

MISHLOVE: You've developed a number of guided meditations for dealing with healing, and part of that process is to really try and feel the pain.

LEVINE: Explore the pain.

MISHLOVE: Explore the pain, and then to know just how we protect ourselves from getting at it—that there's sort of a wall of deadening around the pain, to keep us away from our own pain. It's as if by denying ourselves our own pain, we deny ourselves life.

LEVINE: You're bringing up a really interesting point. The way we respond to pain is the way we respond to life. When things aren't the way we want them to be, what do we do? Do we close down, or do we open up to get more of a sense of what's needed in the moment? Our conditioning is to close down—aversion, rejection, denial. Nothing heals. That is the very basis on which unfinished business accumulates, putting it away—I'm right, they're wrong; no quality of forgiveness. We know many people who are working on sending forgiveness into their tumors, into their AIDS, into their degenerative heart disease. It sounds so bizarre, because our conditioning is to send anger into it, fear into it. Where can there be healing in that?

Most of what we call pain is the resistance that clenches down on the unpleasant. The word surrender is so funny, because most people, particularly in the case of illness, equate surrender with defeat. But surrender is letting go of resistance.

In fact, a really dynamic, practical sense of that is that a lot of the people we work with are not trying to take healing from outside. They're not giving up control to healing. They're participating in it, they're taking responsibility for it—responsibility being the ability to respond, instead of the necessity to react. They look at their pills, and as they take them in, they guide them with loving-kindness into the area, because they've put so much attention into the area they know the inside, the multiple molecular variation of sensation within, the moment-to-moment-ness of that area. They direct it into that area, and

they find, for instance with pain medication, that once the resistance has been gone through, they can decrease the medication. Because I think a lot of medications get used up by the resistance before they ever get to the place that they're being taken to.

MISHLOVE: Our medical system doesn't really encourage people to take responsibility at that level. It's as if we're passive, not only at the hands of doctors, but even at the hands of spiritual and psychic healers.

LEVINE: It can be. We're not saying, "Throw away your other practice." We're saying, "Whatever you're doing to heal yourself, why don't you try to see for your own self what it might mean if you put mercy into that area?" It's so outside of our conditioning. We suggest that people treat their illness as though it were their only child, with that same mercy and loving-kindness. If that was in your child's body, you'd caress it, you'd hold it, you'd do all you could to make it well. But somehow when it's in our body we wall it off, we send hatred into it and anger into it. We treat ourselves with so little kindness, so little softness. And there are physical correlations to the difference between softening around an illness—blood flow, availability of the immune system, et cetera—and hardness. You know, if you've got a hard belly and your jaw is tight, and that hardness is around your eyes, it's very difficult for anything to get through.

MISHLOVE: You seem to be suggesting that that healing is not just for the sick, but is a way of life in general. It's as if moment by moment we make the choice whether to harden or to soften.

LEVINE: Well, the hardening has become involuntary. As for the softening, it takes remembering priorities, that this is the only moment there is, and this is the moment to open. If we're not doing it now, how will we do it at any other time? That's why we suggest, don't wait until you get a terminal diagnosis to start to give yourself permission to be alive, to get on with your life. Now is a good time . . . ☐

Stephen Levine is a poet, an author, a spiritual teacher. He has written numerous books, including Who Dies?, Meetings on the Edge, Healing into Life and Death, *and* Grist for the Mill.
This is an excerpt from the television series Thinking Allowed, *which the Institute of Noetic Sciences has helped to sponsor.*

Cause and Effect in Science:
A Fresh Look

*If we see purpose extending through the whole universe
it leads us to a different view of nature.*

by Rupert Sheldrake

*Rupert Sheldrake presented this talk to the Institute's Board
of Directors, to stimulate discussion on the Institute's new
research program on scientific causality.*

First, I want to say something about the genuine complexity
of the subject which stems, of course, from the genuine complexity of nature and the fact there are a great many con-
tributory influences on any event that occurs. Typically in
science, you isolate just one of these events and then you
conduct experiments in which you hold everything else
constant except for the one variable you're examining. Then
you can see the effects of that very specific single cause. You
leave out the hundreds or thousands or millions of other
causative influences because they are not relevant to your
present considerations.

An example: Consider the cause of the sounds coming from
a radio. One person might say, "It's the electricity. Without
that you don't get the sound. Pull out the plug, the set stops.
Electricity is the cause." Somebody else might say, "No, the
cause is all these components inside the box. Chop out a few
wires and transistors, the sound stops. Put them back in, the
sound starts. So there's the cause." Somebody else says,
"No, no, the cause is what's going on in that transmitter
hundreds of miles away." And still someone else will say,
"But those sounds are part of a program that was drawn up
months in advance by the radio corporation planning department. That program is the cause."

All these things, you see, are causes of the sounds you hear.
And there are many others as well.

Now, in the real world, such questions arise in commissions
of inquiry and in courts of law. For example, there was a big
railway accident in London and everyone wanted to know
what was the cause. Loose wires. And what's the cause of

that? Incompetent management? Bad staff? Government
policy? There was a whole range of proliferating causes that
filled the newspapers for weeks. And in courts of law,
similar issues arise. These issues of causality in fact preoc-
cupy us a great deal of the time in ordinary life. We are all
familiar in real life with this vast complexity of interacting
influences.

Aristotle's "Causes"

The classical discussion of causality was provided by Aristotle and still, I think, provides the best framework from
which to start clarifying this huge and confused area. The
four causes of Aristotle were:

- The material cause—that of which something is made,
  the marble of a sculpture for example;
- The formal cause—the plan or design that it is made
  into by the sculptor making the sculpture;
- The final cause—the purpose of the sculpture;
- The efficient cause, the moving cause—the chisel hitting the marble.

All these are important in this example of the sculpture
being made ready to be put in the marketplace.

This system of considering four kinds of cause—material,
formal, final and efficient—was the standard way of thinking about causation in the classical world and in the scholastic period in the Middle Ages. They had a far broader conception of causality than we now have in science. In their
view animals and plants had souls—and the soul of the
plant, the soul of the rosebush, for example, was what gave
the plant its form. The soul was the formal cause. It was also
the final cause; it gave the rose its purpose to grow into a
mature rosebush and to flower and set seed.

So the soul was that which contained formal and final causes. These were non-material. And the final cause of the whole universe for Aristotle was God. God was the prime mover of the universe—not because He pushed it, but because in a sense He pulled it. He attracted the universe toward Himself. And there's a sense in which final causes—purpose and goals—have this kind of attractive quality. They draw things toward them. Aristotle thought the whole universe moved because it was attracted toward God's eternal state of bliss. This is completely different from the model of things being pushed from behind in the mechanical universe.

Descartes' Mathematical Universe

But with the seventeenth century revolution in science, causation was more or less restricted to material and efficient causes—to matter and motion. Souls were withdrawn from the whole of nature. Animals and plants became mere machines. And although the earlier Platonists had thought the world had a soul—the anima mundi—the soul of the world was now abolished as well.

The soul was also withdrawn from the human body. In the older system, the body was thought to be in the soul, not the soul in the body. The soul was greater than the body. But in the new seventeenth century vision of Descartes, the soul was withdrawn from the whole of the body until only a small part of it was left in some region of the brain, as the rational soul. This kind of rational soul was the only non-mechanical thing left in the whole of nature. Everything else became mechanical, to be understood merely in terms of efficient and material causes.

The purpose or final cause of nature, said Descartes, is God's purpose for the world. But since God is constant, the final cause is constant. So we can acknowledge there is a purpose to it all, but since the purpose remains constant from a scientific point of view we can neglect it; it is not necessary to know what it is.

That got rid of the final cause from nature. And the formal cause, why things happen as they do, interestingly enough was then assumed into the laws of nature. The mathematical laws, which Descartes and the other founding fathers of science thought governed the world, became the causes of why planets move in their orbits and follow the paths that they do. These and other ordered patterns in nature were not given by souls inherent in nature, but by mathematical laws outside nature which were thought of as ideas in the mind of the mathematical God.

Aristotle's Four Causes:

The material cause: that of which something is made—the marble of a sculpture, for example

The formal cause: the plan or design it is made into

The efficient cause: the moving cause—the chisel hitting the marble

The final cause: its purpose

Drawings by Carol Guion

So the formal causes did, in fact, remain. They were in the laws of nature—and they still are from the point of view of conventional science. It is these non-material, mathematical principles which are supposed to give the formal structure to the world.

Fields: The Medium of Action at a Distance

Well, there were problems with this view. The biggest of them was action at a distance. Mechanical causation of the pushing and pulling kind normally, according to common sense, depends on contact. Newton's Law of Gravitation presupposed in effect that causal effects were operating over enormous distances. Between the moon and the Earth, and the sun and the moon, for example. This was a problem.

And of course a similar problem cropped up again in relation to electrical and magnetic phenomena—where, again, there was action at a distance. In order to deal with these the concept of fields was introduced, first in the realm of electromagnetism and then in the realm of gravity. Fields now became the medium of action at a distance. And they also became, as it were, the formal cause of things. The Einstein gravitational field gives the shape and structure of space time. The structure in space time is curved in the presence of matter, and it brings about gravitational effects, such as the orbiting of the moon around the Earth, by acting as a formal cause, or "geometrical cause", to use Einstein's phrase.

> *A field is a region of influence in space and time which has formative influence.*

In the electromagnetic realm too the fields became formative influences. The patterning of iron filings around the magnet depends on the shape the magnetic field has. It's an invisible structure or shape. A field is a region of influence in space and time which has these formative influences on things. And in a sense we can see fields as having taken on the traditional causal roles of souls. Fields have many of the same properties that souls used to have. They're not identical in all respects, but I think they fulfill the same role the souls did in the scholastic view of nature.

Two-Tiered Reality

In the seventeenth century view the abolition of souls left a dualistic or two-tiered structure of reality: spirit and matter. Spirit consisted of God and the rational human mind, and matter became just atoms in motion. The intermediate level of the soul had gone. There were just mathematical laws and inanimate, unconscious, blind matter obeying these laws. There was a cosmic dualism between the material, energetic world and the nonmaterial, nonenergetic, timeless and immutable mathematical laws of nature. How the two fitted together, how one worked on the other, was left unclear. It's still unclear.

The Streams of Prime

—by Tony Basilio

The streams of prime . . .
*   they are underground,*
*   where we don't see them.*
*   But they're there.*

The streams of prime,
they're just behind our wisdom,
*   and sometimes,*
*   when the air is between us,*
*   as a presence*

*   you can feel*
*   the streams of prime*
*   flow.*

The medium through which
*   our feeling flows,*
*   one to the other*
*   these, are the streams of prime.*

*   One to the other.*
These are the streams of prime.

Everything is connected,
*   in the streams of prime.*
We all own all of it,
*   in the streams of prime.*
We share equally in the glory,
*   and in the shame,*
*   in streams of prime.*

The introduction of fields, then, provides an intermediate level. It's the fields which cause one thing to influence another. It's the fields that are involved in the impact of "billiard balls" bouncing off one another. All these kinds of mechanical phenomena are now explained in terms of fields of nature.

The same kinds of problems arise in biology as in physics, but even more so, because one of the problems in biology is to understand the forms of organisms. Why do different species of plants have different shapes? Why do animals have different forms? Why do different animals have different instincts and how are they inherited?

In the older system of understanding, the forms of animals' behavior and the forms of their bodies were said to be determined by non-material causes, formal causes. For Platonists these formal causes were Platonic ideas or forms, eternal archetypes transcending space and time, ideas in the mind of God.

For the later Aristotelians and the scholastics, however, these forms were not *outside* nature, but *inside* nature. They were in the souls of these species, and the souls were in and around their bodies. They weren't free-floating somewhere beyond time and space as with the Platonists.

Then, for the mechanists after the seventeenth century the formal causes were in part dependent on the general laws of nature. But those laws were obviously too general to explain the exact shape of the hedgehog or a cauliflower. So the formal cause had to be supposed to be material structures inside the organism. At first, people thought that these material causes must consist of pre-formed microscopic versions of a finished organism. So a giraffe egg, for example, contained a miniature giraffe. The process of giraffe development simply consisted of inflating this miniature giraffe inside the egg. This was called the doctrine of pre-formation. It was the most obvious materialist explanation of form and formative development in biology.

The logical problem of course is that this miniature giraffe would have to have eggs for the next generation inside it, and that in turn would have to have eggs for the next generation inside that. So one got an infinite regress of "chinese boxes" of eggs within eggs within eggs.

In the eighteenth century illustrations of those tiny pre-formed organisms were acutally published. There were pictures of sperm—horse sperm showing baby

For there are no borders there,
in the streams of prime,
in these dreams of prime.

They don't recognize individual cells
as separate from the Big Body,
in streams of prime.

They say,
One man, contains all men
in the streams of prime.
They say, Every one,
has all possibilities . . .
in them
in streams of prime,
in these dreams of prime.

They know.

All people,
made of people
in the streams of prime.

People.
Made of People,
in streams of prime.

The introduction of fields provides an intermediate level—taking on the traditional causal roles of souls. They cause one thing to influence another.

horses inside them, and donkey sperm showing much the same thing but with bigger ears. People thought that the doctrine of pre-formation had actually been proven and it was widely believed. It seemed to provide a materialistic explanation for the development of form. They got rid of the problem of formative causes by saying that the forms were already there. All materialists in biology have to resort to some explanation of this kind. They have to put the formal or formative cause of the adult organism in the matter of the fertilized egg.

Reinventing the Soul

Of course, the pre-formation theory was wrong. People couldn't find these miniature organisms inside the egg, and it was shown by studying embryology that new forms and structures emerged as the organism developed. The neo-pre-formationism of the late nineteenth century was somewhat subtler. It posited, not that the total structure was there in the fertilized egg, but some other material structure that determined it. This was Weissman's theory of germ plasm. The germ plasm was supposed to generate the organism from its own material structure, in a way that was utterly mysterious!

Now, the vitalist tradition in biology has always said that living organisms are alive, and that what makes them alive is the presence of the soul, or something like a soul, that gives them their form, shape, structure and organization. The mechanistic theory has always denied this. But what in fact happens is that mechanists keep reinventing the soul in a miniaturized form—replacing it either inside the germ plasm, or more recently inside the "selfish" genes which are endowed with all the properties of life and mind. Or replacing it with the concept of the genetic program, which is a purposive organizing entity rather like the entelechies of the vitalists.

The fact it's couched in computer language makes people think it must be scientific. The genetic program is an extremely vague, loose, slippery concept, the vital factor or the soul in a modern mechanistic guise. In fact the computer analogy as a whole, which is so popular nowadays, demonstrates again the intensely anthropomorphic quality of mechanistic thinking, projecting human preoccupations onto the whole universe. It does this in a way, I think, far more insidious than even the worst of the animists. It now takes our current preoccupation with computers and information technology and projects these onto all nature, including ourselves.

Here again we see the same system of causes at work. It's another example of how this older system of causes keeps coming back. The hardware of the computer is the material cause. The efficient cause, the moving cause, is the energy. You pull the plug out and it stops. You put the plug in and it starts again. The formal cause of what the computer does is the program. And the final cause, the purpose or end, is the use or the purpose of the program of the computer.

So you can find all these Aristotelian causes at work in the computer analogy. And the fashionable word for formal cause, or formative cause, is of course "information". The whole world is considered to be permeated by information. Nobody is ever quite sure what this information is. But what it does is to get form into things; it in-forms. It is playing the role of formal or formative cause.

People . . .
  made of people . . .
    got people stuff in 'em.

What any one got . . . concern 'em all.
  in streams of prime.
  either way,
  good or bad,
  in streams of prime.
  (Every body got it all.)

Streams of prime
  are the veins of embodied form.
  The rivers of life
  through which life
    is breathed in to the stuff,
  Where people, is the stuff
  and world, is the body,
    the stuff makes . . .
  As it builds universe,
  as it dances together
    the strands of our pure stuff.

The globe, is our body,
as much as the finger is our body,
  at our pure stuff.
  At the streams of prime.

The Causal Role of Fields

In biology since the beginning of this century, it's become clear to many people that embryological development can't be understood just in terms of the material components of the organism. Since the twenties, the idea that organisms are organized by fields, morphogenetic fields, has been quite widely discussed. These fields are supposed to be within and around these organisms that they organize. There are hierarchies of fields within fields. So in our bodies there is a liver field, a kidney field, an eye field, and so on. And within those fields are the fields for the tissues and fields for the cells—nested hierarchies of fields within fields.

These organizing fields, again, play the role of formal and final causes. They give the developing organism the end or the goals toward which it is developing, and the final form it is going to develop towards. If you disturb a developing embryo, chop a bit off it, very often it can still form a normal organism. So somehow within the field of the organism, it contains the structure of the final form. It can draw or attract the system toward it even though it may follow an unusual route to get there. It has a kind of purposive quality.

These fields also have a holistic property which is not present in chunks of matter. Again, you can understand it by analogy with magnetic fields. If, for example, you chop up a magnet into small pieces, what you get are not just lots of fragments of the magnet or fragments of the field. You get a lot of little magnets, each with a complete magnetic field. This is analogous to what you can do with lower animals like flat worms. You can chop them up into pieces and each piece can regenerate into a whole worm. You can cut up a willow tree into hundreds or thousands of cuttings and each one can form a willow tree. There is something about these organisms that enables them to retain their wholeness even when their material structure is split up into bits. Something in

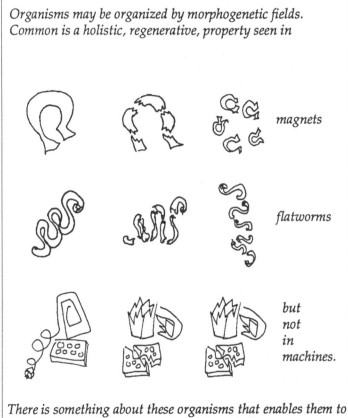

Organisms may be organized by morphogenetic fields. Common is a holistic, regenerative, property seen in

magnets

flatworms

but not in machines.

There is something about these organisms that enables them to retain their wholeness even when their material structure is split into bits, something in field phenomena which doesn't occur in machines . . .

Where the wisdom,
that makes the globe turn
and holds stars, in the skies

also makes residence
in every cell in our body.
And exists
as a plan, we must follow.
These dreams of prime.

The Prime Template, if you will
spiritual DNA;
the Idea for the original form,
the Big Teacher.
Swims in the streams of prime.

Everywhere at once!

And we need to bow,
at the streams of prime.

field phenomena which doesn't occur in machines—if you cut up a Cray computer into lots of little pieces all you get is a broken computer.

This magnetic field analogy helps us to understand how the morphogenetic fields can contain this wholeness—can somehow contain the form and shape of the structure and shape the material system that develops under their influence. This idea is very widespread in biology. The morphogenetic fields give the plans of the developing organism. Your arms and your legs, for example, develop differently according to this view because they do so under the influence of arm fields and leg fields. The DNA, the genetic material, the genetic program is identical in the arms and the legs, and so are the chemicals, the proteins. The fact that you get different shapes depends on the different formative causes in these fields. It's the same in architecture. You can build houses with different plans using the same building materials. The plans play the role of the formative causes.

So I think this is one of the key questions in causality—the causal role of fields and the causal nature of fields. It's a question that Hume never discussed in the eighteenth century, because fields were not then recognized. Because he never discussed it, most Anglo-Saxon philosophers have not discussed it either. The causal role of fields is something grossly neglected by philosophers. And with it, so is the whole question of the nature of formal and final causes, and of patterning and formative influences, and purpose or intention.

> *The causal role*
> *of fields is,*
> *I think,*
> *a big question*
> *in causality.*
> *And with it*
> *so is the*
> *whole question*
> *of patterning and*
> *formative influences,*
> *and purpose*
> *or intention.*

Life is a Gift.
Accept it with Grace.
> *Get down on the ground,*
> *and pray.*

We are the servants . . .
> *of the streams of prime.*
We are the vessels . . .
> *of the streams of prime.*
We are the implements . . .
> *of the streams of prime,*
> *We dance at its urging.*

We are the children . . .
> *of the streams of prime*
> *We can grow.*
> *They give us* <u>*choice*</u> *here.*

Nature Organized by Evolving Fields
So now we come to the question of the nature of these fields, which I call *morphic fields*, fields concerned with form and shape. I'm now talking about fields in biology, and fields underlying patterns of behavioral organization and social organization and, I think also, chemical organization of crystals. How do organizing fields have the structure they do? If they're the formative causes of what's going on under their influence, what forms them?

The conventional answer in science is always to say they must have been formed by some Platonic or Pythagorean set of transcendent mathematical equations somehow beyond space and time. The fields are determined by eternal mathematics in some way that remains unexplained.

That is one way of looking at it. But I myself am very inclined to challenge that view, the idea that nature is governed by eternal mathematical laws. The universe is no longer considered to be eternal. We now have an evolutionary cosmology starting with the Big Bang. The world has evolved. We can ask the

We are the bodies . . .
  of the streams of prime,
  They give us form here.

  We are the Human Aspect,
  of God,
  (Source of the Streams of Prime.)
  . . . at streams of prime.

  We create.
  . . . at streams of prime.

  Or destroy.
  . . . at streams of prime.

  And the difference,
    is at choice!
    At streams of prime.
    They give us that choice here.

  We are the Creators,
  We are the Destroyers,
    it comes with our participation
    in being
    Co-Creators, more fully
    in the game of life.

  Water . . .
  in the streams of prime.

  Flow like WATER
  in the Streams of Prime.

  You ARE
  These Dreams of Prime.

question: If the world is evolving and nature is evolving, why aren't the laws of nature evolving too? Why should we assume that all the mathematical laws in the world were given in advance before the Big Bang? Equations for each of us, equations for the development of all kinds of animals and plants that were already somehow there in advance, before there was even a universe. That's the conventional assumption.

By contrast, I think it is better to think of these fields as having a historical basis, depending on what happened before—containing a kind of memory, representing a kind of habit principle in nature. This is the basis of my morphogenetic hypothesis which I call the hypothesis of formative causation. I think the causes of form are the fields of previous similar things. So the field of the hedgehog contains the memory of all past hedgehogs and is linked to them by a process I call morphic resonance, the influence of like upon like.

I'm suggesting that nature is organized by evolving fields. The fields themselves are habitual in nature. They contain memory, rather than being determined by laws that somehow stand outside space and time.

This doesn't answer the question of how the first of anything comes into being. This theory of habit formation and repetition explains how once something happens and is repeated, it tends to be repeated again and again. It's a theory which is testable and is being tested. It predicts, for example, that crystals should more easily crystalize all around the world just because they've been crystalized already. And indeed they do seem to get easier to crystalize as time goes on. It also predicts that melting points of compounds of newly synthesized compounds should go up. And indeed recent data I have discovered seem to indicate they do so.

So nature may be changing. The causal patterns in nature may themselves be evolving. I think that is how the stability of nature develops in the evolutionery process.

Creativity: The Ultimate Mystery
But again, this still doesn't explain how the first example of any new pattern comes into being. This takes us into an area which is related to causality—namely creativity. How does the first of any kind of molecule or organism or instinct or idea come into being? And where does it come from? It can't be caused just by pre-existing causes in the physical world through a kind of repetition process; otherwise it wouldn't be truly new.

There are a variety of theories of creativity. The one that comes cheapest is the materialist theory: It all happens by chance. For as soon as you've said that, there's no more to be said. It simply says that we can't understand it, it's incomprehensible, there's a complete blank wall beyond which we can never go and there's no point in even trying. It's chance. It's random.

The presiding goddess of chance is the Greek goddess Tyche, or the Roman goddess Fortuna, who is blind. I see the chance-doctrine as a kind of unconscious cult of the goddess Fortune. It doesn't permit any further inquiry. It's a way of getting a cheap answer at no expenditure of energy or effort. But I don't see any particular reason for believing it.

If the world is evolving and nature is evolving, why aren't the laws of nature evolving too?

Then there is the argument that creativity somehow emerges from below. This comes from the archetypes of feminine creativity. It comes out—like a child comes out of the womb. It emerges. As Jungians would say, it wells up from the collective unconscious.

And then, of course, there are top-down theories of creativity, one of which involves our old friends, the Platonic Forms. Everything new that happens already exists potentially in some transcendent realm, awaiting a moment when it can manifest in the physical world. That's another view.

Another way is to think in terms of the whole hierarchical order of nature. There's always a higher level within which something new happens. Human thoughts for example seem to emerge within the context of societies and cultures. Societies and cultures are within the context of the Earth. The Earth is within the context of its solar system. That's within the galaxy. And within each of these there's always a higher level within which something new happens. Thus it's quite possible to think of creativity depending on downward causation, descending from some higher level of organization.

But creativity is ultimately mysterious. It raises the question of causality in a particularly strong, striking, and probably insoluble manner—but one for which we can use various alternative metaphors to try to conceive of it.

Another way of looking at some of the things I've been describing is through David Bohm's theory of the implicate order. Instead of morphic fields as formative causes, he thinks of the implicate order as formative cause. The implicate order can be thought of as having a kind of memory: What happens in the explicate order, in the world we live in, feeds back and influences the implicate world, so that it is changed by what actually happens in the world. This is what differentiates it from the Platonic view. The Platonic ideas or Forms are quite uninfluenced by anything that actually happens. They're beyond space and time, eternally the same. Nothing makes the slightest difference to them.

An Evolving God?

This leads me to the final point I wanted to make: When we think in terms of any possible causative influence of God, or a supreme spiritual reality, we run into some of the same problems. Many traditional views of God have thought of God as being utterly removed, transcending space and time, and utterly changeless. That is the basis for both Platonic theology and the mechanistic theory of nature insofar as it presupposes eternal mathematical laws. This changeless transcendent realm gives a kind of fixed background for causality in the world.

If on the other hand, along with the Process theologians and others, we take the view that God is in some sense evolving along with the natural world, then we have to think of memory as inherent in the divine being. I think in fact on theological grounds we cannot avoid this conclusion. If God is omniscient then He knows past, present and future. And His omniscience must include knowing which things have already happened and which haven't yet happened. To know what has already happened, as opposed to all the things that could happen, must involve some kind of memory, which means that God's mind must change as the universe evolves. There must be some kind of memory inherent in it.

This is just a summary of the particular views I have myself. Whether or not this hypothesis I've put forth turns out to be correct, I think there are big problems with issues of causality. The big problems are to understand the role of formal and final causes, in other words patterns, formative or informative influences on the one hand—and purpose, goals, intentions on the other. These of course are important on the human realm. I think they're also important in the whole of nature. The mechanistic theory restricted final causes to the human realm. Only human beings and God could have intentions. The rest of the world, nature, had no purpose at all of its own. It was simply there to be used by man as he saw fit.

But if we see purpose extending through the whole universe, it leads us to a completely different view of nature. I think this causality project does indeed raise extremely deep and interesting questions. □

Rupert Sheldrake received his PhD in biochemistry from the University of Cambridge. His work has been featured prominently in both scientific journals and the popular press. In May 1989, Sheldrake was named a Fellow of the Institute of Noetic Sciences.

Tony Basilio is a poet who lives in Stinson Beach, California.

How we think about cause and effect influences how we live our lives. How do our concepts of past and future affect us in the present?

Here are some choice words from Rupert Sheldrake and Peter Koestenbaum.

The final cause of the whole universe for Aristotle was God. God was the prime mover of the universe—not because He pushed it, but because in a sense He pulled it. He attracted the universe toward Himself. And there's a sense in which final causes—purposes and goals—have this kind of attractive quality. They draw things toward them. ... This is completely different from the model of things being pushed from behind in the mechanical universe.

—Rupert Sheldrake

The unity of consciousness is not ... one of past, present, and future. In the dimension of time, consciousness is experienced as the eternal present with a strong element of teleology: It is the future that pulls rather than the past that pushes. Some traditional views of man interpret the present as determined by the past. Specifically, these views hold that present events or problems are the workings out of early programing. Maturity then becomes the resolution of childhood conflicts. The present is seen in terms of the categories—persons and feelings—of the past. ...

An alternative interpretation of the situation is to seek ways to *outgrow*, i.e., genuinely *overcome*, a problem. Reliance on the past is based on a mistaken analysis of the structure of consciousness. Genuine growth is the experience of being pulled or attracted by a goal in the future (Aristotle's final cause or *telos*), not that of being pushed into action (Aristotle's efficient cause or *aitia*). And in directing our gaze to the future, we utilize whatever material from the past we deem appropriate, including use of the past to interfere with the future. Under this analysis, the past becomes almost irrelevant in the experience and conception of the present.

Men like Konrad Adenauer, Charles de Gaulle and Bertrand Russell were able to maintain joy, growth, and vigor in old age because the future and not the past was experienced as determining their present.

—Peter Koestenbaum

From *The Vitality of Death: Essays in Existential Psychology and Philosophy,*
Greenwood Publishing Company, 1971.

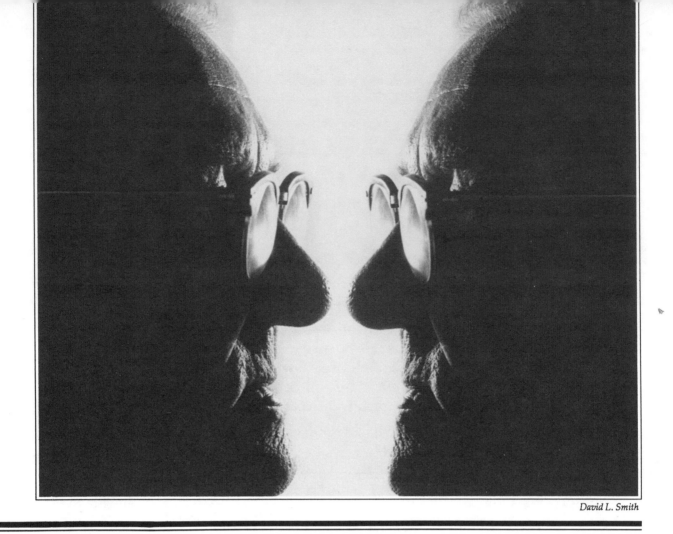

David L. Smith

The Case Against Competition

from a talk by Alfie Kohn

Alfie Kohn is author of No Contest: The Case against Competition *(Houghton Mifflin, 1986), which received the National Psychology Award for 1987 and is being translated into German, Hebrew, Japanese and Swedish. His new book, out in May, is called* The Brighter Side of Human Nature: Altruism and Empathy in Everyday Life *.*

This is a partial transcript of a talk given at the Institute-sponsored symposium, Beyond Conflict:Transcending Us vs. Them, *held June 24-25, 1989, in Washington, DC.*

The title of this conference—Beyond Conflict—gave me pause, frankly, because the way I use the word conflict I don't see much need to move beyond it. But words pertaining to competition, aggression, conflict, cooperation, and so on, are very difficult to get straight, and sometimes we argue when we don't mean to argue about their substance. For example, when students in class help each other in a cooperative fashion we don't call it cooperation in this country, we call it cheating. Other times,

when the word cooperation is used, again in a classroom setting, it is used to mean obedience, as in "I want you all to cooperate now", which means "Do exactly what I tell you".

So let's look at conflict. I don't think there is a need to move beyond it. The question is not will there be conflict, or should there be, the answer to these questions being yes, as far as I'm concerned. The question, rather, is whether that conflict takes place in a context that is cooperative or competitive.

In business meetings and at dinner parties, for example, people raise objections, make arguments, disagree, so that everyone can be exposed to another idea which is seen to be important, so that people can reach some agreement that's more informed. This is cooperative conflict. And then there are people who raise disagreements, open up controversy, just to hear themselves talk, or to show how clever they are. You can smell the difference between these two kinds of conflict.

> *Competition—no matter in what amount it exists—is always destructive. This position, even though it sounds radical, is backed by research.*

Cooperative conflict seems to make a lot of sense: People disagree with each other for a purpose that is productive or that educates. There is a significant research literature showing that this seems to work better than either debate or competition on the one hand, or people all pretending some sort of magical harmony and forced consensus on the other.

In fact, you might even say that this is parallel to what Darwin meant by natural selection. The phrase "survival of the fittest", as you may know, was not coined by Darwin but by Herbert Spencer, who corrupted his thinking. And in fact the idea of survival of the fittest is one that does not involve competition by its nature at all; it merely suggests that creatures that adapt best to a changing environment are allowed to live and reproduce another day. It does not specify what mechanism is used in order to adapt, and thus all of the evidence we just had presented to us at this symposium suggests cooperation as the best way for this amazing concept of evolution to take place. [See "The New Biology" by Robert Augros and George Stanciu in the Winter *Noetic Sciences Review.*] Similarly with conflict. It doesn't specify the mechanism of cooperation or competition.

So cooperative conflict and wrestling with ideas I think is fine, but there is a particular kind of conflict, as I've mentioned, that is especially disturbing, and that is competition.

Competitive Conflict
Basically there are two respectable positions to take on competition in this country. One is unqualified endorsement, and the other is qualified endorsement. Unqualified endorsement is represented in the Vince Lombardi quote, "Winning isn't everything, it's the only thing." It's a dog-eat-dog world out there, or perhaps, given how early it starts now with pre-school, we should say a doggie-eat-doggie world out there, and we've got to get kids primed for as much canine consumption as possible, very early.

The second camp says something like, "Competition has gone too far in this country. We push kids too fast and too hard to be number one. But if we keep things in perspective and don't get carried away, then competition can be natural and appropriate and healthy."

That used to be my position. But in writing *No Contest* I went through more than 400 studies and slowly I came to a third position, which may be occupied only by me at this point. My position is that competition is destructive and counterproductive not merely in excess; it is destructive not merely because we are doing it the wrong way; it is destructive by its very nature. I think the phrase "healthy competition" is a contradiction in terms, and the ideal amount of competition—note I do not say conflict—in any environment, the classroom, the workplace, the family, the playing field, is *none.*

I want you to open to the possibility that all things that are bad in excess are not necessarily good in moderation. That's a surprising concept. I like to confront audiences who challenge me on this by saying: "You know, I agree with you. I think the same thing is true about torturing children. We don't want to overdo it, but you can't have none at all, now, can you?"

The point is that not everything is good in a middle ground. Some things are inherently destructive. This position has not won me plaudits, as you can imagine. I'm alternately called a communist and a wimp as I discuss these things—although never both.

But the position, even though it sounds radical, is one that is backed by research. Competition, no matter in what amount it exists, is always to that extent destructive. Some competitions are worse than others.

Competition: Structural vs. Intentional
I like to distinguish between what I call "structural" competition and "intentional" competition.

By *structural competition* I mean "mutually exclusive goal attainment", which is a fancy social science expression for "I succeed only if you fail". There is a stronger version of this, which is "I succeed only if I *make* you fail".

In the first case you may be talking about golf or bowling. I do something, you do something, I do something, you do something, and at the end, of course, we're Americans, we have to have a winner, we compare scores; but we don't interfere with each other's performance. The stronger version, "I succeed only if I make you fail", we find in war . . . or tennis . . . in which in order for me to do well I have to actively interfere with how *you* do it. So a good shot in tennis, for example, is one that you cannot return; that's true by definition. The goal of the activity is not just to succeed at the end, but in each moment to interfere with your success. That doesn't mean that all tennis players are nasty or neurotic or malicious. It means that the rules of the game, the structure, so to speak, require us to succeed at the expense of other people's failure. And that is what I am arguing is always and by its nature unnecessary and destructive.

By *intentional competition* I mean simply the need for one person to be number one. Here we're talking not about the rules of the game but about the personality.

Can we have this kind of intentional competition without structural? You bet. Some people may have come to this talk today, for example, with the objective of asking the cleverest question, or to be the best dressed, or something of that sort.

You can also have the reverse situation, which I think is worse: structural competition without intentional. This is something we see every day in this culture—individuals who are satisfied with simply doing their best, having fun, reaching excellence, but who have to engage in those goals in a way that prevents other people from reaching theirs.

Success and victory, which are two completely different ideas, have been confused in this society, so we can't understand what it is to reach one without reaching the other. We have to tease these apart. I'm all in favor of success and excellence, as I am of conflict in certain situations. The question is, do we have to do it to the exclusion of other people? I think the answer to that is clearly no.

Let me summarize three consequences of competition and what has driven me to this surprising view that it is always destructive.

Competition: Does *Not* Predict Success
First there is the question of productivity, or excellence, success. This was the trickiest one. To be very honest with you, when I began my book I accepted that competition

was not very good for us psychologically, or for our relationships, but I bought the party line that you needed some competition in order to push yourself to do your best. That there was some dialectical relationship between the two, and we couldn't dispense with competition without there being a trade-off, but maybe it was worth it. Well, I was wrong.

After going through hundreds of studies conducted in classrooms and the workplace I have become convinced of what I will put into one bold and startling proposition: Not only is competition not required for excellence, its absence is required for excellence.

All of these studies are available in any good library, but they don't get read and they certainly don't get talked about in the public arena, or mentioned in popular publications for the most part. We are brought up not only to compete frantically but also to believe in competition. Therefore it is awfully threatening to have people say you have been deluded, that you are barking up the wrong tree.

Not only is competition <u>not</u> required for excellence, its <u>absence</u> is required for excellence.

Researchers have shown repeatedly that cooperation predicts to learning more than does competition or individualized attainment. It's true in rural, urban, and suburban schools; it's true for all ages; it's true for all subject matters. And the more complicated the task is, the worse competition does; the more cognitive problem-solving and creativity is required, the worse competition stacks up when measured against cooperative approaches.

This has been found in the workplace, too, both in terms of structural and intentional competition. There have been studies suggesting that people in cooperative workplaces—real-world situations, not some contrived laboratory setup—do better when they're working together than when they're trying to best each other.

continued on page 89 . . .

Some Questions from the Audience

Q: How would you run a track meet? What would you do instead?

A: I'm not on a crusade for the abolition of track and field events. But if you ask me if there is a way for us to have fun in a way that does not involve trying to triumph over other people, I think the answer is yes. If you ask people if they enjoy playing tennis or squash or watching a track meet they say yes. But *my* question is, when have you ever experienced a non-competitive recreational alternative? Most of us haven't.

The first game I learned was at a birthday party; it was called musical chairs. X number of players scramble for x minus one chairs. A prototype of artificial scarcity. Stop the music each time. Out, out, out. At the end, you've got one kid sitting down, happy, smug, and triumphant. Everybody else excluded from play, losers, unhappy. That's how you learn to have fun in this culture. No wonder we can't think of any better way to enjoy ourselves. We never learned any other way.

There are loads of cooperative games—I can point you to where you can find them—as well as many ways in which we can challenge ourselves, feel that sweaty sense of accomplishment, that ecstatic feeling of transcendence, test our skills and limits, all without competition. You can try to do better today than you did yesterday, or last week. I don't call that competition; some people call it competing with yourself. I don't have any objection to that, unless you get carried away with it to the point you never enjoy yourself. But the need to try to struggle against another person is not necessary for a good time any more than it is to be productive, or to learn.

Q: Aren't some situations inherently unavoidably competitive such as the shortage of jobs for professors? How can we structure things so that people in selective careers are not locked into destructive competitive motivational structure?

A: That's a very important question. There is no easy answer. The first thing to be said is that the arrangement we have that looks like a pyramid, specifically in corporations, and to some extent in our universities too . . . I mean, God did not decree that organizations have to be shaped like pyramids—that in order to do well one must get up into a scarce position. The number of people available to do these tasks and the number of tasks are socially constructed decisions.

I live in Boston, where the parking is even worse than here; there's one space and two cars, and you look at it and say, you know, there's no choice but to compete. Well, yes, if you freeze the frame and only look at that. But you ask, who decided the number of parking spaces? Who decided the quality of mass transit? Who made all of these decisions that led to that situation in which we have two people competing for the same job or two cars competing for the same space? I don't have a recipe, and this goes for business and economic concerns as well. I don't know how we can, in four easy lessons, transform our economic system into one that's cooperative and productive and democratic. I don't know the answer; I'm not satisfied with my own response any more than you probably are, but I know that we haven't even begun to ask those questions.

The service that I perform, if indeed it is a service, is the very modest one of saying let's sweep out the myths that have been keeping us from asking those questions.

Q: Aside from passive resistance such as with Gandhi and King, what non-competitive strategies can we use to alter the behavior of those obsessed with political control, those who use violence to compete for power, as in China?

A: Well, I'm not sure why we should sweep aside Gandhi and King, because I think they have more to tell us than the specific localized strategies that they did give us. There was no one more concerned about conflict than Gandhi, except perhaps King. They were engaged in a kind of fight, a controlled disciplined form of resistance. They just refused to use violence. They showed that we can alter the behavior of other people by bringing it to their attention, and by doing it from the ground up.

That isn't to say that I have an easy solution for the tragedy in China, or for the equally if not greater tragedy of soldiers killing students and children in various US-supported regimes around the world. We need to ask, how can we raise children so they don't grow up reproducing these same ineffective strategies? It is a tragedy that people say, "I agree with you that competition is destructive, but look, you gotta fit in. You gotta raise kids to adapt, to become competitive." This kind of reasoning is why competition endures.

I'll make a crazy suggestion. I think the evidence on competition is so powerful that we should teach kids explicitly about the dangers just as we teach about the dangers of alcohol or drugs or driving recklessly.

Q: How can we address the impact of sex-role stereotyping which particularly expects males to be competitive?

A: I have a whole chapter on this in my book, and I have to say that one of the things that troubles me more deeply than anything else is the idea that women have been urged in the last couple of decades to be as obnoxiously competitive as men under the banner of liberation. I feel that I have, as a man, a lot to learn from some values traditionally associated with women—of relationship and cooperation. It pains me very deeply that that is being turned around, that instead of men becoming the students, they're becoming the teachers. It serves no one's interest, it's not a productive response to sexism to become like the people we are trapped by. In a sentence: Everything that men do is not worth imitating just because men are doing it.

In the early part of this century women said, it's not fair that only men get to smoke. And they were right, it isn't fair. Every single opportunity open to men should be open to women, but we can't leave it at that. It's a hard issue, because I am not by any means urging any kind of reactionary position like telling women to get back to the kitchens where they belong. I'm suggesting that we all need to have those opportunities open to us. But we don't need more competition, we need less of it, by men as well as women. We address the sexual stereotyping by making sure that these norms of cooperation become the norms to which everyone aspires, men as well as women. Now today, to continue that brief metaphor, women have lung

cancer rates that are equal to those of men. That's not liberation, that's not a response to sexism. That's buying into the structure.

These norms go very deep. But there is zero evidence that any of this stuff is inborn or in the genes. I have gone through the literature on sex roles with respect to aggression, nurturing and competition pretty carefully. A lot of studies say that testosterone levels, for example, and other hormonal levels are not merely *causes* of behavior, but the *effects* of behavior. When you change various organisms like some apes and chimps, and move them into different dominance hierarchies, the testosterone level changes. Biology is not merely the cause, it is also the reflection—but that unfortunately challenges our simplistic idea of determinism.

Q: Will you speak a bit about the role of challenge, vis-a-vis competition and/or cooperation?

A: Sure. I'm a big believer in challenge. The only question I ask is whether challenge has to exist at some other people's expense. Does it have to be a zero-sum game? It is competitive thinking that is responsible not only for a lot of obnoxious people that we know, but for the potentially most deadly form of competition altogether, which is the arms race which threatens to extinguish all of us. The assumption that when the Soviets offer us an arms control initiative it's good for them and therefore bad for us is exactly the kind of thinking that will annihilate us. And merely moving that competition to other arenas doesn't change the thinking. We have to do that in other ways. We have to think of challenges we can meet without competition. Sometimes that means working independently. But more significantly, we need to identify challenges we can meet working cooperatively with others.

Cooperation does not require simply working together in one group in order to triumph against other groups. We *can* understand challenge without ever appealing to notions of besting other people, and we can do it even better by working *with* other people to accomplish mutual goals.

. . . continued from page 86
There have also been studies showing that the personal need to compete, what I call intentional competition, gets in the way of success. This counterintuitive finding (for us Americans) has been borne out again and again even when researchers expected to find the reverse; and one after another you find them saying "counter to hypothesis . . .". Why?

I think there are three reasons. I'm oversimplifying here because of the limited time available to me, and also because sometimes I get a kick out of oversimplifying.

. . . It Causes Anxiety
First, competition causes anxiety. When you are trying to beat someone and they're trying to beat you, you are distracted from doing the best job you possibly can because you're afraid someone else is going to step on your face. Not because they're mean, but because that is what competition by its nature requires.

. . . It Is Inefficient
Second, cooperation allows people to share their powers and their skills and their resources in a way that competition never does. I'm always asked, do you think we would have gotten to the moon so fast if we weren't in a race against the Russians? Well, assuming that is a good goal—by the way, a question that is almost never asked when you're in a race—but assuming it is a good goal, I think we would have gotten there an awful lot faster had we been cooperating with the Russians. Because competition among its other faults is redundant, it's wasteful, it's duplicative. They're solving problems we've already solved, and vice versa. Only when you're able to share can you get there faster and more efficiently. You could share in a competition, but you'd be nuts. It's irrational—why should I help you if your success comes at the expense of mine? You can't share in a competitive situation.

. . . It Undermines Intrinsic Motivation
And the third reason is in a way the simplest and most subtle at the same time: not only is the idea of success or excellence completely different from victory or beating other people, not only are they conceptually different, but in actual life they pull in opposite directions. The more I am focused on getting that reward of being number one the less I am concerned about what the task itself has to offer. You remember this kid in school—ooh, ooh, waving her hand wildly, teacher finally calls on her—"What was the question again?" Why? Because she's not thinking about the subject matter, she's thinking about being number one,

and those often are mutually exclusive in practice—in the way they *feel*.

Now competition in this respect shares something destructive with all external or extrinsic reward systems. Whether it's the trophy, grades, or money, the more we think of ourselves as working for that outside goal, the less we are concerned about the intrinsic motivation—what's there in the task itself.

Not only are external rewards such as competition less effective as motivators, but in fact they *undermine* intrinsic motivation, so that people who used to find something very interesting in its own right, once they start doing it in a competitive fashion or for money, they suddenly lose interest in it. There's an important literature on the social psychology of this—the way parents and teachers and managers have been leading their organizations or their homes. In the process of trying to encourage success, they have been systematically undermining curiosity, the single most important predictor of success.

So those are the three reasons I think the research shows with surprising uniformity that competition does not predict success.

Competition: Destroys Self-Esteem
But competition is destructive in another respect. And that is that competition does not create "character", whatever that means. If we mean by that something like self-confidence, self-esteem, the evidence is crystal clear here. I like to say that competition is to self-esteem as sugar is to teeth. That's what the evidence shows.

The solution is the problem. The emotional needs that we attempt to meet through competition are exacerbated by competition. They make us more dependent, they make our self-esteem more contingent—I am good insofar as I beat these people in these activities. There is no winning there. It is not the way to solve those emotional problems.

Competition: Poisons Relationships
Competition also poisons our relationships with people. We are envious of winners, which is not a pleasant emotion, and we are contemptuous of losers. If you think about it there is no nastier epithet in the American lexicon than "loser". And we are suspicious of just about everyone, hostile toward them, because even if you are not my rival today, you could be tomorrow, so I am going to hold you at a distance from myself, I am going to hold a part of myself in reserve. Why should I trust you, if you're my

competitor? People who compete and people in competitive situations communicate less effectively, are less trusting, less sensitive to other people's needs and less able to take their point of view. Kids or adults who are cooperative find that those skills are all increased in amazing ways.

People sometimes ask, does competition cause aggression? Competition *is* aggression. The only question is whether it will occasionally manifest itself in outright violence. It is an *against*-ing process. We are at loggerheads, we are working at cross-purposes. We do so in sports and we do so in the classroom—with both spelling bees and competitive grading systems. Long after kids forget how to spell some long word or forget who was the twelfth president of the United States, they remember the fundamental lesson of any competitive classroom, which is "other people are potential obstacles to my success".

That's why I am suggesting that we have to work not merely to change our individual selves, not merely to go to psychotherapy and look deep within to find why we're being competitive. I'll tell you why you're being competitive—because you live in a society that demands it of you every day of your lives. And until we make structural changes it is self-deluding to talk about the prospect of merely working from within out. That's good, too. I heartily recommend to you that you stop yourself and say, why did I interrupt him again? Why do I see this need to prove how clever I am? Why don't I just sit and listen and maybe learn something?

That's great stuff. But it's not going to get very far until we change our recreation and our workplaces and our families so that competition is no longer required. Now that's a harder task.

We Americans are very suspicious of any kind of structural change. We love to blame individuals. You're poor? You're just lazy. Get a job. You commited a crime? You're evil. Put you in jail for the rest of your life. Kids aren't learning in school? Teachers aren't any good. You need more homework. Et cetera. This lets us off the hook very easily. Instead we need to look at the deeper social, economic causes of these kinds of attitudes, and these kinds of behaviors; that's what we have to change.

And I'm afraid I have to take issue as well with those who say we should change the competition between the Soviet Union and US so we start competing about good stuff, like who can feed kids most. The answer to competition is not more competition. Any kind of competition, even in something that appears to be relatively salutary, something felicitous, something whose goal we all agree on, is going to fortify those underpinning structures that say we have to see who can be number one.

The genuine alternative to being number one is not being number two. It's being able to dispense with these self-defeating rankings altogether. A lot of people say, that's all nice to talk about, what a charming thought, but competition is just part of human nature. Usually with a shrug, and slightly patronizing smile. What a charming thought, but unfortunately it's just human nature to be competitive, or aggressive, or stubborn, or territorial, or lazy, or selfish. Nobody ever says, why of course she helped him, it's just human nature to be generous.

This is why I moved on from my work on competition and cooperation to my next book, *The Brighter Side of Human Nature*, which will be out in the spring, which deals with issues like altruism and empathy, and the extent to which this part too is just as real, just as natural a part of human nature.

I think the overall message I'm trying to urge with respect to competition and "human nature" is not only that we *should* change, but that we *can*.

Where does competition come from? I have been working on this topic for about seven years, and I have not found a shred of evidence to support the common assertion that competition is an inevitable part of "human nature".

*The genuine alternative to being number one
is not being number two. It's being able to dispense
with these self-defeating rankings altogether.*

A woman and two little boys in their swimming trunks got on the hotel elevator I was riding, obviously on their way to the pool. She said to them, "So, who's going to jump into the pool fastest?" And they said, "We both are!" I thought, How long can they hold out?

Where does competition come from? I have been working on this topic for about seven years, and I have not found a shred of evidence to support the common assertion that competition is an inevitable part of "human nature".

We have all the evidence we need to explain the way we subtly (and not so subtly) make sure it's reproduced from generation to generation. You heard the evidence about nature [see *The New Biology* by Robert Augros and George Stanciu in the Winter *Noetic Sciences Review*]. We can't appeal to nature to justify why competition exists—in spite of those exciting nature documentaries on TV.

(When I'd watch these shows, I'd think, well, nature is certainly red in tooth and claw—look at them going at each other. Of course, I'm not suggesting those things shown on TV didn't really happen; it's not like they had highly paid stunt wolves or something.) One reason we persist in the belief that competition is natural, despite all the evidence to the contrary, is that scientists live in this culture just as you and I do. *We take our understanding about social interaction and project it onto nature, and then read it back from nature to justify our own cultural practices.* Friedrich Engels said that a hundred years ago, and it's no less true today. You can't use nature to explain competition.

If you look at cross-cultural evidence you find the same thing. There are some cultures without any competition—in recreation, in education, in economics. Those cultures are sometimes rather rudely called primitive cultures, or, as I prefer to call them, non-VCR cultures.

This doesn't mean that we can or should be like them. What it does mean is that we need another explanation besides "something innate about us" to explain competition. If anything, we'd expect them to be closer to nature, so if it were indeed in human nature to be competitive and aggressive, they should be more so, not less so, as Erich Fromm pointed out. In other words, *ours* are the primitive cultures.

Needed: Another Explanation

The idea that aggression too is a part of our nature and thus unavoidable makes about as much sense as saying that because oxygen blankets the Earth and fires need oxygen that it's the nature of the planet for buildings to burn down. It makes no sense.

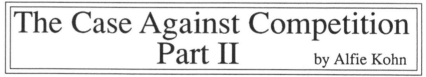

The Case Against Competition
Part II
by Alfie Kohn

Even if aggression were universal, we could not conclude from that universality that it's in the genes; that's just a clever and facile way to explain things away. Certainly there are some parts of the brain that, when stimulated, make humans or other animals more aggressive, but that doesn't mean that it is a matter of self-enclosed organisms with a self-contained reservoir of aggressive energy that has to be let out somehow. That notion, popularized by Freud and Konrad Lorenz, has been more decisively refuted than any other single old wives' tale on human behavior I know.

And the idea that war is just part of human nature—that is even more absurd. Rousseau said that war is not a relation between man and man, but between state and state, and individuals are enemies accidentally. That's why propaganda is needed, because otherwise we wouldn't be inclined to kill. There is no innate need for an enemy. There is a need to understand social and political and economic structures, and why states get involved in this sort of process.

The Institute is especially grateful to the Washington, DC, members and the symposium speakers who gave so generously of their time and resources to make this meeting a success.

But even if we move beyond competition and aggression, we need to be very careful about the way we use that phrase "human nature". Whom does it benefit? Arguments that competition and aggression are part of human nature are profoundly conservative arguments masquerading as realism. Human nature arguments are used to silence dissent. "I like your idea for changing the way we do things, but the way we do things has been legislated by nature. It's just *the way life is.*"

Why do we think this? For one thing, it's the easiest assumption available to us. If you look around and see everybody around you living in a particular way, you say, well, it must be human nature to live this way.

Another reason is that the people turning out the studies have been trained in terms of genes and hormones and neurotransmitters, and, as Abe Maslow used to say, if the only tool you have is a hammer, you will treat everything as if it's a nail.

The media are partly responsible, too, and to the extent that I write articles for popular culture I try to make a point of addressing this fact.

In 1986 experts in all social and natural sciences from more than a dozen countries met in Seville, and concluded that aggression is not an innate fixed form of human nature. Have you heard about the Seville statement? I sure hadn't. That's because nobody in the media was interested in covering it. One of the organizers told me that when he talked to reporters about the importance of this finding, one of them said to him, "Call us back when you find a gene for war." That is the bias that we keep getting.

As Jeff Goldstein of Temple University says, "If all you know about aggression is what you see on TV, what you know is nineteenth-century biology." That's what we get. There are many other, complex reasons as well.

The Reasons for Our Cynicism
Not only do we assume that there is a fixed human nature, we also assume there is a bad human nature. It's a two-step argument. The first is a kind of crass biological determinism, and the other is the specific belief that this nature we have is fundamentally flawed. You will recognize some of the contributors to the latter, in various ideologies ranging from orthodox psychoanalysis to Konrad Lorenz—to the notion of original sin, for that matter.

Leon Eisenberg, in an article in *Science* in 1972, put it very well:

> To believe that man's aggressiveness or territoriality is in the nature of the beast is to mistake some men for all men, contemporary society for all possible societies, and, by a remarkable transformation, to justify what is as what needs must be. Social repression becomes a response to rather than a cause of human violence. Pessimism about man serves to maintain the status quo. It is a luxury for the affluent, a sop to the guilt of the politically inactive, a comfort to those who continue to enjoy the amenities of privilege.

It's not only a mistaken belief but a politically loaded belief.

It has become cool to be cynical. You really risk if you say, I think there's something good here—that empathy, that helping, is as natural as hurting.

Dostoevski had one of his characters say, "The higher the stage of development a man reaches the more prone he becomes to cynicism, if only because of the increasing complexity of his makeup." A lot of us believe that to be "cool", in the sense of fashionable, is also to be "cool" in the sense of disdainfully skeptical.

And then there's a false dichotomy we set up. On the one hand we have those people who say that we're basically bad by nature. On the other hand we have smiley-faced Pollyannas who say everything is lovely and human nature is terrific, and anybody who acts badly just hasn't gotten in touch with his or her real nature.

We have to eliminate this false dichotomy. We have to understand that we're not denying the real evil that is done in our society and in other societies by affirming that there is more to us than just the competitiveness and the aggressiveness and the selfishness. It's time now that we debunk the debunkers. ☐

The audiotape of this talk and others from the Beyond Conflict symposium are available through the Institute's mailorder service. Please write or call the Institute for ordering information.

See page 93 for a response from Olympian competitor Marilyn King.

Letter to the Editor

I am concerned that Alfie Kohn, in his article "The Case Against Competition" [Spring *Noetic Sciences Review*] perpetuates erroneous notions about the true nature and value of competition. One of the things he says is that competition is destructive by its very nature. This argument is based on the premise that no amount of competition is healthy.

I think his definition of competition as "mutually exclusive goal attainment" is a pretty narrow one. It's based a lot on the popular culture which is perpetuated by a media whose main purpose is selling air time or magazines, and that definition of competition has gotten us into a lot of trouble.

A perfect example of that occurred the day that Carl Lewis and Ben Johnson both broke the world's record in the 100-meters. What the media emphasized was the *winner*. In fact, both men had run faster in that race than any one man had run in the *history of the world*. All the media portrayed was the winner/loser aspect of it. I propose that that's where the problem is, not in the nature of competition but in the context within which competition occurs.

This problem is pervasive in our culture. In his article, Mr. Kohn is taking something that is not inherently good or bad, and taking it to its worst extreme. He makes some very valid points about competition. If you set it up as winner/loser, then yes, it is bad in that sense. And I certainly do not want to perpetuate that approach.

But I have derived a wholly different notion about competition based on my experience as an athlete. I would define competition as using your environment—whether it's the space race, or another athlete—to help extract your "best self". I was not particularly a gifted or talented athlete, but I was a great competitor. I knew that the reason I would compete at the highest levels of my sport was how I thought about things, how I used my mind.

For example, when Mr. Kohn talks about competition poisoning our relationships, I am reminded of the Olympic trials of 1976. In order to be in the Olympic Games you have to place in the top three; but in the trials my primary competitor was a woman who placed first most of the year that I competed. She was a taller, stronger, bigger, better athlete than I and she usually beat me. But she began to miss her high jumps. By then it was only the two of us left in the competition. When she missed on her third attempt I went across the field to her and said, "Jane, what are you doing? You left me here by myself. There is no one else in the competition for me. What am I going to do? *I need you in order to jump higher!*"

How many times have I seen two athletes— who have been pitted against each other for four years for the Olympic gold medal— cross the finish line at the Games and not just shake hands and walk away, but embrace each other? On some level they know that the other person is responsible for their being as good as they are, that without that other person they would not have pushed and become as good.

Being in my first Olympic competition (Munich 1972) was the highest attainment that I could even imagine. Winning a medal was not even in my thoughts—the East Germans, the Russians, were much bigger, stronger, faster. But just to be on the Olympic team was to me a tremendous accomplishment, it was my goal.

But if you frame competition in the context where there is only one gold medal and everybody else is a loser, I would agree that competition is destructive. When I came back from Munich, friends would introduce me: "This is my friend Marilyn King. She was in the Olympics." Of course, my chest would swell with pride. But the next question people would ask was, "Oh, you were in the Olympics. Did you win a medal?" When I said I didn't win a medal, they didn't have anything else to say—that

was the end of the conversation. And as a 19-year-old I was pretty devastated by that.

An example of how competition can be healthy is the Special Olympics, where *everybody* gets awards and medals and congratulations for just crossing the finish line, for just participating.

When you contrast competition with cooperation, I agree with Mr. Kohn that in many instances, cooperation fosters good things and many times competition can be very negative, destructive and inappropriate. But I believe that cooperation and competition are called for at different times; they are processes that are appropriate in certain instances and not in others.

—Marilyn King

Alfie Kohn responds:

King's argument turns entirely on her definition of competition as "using your environment— to help extract your 'best self'." This definition seems dubious to me, first, because it is so broad and elastic as to include lots of things unrelated to what we normally think of as competition and, second, because it makes competition valuable by definition instead of relying on arguments or evidence to prove its value.

Maintaining a constructive attitude toward opponents (or focusing on personal excellence instead of victory) is a lovely ideal; unfortunately, it runs smack against the built-in requirement of any competition, which is to win. The structure inherent in contests ranging from spelling bees to the Olympics specifies that one can succeed only if others fail. It is this structure, and not merely our individual attitudes, that will have to be changed if we seek a healthier and more productive way to work, to play, to learn, and to live.

We welcome responses to any articles featured in the Review. *The editor reserves the right to edit any letter we choose to print.*

Energy Medicine In China:

Calvin Yau Ching

Defining a Research Strategy Which Embraces the Criticism of Skeptical Colleagues

from a talk by David Eisenberg, MD

Presented at The John E. Fetzer Foundation Conference: "Energy Fields, Meridians, Chi and Device Technology" May 11-14, 1989

David Eisenberg, MD, is Instructor in Medicine, Harvard Medical School, Associate in Medicine, Beth Israel Hospital, Boston, and is author of Encounters With Qi: Exploring Chinese Medicine. *Dr. Eisenberg was one of the first American medical scholars to be invited by the People's Republic of China to study medicine in that country.*

I wish to begin with two quotations which highlight the challenge to our scientific understanding of energy medicine.

Vine Deloria, writing about the evolution of medical systems prior to the one currently in use, made the following observation:

> For primitive people the presence of energy and power is the starting point of their analysis and understanding of the natural world . . . primitive people felt power but did not measure it. Today we measure power but are not able to feel it.

René Dubos, commenting on modern scientific principles, has reminded us that:

Sometimes the more measurable drives out the most important.

Researchers of so-called energy medicine are a curious lot. We unearth ancient practices, dust them off, clean them with modern solvents and study them under the lens of high technology. All the while, we seek to distill simple truths about health and illness.

Traditional Chinese Medicine

China is a nation of 1.1 billion people where more than 800 million people reside in rural areas. These individuals lead a lifestyle not altogether different from the lifestyles of their parents, grandparents and distant ancestors.

It is said of rural China that the three greatest changes in the past century are the introduction of the bicycle, of the thermos bottle and, most recently, the absence of war for more than a quarter century. Chinese customs have changed relatively little. Children, in the eyes of the Chinese people, remain the most precious gift of nature and the source of hope for future generations. But a Chinese child growing up in the latter portion of the twentieth century will surely face tumultuous change. By law, a Chinese family can have only one child. As such, an entire generation of Chinese children will grow up without an understanding of what it means to have brothers and sisters. Moreover, Chinese children will witness a rapidly changing economy and a volatile political atmosphere—one which is struggling to embrace democracy and Western attitudes without destroying its own cultural heritage.

Furthermore, Chinese children growing up in the 1990s will live in a country where there are two distinct systems of medical care. One system, traditional Chinese medicine, is likely favored by the children's grandparents and rural neighbors. The other system, which we refer to as "modern Western medicine", is likely preferred by the parents, educated relatives and urban neighbors.

Traditional Chinese medicine evolved over two thousand years under the influence of Buddhist and Taoist priests. This medical system emerged in isolation from Western science as we know it. Not until the middle of the nineteenth century were principles of the scientific method introduced to China. This occurred as a result of education offered by medical missionaries from Europe and the United States.

By the turn of the century American and European missionaries had established medical clinics, hospitals, and several medical schools on the Chinese mainland. Prominent professors from universities such as Harvard, Yale, and Johns Hopkins lectured at the newly created Chinese medical schools.

Western medicine became extremely popular with China's intellectuals and with its governmental leaders. In an effort to promote Western medicine the Nationalist Government in the 1920s went so far as to outlaw traditional Chinese medicine on the grounds that it was "backwards and superstitious". This effort failed, as the Chinese people perceived Western medicine to be alien, crude, and highly unnatural.

In 1950, following the establishment of the People's Republic of China, Chairman Mao Tse-tung was faced with a political dilemma: There were approximately 500 million people in China but only 38,000 Western-style medical doctors. At the same time, however, there were approximately 500,000 traditionally trained Chinese doctors. Understandably, Chairman Mao launched a political campaign to "unite medical workers young and old of the traditional and Western schools to organize a solid front". For the past four decades this call for unity and integration has persisted in the People's Republic of China.

However, if one reviews statistics from the Chinese Ministry of Health regarding medical manpower throughout the People's Republic of China today, it is clear that over the past three decades the pendulum has shifted from traditional medicine to modern Western medicine. Today Western-style physicians outnumber traditionally trained medical doctors six to one and Western-style hospital beds outnumber those in traditional Chinese hospitals by thirteen to one. This trend toward a dominance of modern Western medicine will continue for the foreseeable future.

And Its Introduction to the West

What about the introduction of traditional Chinese medicine to the West? In the United States the turning point, I believe, was a single newspaper article written by a prominent journalist from *The New York Times*, James Reston.

In 1971, while accompanying the Nixon-Kissinger entourage, James Reston wrote an article entitled "Now Let Me Tell You About My Appendectomy In Peking". Reston developed acute appendicitis while visiting Bejing and was operated on using Western anesthesia. The surgery was uneventful; however, he suffered profound postoperative pain in the area of his incision. The Chinese medical authorities summoned two prominent acupuncturists to treat these symptoms. Their treatment consisted of inserting several needles. So prompt and complete was Reston's pain relief, that he could barely contain himself from describing this curious technique in detail. This description introduced the West to a therapy which the Chinese referred to as "acupuncture anesthesia".

James Reston's article triggered an enormous surge of interest in this therapy. Medical teams composed of experts traveled to China to witness surgical procedures involving it. Many of these experts returned to the United States utterly convinced that acupuncture anesthesia was a real phenomenon, not merely hypnosis or sham.

I was a college freshman at that time and elected to do an independent study project regarding acupuncture anesthesia. Little did I know that none of the 100 libraries at Harvard University contained a single page describing it.

Acupuncture had been used to treat common illnesses for more than 2,000 years; however, its application as a surgical anesthetic was new. This had to do with the fact that there was no major surgery in traditional Chinese medicine. Major surgery was considered to be a mutilation of the body and the body was considered to be the ultimate gift of one's parents. Filial piety dictated that one never deface the ultimate gift of one's ancestors. Therefore, there was no major surgery in China—only the sewing up of superficial wounds and stabilization of bone fractures.

Acupuncture was not applied to the surgical amphitheater until the late 1950s, as a direct consequence of Chairman Mao's political directive that physicians from Chinese and Western backgrounds work together to "form a united front".

In 1972, when I became interested in acupuncture, there were no English translations of Chinese experimental texts dealing with acupuncture as an anesthetic. Instead, I stumbled on English translations of famous reference texts of traditional Chinese medicine. Chief among them was a book entitled *The Yellow Emperor's Canon of Internal Medicine* (see quote, right). It is still used today as the primary reference for traditional Chinese medicine.

This ancient text helped me understand the basic theoretical differences which distinguish Chinese (that is, Oriental) medical systems from those used today in the West. Specifically, traditional Chinese medicine emphasized prevention over intervention. It also emphasized that one's lifestyle, including diet, exercise, thoughts, and emotions, plays a critical role in the natural course of illness and one's ability to maintain health.

Calvin Yau Ching

"To administer medicine to diseases which have already developed and thereby suppress bodily chaos which has already occurred is comparable to the behavior of those who would begin to dig a well after they have grown thirsty, or those who would begin to cast weapons after they have engaged in battle. Would these actions not be too late?

"... I have heard that in early times the people lived to be over 100 years old. But these days people reach only half that age and must curtail their activities. Does the world change from generation to generation or does man become negligent of the laws of nature?

"... Today people do not know how to find contentment within. They are not skilled in the control of their spirits. For these reasons they reach only half of their 100 years and then they degenerate."

The Yellow Emperor's Canon of Internal Medicine, c. 400 BCE

I was intrigued by the basic principles of Chinese medicine and set out to learn the Chinese language in the hope that some day I could study both traditional Chinese and modern Western medicine.

In 1979, when I was a fourth-year medical student at Harvard Medical School, the United States normalized relations with the People's Republic of China. The National Academy of Sciences selected me to serve as the first US medical exchange student to China. In 1979 and 1980, I studied Chinese medicine at the Beijing College of Traditional Chinese Medicine.

I was not prepared for the education I received in Beijing. Without realizing it at the time, I was receiving my initial formal education in "energy medicine".

I was fascinated by the principal methods of physical diagnosis: tongue and pulse examination. It was hard to imagine that each radial artery could be successfully palpated in six separate locations (three superficial and three deep) and that a masterful clinician could differentiate among 40 different pulse variations at each of the twelve pulse points. More spectacular still was the claim that these subtle pulse variations enabled the clinician to know with accuracy the etiology and extent of the patient's pathology within specific internal organs. Such correlations were unknown to me.

More peculiar still was the Chinese diagnostic approach using the tongue. Students of traditional Chinese medicine were required to master several hundred tongue variations. The size, color, coating, tooth indentation, etc., of each tongue type was said to enable the clinician to make a specific diagnosis in terms of location and etiology of pathology. Again this claim seemed utterly fantastic and new to me.

Not only were the diagnostic approaches to the physical examination alien, so were the specific therapeutic interventions within traditional Chinese medical hospitals. Each, I came to learn, was based on an "energy" system.

Treatment
. . . Acupuncture
For example, acupuncture, known in the West primarily in regard to surgical analgesia, was used daily in the treatment of almost every medical, surgical and psychiatric illness known. Its application as a means of "restoring energy balance" was yet another new observation for me. Clinicians spoke of "putting energy through the needles" and "taking energy out of the body" in a language which was alien to me.

. . . Acupressure Massage
Acupressure massage, based on a system of points and meridians identical to acupuncture, was yet another unexplored modality. Again, claims of energy transfer were used by my mentors in describing what they were doing in diagnosing and treating patients on the massage table. I was impressed clinically by the extent to which patients with acute musculoskeletal pain and/or pain in association with chronic neurologic or musculoskeletal problems found relief from massage therapy. More importantly, in many instances patients' relief was not short-lived but, rather, lasted for days, weeks or months in a fashion which I could not explain. These were among my most humbling observations.

. . . Herbal Medicine
The principal mode of Chinese intervention is not acupuncture or acupressure but herbal medicine. Over the past two millennia the Chinese have developed a vast pharmacopoeia of plant, animal and mineral substances based on empirical observation and clinical experience.

Herbal therapy is unquestionably the most respected and difficult of all Chinese interventions because it requires the study of hundreds of herbal preparations used in complicated combinations specifically for the purpose of rebalancing bodily excess, deficiency or stagnation. Without a mastery of classical Chinese, pulse and tongue diagnosis and insight into Chinese pathophysiology, herbal therapy is a foreboding if not impossible discipline.

. . . and "Energy": Qi Gong
The other Chinese medical therapy which is most closely related to the notion of Western "energy healing" is that of "Qi Gong" (pronounced "chē gōng").

Qi Gong is a martial art, arguably the oldest and most important martial art, from which other forms of martial arts have evolved. The physical movements of Qi Gong, which are circular, symmetrical, and slow, are similar to those movements used in other martial arts (such as Tai Chi Chuan and Kung Fu). However, in addition to the physical movements, the Qi Gong practitioner is instructed in the art of centering, of achieving a particular state of physical balance, and, simultaneously, to meditate.

The practice of Qi Gong involves some of the key elements found in Western relaxation training. These include paying attention to one's breathing, establishing a passive disregard toward one's thoughts, and—unique to Qi Gong—instructions in techniques to sense the source of one's Qi (vital energy) at a point below the navel and to learn to move it through one's body. I will return to this unusual aspect of Qi Gong.

It is said that anyone can learn Qi Gong exercises and that it takes approximately three to six months before one can "feel one's Qi" (in the form of heat or fullness) and begin to move it at will.

The practice of Qi Gong, when analyzed from a Western perspective, may be thought of as a combination of behavioral techniques. These are typically performed for 30 to 60 minutes every day of the year. The behavioral components of Qi Gong include the elicitation of the relaxation response and/or other aspects of relaxation training, aerobic exercise, progressive muscular relaxation, guided imagery, and elements of the placebo effect. In China, where an estimated *50 million* persons practice Qi Gong every day, there is an unprecedented opportunity to investigate the impact of behavioral (that is, non-pharmacologic, cognitive) therapies as they relate to a multitude of illnesses.

The Concept of Qi

There is a single fundamental concept of traditional Chinese medicine which helps clarify the seemingly disparate diagnostic and therapeutic techniques I have summarized. This concept is called "Qi" (vital energy).

"Qi" is said to be that which differentiates animate from inanimate. The body is viewed as a complicated series of conduits through which Qi flows. These conduits are the acupuncture meridians referred to in Chinese diagrams depicting human anatomy. Pathogenesis relates to the excess or deficiency inextricably linked to the force of Yin ("female", "cold", "hollow", etc.) and its opposing force, Yang ("male", "hot", "solid", etc.).

The Chinese clinician's task is to identify where the Qi exists in excess or is deficient. This is done chiefly by means of taking a history, observing and using pulse and tongue diagnosis. The diagnostic label used by the Chinese clinician refers to the specific imbalance which has been noted on physical examination. Each therapy, whether it includes needles, herbs, changes in diet or meditation, is aimed at reestablishing the balance of Qi.

There is one more piece of traditional Chinese terminology which is worth mentioning. "Internal Qi Gong" or "Soft Qi Gong" refers to an individual's ability to sense and move his/her own Qi within his/her own body. "External Qi Gong" or "Hard Qi Gong" refers to the (alleged) ability of some Qi Gong practitioners to emit their Qi externally so as to influence other animate or inanimate structures.

The notion of emitting energy from the human body is yet another example of how traditional Chinese medical thought

---

A summary of the major assertions regarding Chinese energy medicine ("Qi Gong"):

1. **"Qi" (vital energy) exists as a physical entity.** The Chinese claim the Qi can be measured, controlled and has biological and clinical significance.

2. **"Qi meridians" ("energy fields") exist as physical entities.** The Chinese claim that meridians are measurable, and necessary for pulse, tongue and energy diagnosis. Furthermore, Chinese theory suggests that meridians can be predictably influenced by acupuncture stimulation, herbal therapies, massage, Qi Gong or other cognitive interventions.

3. **Tongue, pulse and energy diagnoses are reliable and may help to elucidate important physiologic relationships.** The Chinese claim that subtle variations noted on the radial artery, the tongue and along acupuncture meridians can elucidate the location and severity of internal organ pathology.

4. **Internal and/or external manipulation of "Qi" can alter the natural course of illness.** The Chinese specifically assert that Qi Gong therapy can alter illness patterns in malignant cancers, chronic diseases (for example, renal failure, chronic obstructive pulmonary disease, arthritis, etc.), psychiatric disorders (such as anxiety, depression and schizophrenia) and immunodeficiency (for example, AIDS).

5. **Paranormal (that is, psychic) abilities are "Qi related" phenomena.** There is a long-held Chinese claim that individuals who practice and become masterful at manipulating internal or external Qi are capable of unique paranormal skills.

> *Without prospective randomized trials producing convincing data, so-called energy medicine will not be accepted by mainstream health-care providers.*

diverges radically from that of conventional Western medicine. Traditional Chinese medicine asserts that Qi Gong masters can emit Qi at will and use this energy as a treatment for common illness.

The notion of "Qi" is not unique to China. It is found within the medical systems of Tibet, India, ancient Greece, branches of the Catholic Church, and also has similarities to more recent theories such as that of "animal magnetism" proposed by Mesmer in the eighteenth century.

In the late 1970s and early 1980s the masters of Qi Gong reemerged and began to perform publicly throughout China. They had all "gone underground" during the 1960s and '70s as a result of the cultural revolution's ban on Qi Gong (which was labeled "superstition" by China's political authorities). These individuals claimed to have practiced Qi Gong from early childhood and proudly displayed their seemingly supernatural skills to audiences as large as 50,000 persons. Qi Gong masters split stones with their hands and their foreheads, had trucks drive over them, had massive stone slabs lowered on their bodies by cranes, claimed to be able to see within human bodies and to move inanimate objects at will. The claims seemed carnival-like and appeared to be well-rehearsed circus acts.

Researching Qi Gong

My personal interest in Qi Gong was sparked as a result of a television broadcast in 1980 which suggested that scientific laboratories in Beijing and Shanghai were applying rigorous methods of investigation to the physiologic changes produced by Qi Gong masters. First among these observations were reports of thermal change in surface skin measurements of Qi Gong masters who were "emitting Qi". Thermally sensitive films suggested that when Qi Gong masters emitted energy, the energy tracked down lines in the forearms and legs which were similar to classical acupuncture meridians.

A second series of publications in the area of microbiology were more fantastic still. Professor Feng Li Da of Bejing published an article pertaining to the predictable change of bacterial cell growth in response to external Qi emission by Qi Gong masters. Her paper reported on the ability of several Qi Gong masters to increase or decrease bacterial cell growth in a variety of common bacteria. Dr. Feng claimed to have replicated these experiments on numerous occasions in multiple laboratory settings and seemed confident of her results.

A more recent series of assertions has to do with the claim that certain Qi Gong masters can modulate AC electrical current from any common wall socket and act as a "human rheostat".

After attending a conference in Beijing in October 1988 I was asked by a Qi Gong master if he could demonstrate his skill to me on a visit to my hotel room. He came equipped with an electrical volt meter and a simple wiring device. The device was no more than a plug attached to two wires with live ends. He put the plug in the wall and demonstrated its current by lighting lightbulbs and then tested the current on his hand-carried volt meter. He then licked his thumb and forefinger of both hands and grasped the two live wires. I was horrified and worried he would quickly be electrocuted before me. He was not. Moreover, he convinced me that he could light a lightbulb by touching it with other fingers from both hands. More curious still was his ability to regulate voltage across his two hands, at will, simply by touching the volt meter with the ground in one hand, the meter device in the other. On several attempts he regulated the voltage from 0 to 220 volts, or held the voltage constant, at will, upon my request.

Because I have grown increasingly skeptical of such provocative claims, I asked him how I could be certain he was in fact conducting electricity and not simply fooling me by means of some extraordinary high technology trick. He offered to touch me with his hands while he was connected to the wall socket. I declined, but a colleague with me at the time volunteered. When touched on the shoulder by the Qi Gong master, my colleague's trapezius and biceps muscles went into spasm. Moreover, the Qi Gong master could control the electrical current so as to induce the spasm or not. I allowed the Qi Gong master to touch me for a split second, long enough to feel the live current emanating from his forefinger. He was "live" all right.

In a final demonstration the Qi Gong master took two metal skewers along with a one-pound pork steak which he had brought with him. He put the two skewers through the steak then grabbed the skewers, one in the left hand and one in the right so as to complete an electrical circuit. Having grasped the wires along with the two skewers the circuit was engaged and the pork chop began to smoke and flame. Within minutes there was a medium-well-done pork chop which my Qi Gong friend sliced and offered to serve! I was astounded by this demonstration and have no adequate explanation for why the Qi Gong master did not injure his skin, or cause a serious heart irregularity, seizure or other damage to his own person.

Such feats are no more than a tantalizing introduction to the many provocative clinical applications of so-called External Qi therapy. For example, Lin Ho Sheng, a Qi Gong master in Shanghai, claims to have emitted Qi directly to the acupuncture points used for acupuncture anesthesia. As reported, this type of Qi Gong anesthesia was successfully used in several dozen operations involving the thyroid

David Eisenberg

gland or abdomen. There is no explanation for this kind of claim. Hypnosis has been flatly denied by the Chinese. I am unaware of any replication of this kind of analgesic technique outside of Shanghai.

Qi Gong masters throughout traditional Chinese medical colleges in the People's Republic of China are using External Qi Gong as a treatment for a wide variety of illnesses. They typically treat patients with chronic neurologic and musculoskeletal disease, including multiple sclerosis.

More spectacular still is the observation that large numbers of patients said to have biopsy-proven, non-malignant can-

cer are being treated with a combination of Internal and External Qi Gong therapy. Hundreds of purported cancer patients meet at dawn each morning for the purpose of practicing Internal Qi Gong and receiving External Qi Gong therapy from a Qi Gong master. Moreover, the Chinese lay press frequently displays headlines such as: "Qi Gong Defeats Breast Cancer". These articles tend to summarize anecdotal case histories and are rarely if ever substantiated in medical journals.

I wish to point out that recent estimates suggest that 50-60 million Chinese practice Qi Gong at dawn each day for the purpose of disease prevention or in an attempt to alter the natural course of serious or lethal illness.

A Proposed Research Strategy

I would like to offer a strategy for experimental validation of assertions regarding Chinese energy medicine (see box on page 8).

- My opinion is that we should emphasize basic science experiments before attempting to design and implement clinical trials involving human subjects. My rationale for this is based, in part, on the fact that clinical subjects committees in hospital and academic institutions are unlikely to approve human subjects experiments if they have insufficient basic science data to support their objectives.

- A specific list of basic science experiments pertaining to energy medicine should include demonstrations of the effects of Qi on a variety of electromagnetic fields, bacterial growth patterns, cell and tissue culture models, and plant and animal physiology. Without measurable, predictable and reproducible evidence in these areas, clinical research will be difficult if not impossible to promote.

- With regard to clinical investigations, the first category is that of diagnosis. An effort should be made to assess, in a critical fashion, the diagnostic acumen of "gifted healers". They should be tested in comparison to the diagnostic acumen of modern technology. Moreover, there should be an attempt to describe inter-rater reliability as well as test-retest reliability among so-called "Energy Diagnosticians".

- The same general philosophy should ideally be applied to devices and machines which claim to be based on "subtle energy" mechanisms. These should all be subject to controlled study in a rigorous fashion.

- A separate set of experiments should ideally assess the ability of healers and/or energy devices to induce *acute* physiologic change in human subjects. For instance, can healers or "energy devices" predictably alter organ function (for example, renal flow or cardiac output) in a fashion which is safe and reliable?

Once demonstrations of acute physiologic change are completed, experiments should be designed to document *sustained* physiologic change. Claims of altering the natural course of illness will likely only be accepted if and when evidence of sustained physiologic change can be supplied.

- If clinical therapeutic trials are to be implemented, they will need to meet rigorous clinical epidemiologic criteria in order to demonstrate efficacy and effectiveness. Ideally, such studies should avoid anecdotes and case studies in favor of randomized controlled trials. Designing such trials will be challenging in that they will need to include non-biased patient populations, controls for confounding variables (such as co-intervention, contamination, experimental bias, etc.). The confounder which is most apt to cause methodological difficulty is that of expectancy of relief (for example, placebo effect). Without careful assessment of expectancy factors prior to, during and post intervention, these studies will likely be subject to savage criticism. Statistical methods will need to include meticulous sample-size calculations and attention to both statistical and clinical significance.

- If and when clinical trials involving therapeutic modalities such as acupuncture, herbal medicine, energy emission devices and/or Qi Gong are implemented, these trials will likely need to involve multiple centers, hundreds of patients followed over months or years and strict outcome parameters which include objective variables such as health costs, days of work lost and overall medical expenses. Such studies may require the professional involvement of dozens of skilled researchers and will likely cost hundreds of thousands or millions of dollars to complete. Without prospective randomized trials producing convincing clinical data collected under rigorously controlled conditions, so-called energy medicine will not likely be accepted or promoted by mainstream health care providers and third-party insurers.

Utilizing Constructive Criticism

I have a number of suggestions whereby energy medicine researchers can work together to build credibility by inviting constructive criticism from qualified skeptical colleagues.

The first priority might be to create professional forums wherein debate pertaining to energy medicine basic science and clinical investigations can take place. Such debates may take the form of prioritizing research projects, the utilization of financial resources, popularization of ongoing research and a more meticulous review of work in progress.

We should consider identifying and electing appropriate experts to serve as mentors and scientific advisers with regard to energy medicine research. Such individuals might offer constructive criticism to protocols prior to their implementation. Once successfully implemented, this mentor (or scientific advisory) group could assist in refining data analyses and perhaps attempt to implement a replication of successful experiments in the laboratories of qualified skeptical colleagues.

Ideally, if experiments can be critiqued and replicated in the laboratories of critical colleagues, they would stand a far greater chance of being accepted in peer-reviewed journals. Moreover, having engaged qualified skeptical scientists prior to publication, professional criticism post-publication is apt to be predictable and more easily handled. This group might also consider a formal pledge to avoid public disclosure of critical experiments and/or manuscripts prior to acceptance for publication in peer-reviewed journals.

Last, scientists investigating energy medicine-related phenomena should be encouraged to share and publish experiments which have resulted in negative findings as well as those with positive results. Only in this way will the field gain credibility and will researchers be properly informed so as to avoid nonproductive methods of inquiry.

I conclude my remarks with a Chinese proverb: "Real gold does not fear the heat of even the hottest fire." Qi and Qi-related phenomena, if real, are like precious gold. Undoubtedly, once subjected to the heat of criticism, they will be reshaped, recast, but not destroyed. This process of enrichment will enable investigators to demonstrate more clearly the value of "energy"-related biological phenomena. □

"Real gold does not fear the heat of even the hottest fire."

Chinese proverb

*It's possible
that there is no minimum,
there is no smallest thing.
It's possible that [the universe]
is like an infinite onion
that you can keep on
peeling layers off,
and every time you probe
to smaller distances
using a higher energy tool,
you'll discover still another
layer of the onion.*
Burton Richter, Director
Stanford Linear Accelerator Center

*There is nothing so small
but that there is something smaller.
There is nothing so large
but that there is something larger.*
Native American saying

photo by Steele Photography

A Native American Worldview

Based on a Presentation to the Board of Directors of The Institute of Noetic Sciences

by Paula Underwood Spencer

Paula Underwood Spencer is responsible for one traditional way of knowing. Passed down with what she calls "meticulous care" from her grandfather's Oneida grandmother, this tradition contains vast oral histories, some related to the first settling of North America; an extensive educational structure, part of which has been declared "an Exemplary Educational Program" by the US Department of Education; and a specific shamanic tradition called The Strong Spirit Path. In this article she relates her Native American educational and shamanic trainings to Western science. Paula Spencer also holds an MA in International Affairs/Communications and has extensive experience with organizations and government in Washington, DC. She describes herself as "still looking for words and phrases with which to share more effectively the ancient tradition".

First I want to explain to you the base from which I'm speaking. My grandfather's grandmother was Oneida. She became responsible for an ancient tradition and for passing it along. She did this because she was both a Healer and a Spirit Healer. During what was, in effect, her internship, she was assigned a man who was slowly dying. That man, as it turned out, was dying of grief. She learned this very quickly.

This was a test for her, by the equivalent of the Community Medical Board, to determine what kind of healer she was, and what she would do.

She pinpointed the cause of his grief: He was the Keeper of the Old Things. He had not been able to find, during his very long life, anyone at all who would take the time to sit with him and learn all of these ancient treasures. This was because of the oncoming tide of the Pale Ones.

Therefore as part of this man's therapy, my grandfather's grandmother began to learn these things from him. And immediately his condition improved. He got better and better.

Now her purpose in life had always been to be a Healer. So during this therapy she thought she would find somebody else to learn all these things from him and pass on the responsibility. But she was never able, in three decades of trying, to find anyone at all who could learn this from him or from her. So she finally accepted maintaining this tradition as a family responsibility. The idea was to perpetuate this ancient wisdom as far into the future as necessary, until Earth's children grew Listening Ears.

Black Elk, whom some of you will know, said that it was the fifth generation that would grow Listening Ears. In this specific tradition, I am the fifth generation. In my own lifetime I have discovered that people have indeed grown Listening Ears.

Now—my father's idea was that I should wait until I developed some grandmother wisdom before writing this down. In other words, I needed to live through the life cycle before trying to commit to paper all of these ancient understandings. My grandfather had given up a career in medicine to spend his time learning all this from his grandmother. He then passed it on to my father after a great deal of testing.

I don't want to give you the impression that this transmittal is based on automatic lineal descent. It's not. In this tradition a man learns these things from a woman, if possible, and a woman learns them from a man. That way you keep things in balance. It gives you an understanding of the other half of life and prevents some of the competition that can often come in when you learn from someone who is also male, also female.

My father's responsibility was to find someone who would have the natural proclivity, the motivation, and the latent skills to learn all this. I went through extended periods of testing with my father, not pass/fail tests, but evaluations. There's a lot of evaluative testing that goes on in this tradition. (See accompanying box.)

As a result of 15 years of careful exploration of ways to share these things, the first book to be published out of the three Basic Learning Stories has received three national awards, one of them being recognition by the US Department of Education as part of an Exemplary Educational Program. The three Learning Stories represent Body, Mind, and Spirit. We hope to publish them together soon.

Learnings in Sensitization

There are many kinds of sensitization processes that you have the opportunity to go through if you choose. You get many kinds of testing to evaluate how you think. The idea is that everybody learns, but you need to figure out *how* a child learns in order to design a learning circumstance in which each individual can teach themselves. The idea is always to teach yourself. In fact there is no word "teach", or there didn't used to be, in the fundamental language.

Then you go through mind transfer situations. One of the ways oral history can be handed down is in visual form. How do you do that? When my father was teaching me we sat in the garage. You have to have a sacred place for learning, and the fire laws of California prevented us from having a traditional sacred place, so we had to settle for the garage. My dad would be just sitting there staring at the back wall, and he would say, "What am I looking at?" It wouldn't take me very long to figure out he wasn't looking at the wall, and he wasn't looking at the gunny sack that was hanging there, or the hoe, or the rake, and all of a sudden I said, "Oh, you're looking at a mountain." "What kind of mountain?" And then we would go through a long process of description of every inch of the mountain.

Then, he would say, "Try this," and all of a sudden I realized I was looking at a tree, one I hadn't seen before. Then he would take me for a little walk maybe several days later, and all of a sudden I would say, "Oh look, there it is!" So, you test whether this is working all the time. Then he would come home from work and he would say, "You know what I was thinking about today?" and that would just click and I would say, "Yes I do—you were thinking about . . ."

My dad was functionally illiterate, he was so dyslexic. This worked out very well because his mind wasn't distracted with academic things, as my grandfather's mind had been, because he was a very educated man. My father had a very simple job, where he didn't have to do anything but physical labor. He'd get himself into the swing of his work, and then he'd just start figuring things out, maybe my lesson for the next day, or maybe "Let's see if she can pick this up." So the thought would just come to me. And then he would find some way of establishing whether or not I had picked up his thinking accurately.

Then at that point, when you've checked, double checked, triple checked, quadruple checked, at that point you begin trying to hand down some of the visual information. So I have stored visual information to which I would give a very high probability of accuracy, maybe 96%. And I went through all these excruciatingly detailed testing processes first.

The Consensual Oral History, under the title *The Walking People*, has also been written down. It is about 700 pages long. It goes back to before what logically must be the crossing of the Bering Strait, which was called at that time Walk by Waters. There is a great deal that precedes that event, so it is indeed an ancient history, which has been maintained down all these generations.

Now—one of the difficulties of my path through life has been to find ways to express these ancient ways of knowing. I knew from the time I was a child that I would need to take the step in my generation of stating these things in English. I wrote a thought piece a while ago which refers to the problem of "catching a concept in a net of sound patterns called English". Sometimes you can do that and sometimes you can't. I want to speak to that briefly.

Years ago I took a class in parapsychological research. The idea was to get an updating on all of the latest in Western scientific studies. I had a terrible time. I wanted to get up and run screaming from the room. Often! And I thought, what's going on? What is my problem?

Then I realized that the problem was language. The language was driving me crazy. In my tradition, for instance, the process of going somewhere when your body stays here is called Spirit Walking—because that's what happens. The Spirit Walks. It *feels* like moving forward, like walking. In English it's called Out-of-Body Experience. Well, in my tradition, that's considered dangerous. You don't want your whole Spirit out of your body because you may not find your way back. You handle it in a different way and you speak in terms of Spirit, rather than Body. So, all of these body-related terms bothered me.

Finally I went to the teacher and told her my problem. She asked me to make a presentation to the whole class explaining this. The whole class spent some time making up new terms in English. Over the years I have found ways to deal with this, which do not include leaving the room. And this has worked reasonably well.

When you talk to Native American people you need to understand that most Indian languages are much more verbal—that is, verb-oriented—than English. English has worlds of nouns. The Iroquoian languages—which is my tradition—have nouns also, but not so many. The Hopi, I understand, have no nouns at all. Everything is described in verbal terms.

You would not for example call Paul Temple over there the Chair as much as you would call him Man who sits at head of table. This tells you something. You go through the thought process of placing him at the head of the table (in the North) and thinking about his behavior, rather than just announcing who Paul is, what

his title is. It becomes extremely difficult, painful, agonizing sometimes, to try to say things in English, because you're forever jamming things into categories that don't work and making yourself think in ways that aren't natural to you.

Now—the tradition that I come out of says: If you want to be truly understood, you need to say everything three times, in three different ways. Once for each ear . . . and once for the heart. The right ear represents the ability to apprehend the nature of the Whole, the wholeness of the circumstance, the forest. The left ear represents the ability to select a sequential path. And the heart represents a balance between the two.

How do you choose a Path if you haven't looked at the Forest?

If you've only admired the Forest, where are you going in Life?

The distinction that I want to make between Western science and the approach to science which my tradition, and perhaps other Native traditions, have found useful . . . is that first you look at the Forest . . . and *then* you look at the Path. We had a speaker earlier, Michael Murphy, who described a process of acquiring sensory data and then testing it. This is the reverse of my tradition, which is that you first acquire an intuitive, whole understanding, and then you focus on a Specificity and examine it, and then you *always* put it *back* into the Whole.

Now—when you examine anything, you examine it first with your mind. When I was a child, if I were trying to understand the process of a leaf growing, for example, the idea was to sit and think, allow my thoughts to flow into the leaf. Only after I was completely satisfied with my explanation would I ask the plant's permission and hold it in my hand. So you go through sort of a mirror image, a reversed image of the process of Western science.

We were talking earlier about the difference between the Western way of understanding, the Eastern way, and the Indigenous way—the Native American perspectives and approaches. It strikes me that the Western tradition represents body because it's always looking at things out here at arm's length. It's using microscopes, it's using all kinds of tools to look at things, to take them apart. That's changing, but this has been the understanding. The Eastern approach uses Spirit—you meditate, you breathe, you apprehend the nature of the Universe through your Spirit. I think the Native American tradition, at least the one that I understand and grew up in, represents Mind. Because, as I say, you let your thoughts precede you. You let your thoughts flow into that circumstance to understand it.

to page 107 . . .

Hawk and Eagle
Both are Singing

A Comparison Between Western and Indigenous Science
—in which the author attempts to share the relevance of her shamanic training to Western science—

As a part of the Native American training I received from my father, one of the aspects of perception that I was asked to understand was the distinction between Hawk and Eagle, between the way Hawk perceives and the way Eagle perceives. In this shamanic tradition, you gain that appreciation by what is considered to be direct experience. However, the distinction—once learned—is easily translated into Western logical sequential language structure.

> Dictionary definition of "science" -
> "Originally, state . . . of knowing"

When hunting, Hawk sees Mouse . . . and dives directly for it.

When hunting, Eagle sees the whole pattern . . . sees movement in the general pattern . . . and dives for the movement, learning only later that it is Mouse.

What we are talking about here is Specificity and Wholeness.

Western science deals from the specific to generalities about the whole.

Indigenous science begins with an apprehension of the Whole, only very carefully and on close inspection reaching tentative conclusions about any Specificity.

Indigenous science is based on a profound immersion in and awareness of the whole circumstance. Rather than mistrusting personal experience, Indigenous science has learned to thrive on it. The standards for personal honesty are excruciatingly exact and taught from earliest childhood. Educational structures like the Vision Quest have as one goal coming to terms with accuracy outside of or devoid of your own assumptions or the assumptions of your society. The idea is that you are always — if you are wise — moving toward enhanced accuracy. You will never entirely arrive at complete accuracy, but you are constantly trying to move in that direction.

As to the efficacy of Indigenous science, let me give you one example.

Since Universe is Energy, part of the process of understanding, at least as I experienced it, is to learn to "see" flows of energy and specificities of energy. Both are necessary. Because, you see, Universe is both Whole and Specific. Western science is beginning to understand this through explorations of theories about particle and wave. Both the particle/ particularity/specificity of Universe and the wave/flow of Universe were aspects I was encouraged as a child to apprehend and understand. I was asked to "see" the "dancing points of light" and then to apprehend the shift from location to flow. Much of shamanic practice has to do with developing the ability to enter and use this shift.

So when I read that the Western science of physics was looking at particle/wave theories, I had no trouble with that at all. Instead of being startled or surprised, I was given a wonderful gift—the ability to communicate more easily some of the things I learned in the shamanic process of understanding Universe.

> To the extent that Universe is Whole,
> location/time is irrelevant. To the extent
> that it's Specific, relationship is a better
> construct than either time or location for
> purposes of accurate understanding.

The process of Indigenous science allows you to learn about and to experience the flow of Energy through Universe. You quickly come to understand (well, maybe it takes a while!) that Universe has a kind of binary on/off structure, which can certainly be stated as particle/wave. In the particle state, particles can be understood in terms of "location". But "location" requires a point of reference which is more or less fixed in relation to that particle.

Tell me now, where is that point of reference? Is it not also moving? Are you not also moving?

The Indigenous scientific approach understands Universe—or All Things—as constantly in motion. Even the particles are "dancing", already moving toward the flow state. Since everything is in motion all the time (oops, time is irrelevant!)—since everything is constantly in motion, any location is in constant flux in relation to everything else.

Ah . . . in relation to!

"All Things, All Things, All Things are Related" is not just a charming chant, designed to put you in touch with "all your relations", it is a profound evaluation of the nature of Universe. ➤

There is a great contrast between Native American languages in general and that logical, sequential construct called English. In general, it can and has been explained that Indian languages are much more verbal—that is, verb-oriented—than English. English uses an extensive noun/category structure which requires you to constantly decide which "category" whatever you are describing belongs in. Thus, in English, we constantly divide a whole Universe into semi-relevant parts. Indian languages in general don't do this.

Language predicts the conclusions reached therein. Understanding this, my ancestors consistently examined new words the way the Commerce Department examines applications for new patents, except that their usefulness was also explored, as was their impact on the culture as a whole. The Academie Francaise limits itself to examining the accuracy of French. My ancestors required a detailed cultural Environmental Impact Report!

That which enables, disables also.

From an Indian perspective, the "priesthood" nature of Western science is anathema. My own tradition disbelieves in "experts". "That which enables, disables also" means that a physicist will fail in understanding in many other areas, perhaps in too many other areas, precisely because of the amount of time she/he spends on physics and therefore not on other things. Such people are not considered "experts", but "those extensively informed on part of the whole". They are listened to not on a priesthood basis, but on the basis of their having information others may not yet have—just as vice versa.

The search for greater wholeness—which has no room for "expertise"—is unending!

Any highly trained person will of course have a particular view—and therefore has a *special* responsibility to listen before speaking in any discussion of what the people may choose to do. Any person in a group who gets out of touch with his, with her community, is separated therefrom. Although I don't think there is the same negative connotation as there is in English, a shaman out of touch with her, with his community takes on aspects of the wizard—an isolated person who can inadvertently or on purpose do things that are harmful to the community. The process of Western "expertise" would be seen as a process of encouraging people to be isolated from the rest of their community in some way.

If Universe is Whole, what causes what?

As I have said, Universe in its particle state has the quality of relatedness. Universe in its wave state partakes of flow. The particle state can be said, then, to have a quality of location. The wave state can be said to have a quality of direction. It is this movingness of Energy, this direction, that produces Change.

But look, if everything is in motion, what causes what? How can we say that this drop of ocean water pushes that drop of ocean—and that's why it moves! Rather, direction, flow, the movingness of Energy of its nature produces Change.

And here we have a problem with English. "Produces" means "causes". It doesn't mean that in my tradition. There is more a sense of evolution, a sense of cooperative evolvingness, of the Universal Reality acting through you and with you and with everything else— all at once. Perhaps "engenders" is a better term. Perhaps a better term has yet to be invented. In any event, in any shift from one language to another, much is lost in translation.

It seems to me that there are two aspects here that make Western science's preoccupation with causality sometimes counterproductive. (Remember, that which enables, disables also.) One is the probability of multiple causation. Laboratory experiments obsessively select out "causative" factors for experimental demonstration. This clarifies and obscures, both at once. It leads to situations in which, for example, a blood test run to determine "causation" of some dis-ease may not reveal the culprit, as "we weren't screening for that condition"!

It also leads to situations in which the results of isolated experiments are applied to the broader community with disastrous or semi-disastrous results. Mistakes are not ruled out by any discipline. But this kind of mistake (Love Canal, nuclear waste disposal) would be less likely in any Indigenous, Whole way of understanding the Universe in which we exist.

The other aspect I see that seems to me to question the relevance of Western science's preoccupation with causality, is: In a sea of constant movement/change— which the wave aspect of Universe certainly seems to imply—is causation a really viable way of understanding? ➤

So Hawk—the tendency to look at the Specific—and Eagle—the tendency to look at the Whole—have something to say to one another. And if they both listen, what is engendered is what is called in my tradition an Interactive Circle. Like Yin-and-Yang, each encourages the other toward heightened acuity.

In cultural terms, this has been going on for a long time. Renaissance Europe was preceded by the Crusades, during which Europeans developed a taste for foreign knowledge/science and technology—and they just kept it up! Much of "Western" science is truly based on earlier explorations by other peoples—Chinese, Muslim, Native American. According to my own oral history, for instance, Benjamin Franklin's famous key-and-kite experiment was his effort to try to demonstrate and understand better what he was hearing from some of his Iroquois friends—which was that Universe is Energy . . . and so on.

To learn to demonstrate through replicable, quantifiable experiments to those unwilling to spend the time to acquire shamanic skills—or whose culture has chosen to forego these skills—some of the things that can be learned through this Whole approach to Life . . . is no small thing! It is an invaluable contribution to human understanding . . . a second eye opened on the Universe to help give us some greater depth perception.

For me, Western science was and is that second eye.

Perhaps Indigenous science can provide that second eye for the West, to the greater benefit of one and all.

Hawk and Eagle—both are singing.

Let us hope they are listening to one another.

Kind thoughts come . . .

. . . from page 104

Specificity and Wholeness

Now—there are general similarities in Native American approaches to life. But they are similar the same way European circumstances are similar as you go from Ireland to Turkey. There are enormous variations. But to a certain extent it's the same dance, from one end of Europe to the other. The similarities I see in many Native American cultures include such things as an absolute sense of the Wholeness of Things. One of the problems that Indian children often have in this educational system is that in school people are always talking about specific and separate things, but the Indian children may understand that it's really one interrelated whole. And this passion for separation just sounds crazy. You try to translate it from English into an Indian language and it literally sounds crazy.

So it's very hard for them to take this seriously. Very difficult. This was hard for me, when I began school, but my father kept saying, learn the system, learn the system. How can you learn to say what we understand in an intelligible way if you don't learn the system? So the idea is, learn the system and contribute in that way. And it is a very viable way of understanding life. What becomes dangerous is when any one way of understanding life is considered to be the only way, or the Right Way.

The idea of relatedness runs throughout all Native American thinking. Everything is related to everything else, everything is attached to everything else. So everything affects everything else. This gets into the causality issue that you've been examining here at the Institute. The idea that this-causes-that is simply impossible in Indian understanding, because everything is attached; everything has its own gravitational attraction. So you

can say what I say comes out of my tradition, but what Michael said this morning has already affected what I say and the presence of the people on each side of me also affects what I say in an ongoing way, and that's the way the world works.

The way that this is stated in mythic terms is that Spider Woman created the world, and she did it in this way: In the beginning all that existed was Thought Woman. She was the totality of all that existed until Spider Woman came and took from that Whole Thought the specificities that were implicit in it and from these she spun the world in which we live.

You see how it is? Every place where a thread crosses a thread, that is an Individuation. And the continuing thread connects every Individuation to every other.

The idea of how Universe functions that comes out of my tradition, and I hear echoes of it in other Indian traditions, is that Universe is Space which contains Energy. Energy of its nature moves. As it moves it produces Change.

In the Western world we call that Change "time"—past, present, and future. But the idea is that it isn't time at all. It is Change—it was, it is, it will be.

Part of the process I'm describing is what I hear discussed in scientific terms at the present time as the distinction between wave and particle—is it wave or is it particle? And the answer is: yes!

In the shamanic tradition you understand the distinction and the interrelationship of Specificity and Wholeness. Particle is Specificity. Wave is Wholeness, the direction that the energy takes. And you spend a great deal of time looking at each. I can't speak for all shamanic traditions. I suspect there may be something similar. But in the shamanic tradition that I'm familiar with you understand the world as binary. Now that's not good/evil, any more than light is right and dark is wrong. Dark is not wrong in relation to light. Light is not wrong in relation to dark. In fact, we need both. We need both.

So the binary nature of life gives us a multiplicity of yes/no choices from which we choose our path, constantly branching in the direction of our yes decisions. Each minute yes/no decision is a binary decision. Understanding this helps you understand another binary, co-equal aspect of Life. When you want to enter a different aspect of Life, you wait for the point at which Particle becomes Wave. And just at that split second before the Particle is gone and the Wave takes over, you enter between, and you become Energy. At the point where the wave becomes Particle again, you enter between, and you re-become who you were or you make a different choice. Which is also possible. I think it is that space in which healing occurs.

The critical thing is to understand that Particle and Wave co-exist.

In one of your papers on Perennial Wisdom it says that the Native tradition is nature-focused. I would like to modify that a little. I would like to say that Indian traditions are nature-inclusive. You do not see man and nature as separate from each other, but you see yourself in the context of an interrelated whole instead.

The Rule of Six
One of the attitudes taught in my tradition is the Rule of Six. The Rule of Six says that for each apparent phenomenon, devise at least six plausible explanations, every one of which can indeed explain the phenomenon. There are probably sixty, but if you devise six, this will sensitize you to how many there may yet be and prevent you from locking in on the first thing that sounds right as The Truth.

But your task isn't over yet. Because you can't just float on a multiple option basis. Now your task is to apply your life experience, which is unique to yourself, and use it as a base to evaluate each of those options. Now you assign a probability factor. That probability factor can never be 100% . . . and absolutely never zero.

You keep a floating attitude toward life, but you constantly know where you are in that context.

When I was very young my father would stand me on my left foot and say, "Answer this question in the manner of the people." Wholeness. And then he would stand me on my right foot and say, "Explain this in a way that your mother would understand." Sequence.

Then he would stand me on both feet and ask, "What do you see now?" Because it isn't enough to do only one, only the other. The critical thing is to strike a balance between the two.

In my tradition you get mind puzzles a lot. One of the questions that my dad gave me as a mind puzzle was, "What is the sound of one hand clapping?" When I discovered that that is also a Zen question, I was delighted. I'm reasonably confident that they come from the same source. I spent months trying to come up with an answer, and I came up with all kinds of different things. My father would say, "No, that's not really the sound of one hand clapping, that's . . ." Then, "No, that's not really the sound either." And finally he suggested to me the kind of clue that you get under this pedagogic structure—"Maybe Eagle has the answer." And I knew immediately he was right, because of course Eagle would understand the sound of one hand clapping.

As with all of his suggestions, I taught myself. This process is called go-and-be-Eagle. You become Eagle in your mind and heart, and look at the world from Eagle's perspective. As a result of that, you may come up with an entirely different concept of what the answer might be, which limited to *this* body you could not have come up with, because this body doesn't work that way.

In this pedagogic tradition, nobody tells you what to think or how to process information. Instead, you discover it for yourself, you keep discovering it for yourself. And only at the other end of this long process of self-discovery would my father say, "That's another generation that's reached that conclusion." In this case, however, he said that my answer was a whole new answer, that he knew of eight others, but that was a whole new answer to the question. He didn't tell me what the other eight were at the time, and I won't tell you what mine is now, because if I did, that would prevent you from ever discovering it for yourself.

The basis of the learning, the basis of the pedagogy, is to cease preventing people from learning things for themselves. This way of thinking, what goes on in here, can really be taught only from the inside out. When it's taught from the outside in, someone else comes between you and yourself, and that's not considered a wise idea. That's the tradition. □

Universe

is Space
which contains Energy

Energy
of its nature moves
as it moves
it produces Change

Change is
it was<>it is<>it will be

sometimes we call this past, present, future
and we say it is Time
it is not Time
it is Change

you see how it is
how everything in Universe
is Energy
flowing from one place to another

what we call Matter
is merely a relatively stable form
of Energy
which is also changing
also moving
only more slowly
like Earth and Ocean
each at its own pace

all things that contain Energy
are alive
as all things are formed of Energy
all things are alive
and all things are related
each to the other
always

*

*from the Strong Spirit Path
a Native American tradition*

*and expressed in English by
Paula Underwood Spencer*

Reconciling SCIENCE

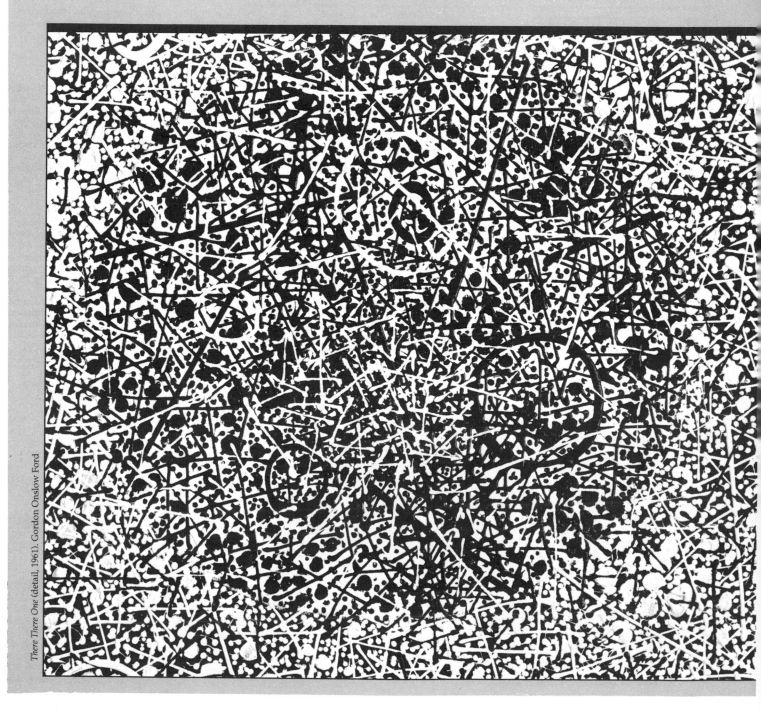

There There One (detail, 1961). Gordon Onslow Ford

METAPHYSICS

The Union Whose Time Has Come

By Willis W. Harman

According to the dictionary, the word "metaphysics" has two quite different meanings.

• The first meaning is a branch of philosophy comprising both ontology, dealing with the question "What is reality?", and epistemology, concerned with the question "How do you know?". (As one of our consultants wrote: "When the soprano sings 'I know that my redeemer liveth . . .' the ontological question is 'Who is your redeemer?' and the epistemological question is 'How do you know?' ")

• The second meaning is the study of the transcendent or supersensible, the contacting of the reality that lies "beyond the physical". This meaning, which has come down through the ages, is essentially the "perennial wisdom" of the world's spiritual traditions—the kind of knowledge that comes from inward-looking disciplines like yoga and meditation.

We use both meanings in this article as we explore what Henri Bergson called "the much-desired union of science and metaphysics".

Willis W. Harman is President of the Institute of Noetic Sciences.

Scientific inquiry is set in the context of the activity, values and assumptions of science.[1] An IONS-sponsored research project is examining the third aspect—the adopted assumptions of science.

1. *The activity of science.* Creating, testing, and applying conceptual models is the chief *activity* of scientists. It is not unique to science; the main way in which little children learn about their environment is to create mental models and test them by experience. The uniqueness of scientific inquiry lies in the next two aspects.

2. *The values of science.* Chief distinguishing values are openness of inquiry, healthy skepticism, and public validation of knowledge.

3. *The adopted assumptions of science.* Modern science tends to be characterized by certain basic ontological and epistemological assumptions which are the result both of long-standing characteristics of Western culture and of the tension between science and the Church around the seventeenth century.

It is these adopted assumptions which tend to preclude any "union of science and metaphysics". Also it is here that our present form of science is most vulnerable to challenge.

Among the metaphysical assumptions which have been assumed intrinsic to modern science, the most important are

> *Objectivism*: the assumption of an objective world which one can hold at a distance and study separately from oneself;
>
> *Positivism*: the assumption that the real world is what is physically measurable; and
>
> *Reductionism*: the assumption that we come to really understand a phenomenon through studying the behavior of its elemental parts (for example, fundamental particles).

By the middle of this century there was almost complete consensus that these are the proper foundational assumptions for science. These are essentially the assumptions of *logical empiricism*. They amount to the premise that the basic stuff of the universe is what physicists study, namely, matter and physical energy—

ultimately, "fundamental particles", their associated fields and interrelationships.

To be sure, these underlying assumptions have been modified with the advent of quantum physics. That modification has been much discussed[2] and it would be presumptuous to think of adding significantly to that dialogue. I want to point, instead, to the possibility of an even more fundamental change—change at the level of underlying metaphysics (first definition, page 5).

Underlying these (modified) classical assumptions is an ontological assumption of separateness: separability of observer from observed; of man from nature; of mind from matter; of science from religion; separateness of "fundamental particles" from one another; separability of the parts of a system or organism to understand how it "really" works; separateness of scientific disciplines and of investigators, competing over who was first discoverer.

The assumption of separateness leads to the hubris that humankind can pursue its own objectives as though the Earth and the other creatures were here for its benefit; to the myth of the "objective observer"; to reductionist explanations; to the ethic of competition. It implies the locality of causes, that is,

it precludes "action at a distance", either in space or time.

THE CONSCIOUSNESS PUZZLE

A major Noetic Sciences research project, analyzing causal models in science, has identified a number of research findings which seem at odds with a metaphysical assumption of separation. Two areas are summarized below. A more complete discussion is available from IONS.[3]

The Concept of the Self

The self constitutes a particularly challenging aspect of the consciousness puzzle. The conscious self is ineluctably involved in observation; yet the science constructed from those observations contains no place for the self. Psychologist Gordon Allport wrote in 1955, in a little volume entitled *Becoming*, "For two generations, psychologists have tried every conceivable way of accounting for the integration, organization and striving of the human person without having recourse to the postulate of a self." The issue remains controversial to this day. Consider the implications of the following:

I n his Introduction to Metaphysics *early in this century, the eminent French philosopher Henri Bergson said of the "much-desired union of science and metaphysics" that it would "lead the positive sciences, properly so-called, to become conscious of their true scope, often far greater than they imagine." I have come to believe that the time for realization of that dream has arrived.*

As a matter of fact, it might be more accurate to speak instead of the reunion of science and metaphysics, for throughout the early history of science the two were strongly linked. The Royal Society, founded in 1660, greatly influenced the early development of science; during this early period science and metaphysics were so intertwined as to be two aspects of a single endeavor. For the first three decades of the Society's existence "'Rosicrucianism', Freemasonry, and the Royal Society were not just to overlap, but virtually to be indistinguishable from one another."[4] The founders of the Royal Society, including Robert Boyle

and Christopher Wren, and the first President, Robert Moray, were steeped in the esoteric metaphysical traditions of Freemasonry, Rosicrucian, Neo-Platonic, and Hermetic thought. Isaac Newton, President of the Royal Society from 1703 to 1727, was strongly influenced by the Hermetic tradition throughout his life. When Benjamin Franklin was inducted into the Royal Society, in 1756, it was still strongly oriented towards the worldview of Freemasonry.[4]

The term "metaphysics" has two very different meanings. The first refers to a branch of philosophy, the second to the study of the transcendent or supersensible reality. It is the second sense to which Bergson was referring in his statement, and to which the early members of the Royal Society were aligned. But for the union to take place, it turns out to be necessary to start by re-examining the metaphysical (first sense) assumptions underlying modern science.

—WWH

- Research on the well-documented placebo effect implicitly assumes that there is a "self" which believes in the efficacy of the placebo.

- Research on subliminal perception, hypnosis, psychotherapy, and other areas reveals that there is a "hidden mind" ("unconscious processes") which basically does all the things the conscious mind does—and possibly much more.

- Research on hypnosis reveals that there is within the human mind an "inner observer" which is not deceived by the suggestions of the hypnotist (or, presumably, by the "suggestions" from the person's cultural surround).

- Research in the area of psychic phenomena, although results are admittedly erratic and findings are controversial, seems to suggest that at some deep level our minds are interconnected in some nonphysical way.

- Research on creativity and intuition reveals that the capabilities of the "hidden" creative/intuitive mind appear to be influenced by beliefs and by the extent to which one trusts in and depends on that part of the mind. Thus we do not know what are its ultimate limitations (if any).

- Research on out-of-body experiences and near-death experiences seems to suggest that consciousness is something other than just physico-chemical processes in the brain.

- In research on "multiple personality disorder", the shift from one self to another may be accompanied by measurable physiological changes, suggesting that "personality" is a holistic, non-reducible concept that can have real effects in the world.

- In such cases of multiple personality there appears to be, in every case, one alternate personality which is different from the rest in that it claims to neither be born nor die, but to simply "be".

- Research on children's recollections of past lives seems to show that these can sometimes be successfully checked for veridicality, lending strength to some concept of reincarnation.[5]

- There exists a great body of evidence, some meticulously gathered, that suggests that the personality in some sense survives the phenomenon of physical death, and may subsequently communicate back to living persons in various ways. Although science by and large ignores this evidence and its implications, to most who have chosen to look

Throughout its early history, science was strongly linked with metaphysics.

deeply into the subject, the amount and quality of the evidence are quite impressive.

- In studies of comparative religion it appears that, besides the many exoteric (public) forms, there is within any of the major traditions an esoteric or "inner circle" form, which is essentially the same for all traditions. This "perennial wisdom" seems to recommend an inner search involving some sort of meditative or yogic discipline, and discovery of and identification with, a "higher" or "true" Self.

The typical scientist at some point gets off this train of argument. But on what basis? This relates to the implicit metaphysical assumptions, as further discussed below.

Action at a Distance

Another persistent puzzle is that of "action at a distance" or **non-local causality**. This shows up especially in the far reaches of quantum physics and in the area of what John Beloff calls **"meaningful coincidences"**[6], where "meaningful" may refer to the subjective judgment of the observer, or to a judgment based in historical data (as in the case of astrology or the I Ching). Use of this term is intended to include Carl Jung's "synchronicity"[7] and most of the range of the "paranormal"; its advantage is that it does not imply any particular kind of explanatory conceptual framework.

Examples of "meaningful coincidences" include, for example, apparently "telepathic" communication, seemingly clairvoyant "remote viewing", and the "coincidence" between the act of prayer and the occurrence of the prayed-for, such as healing. Another example is the feeling of having a "guardian angel" when a person feels warned about a danger, or is provided with a particularly fortuitous circumstance in life. Other examples are in the area of "miracles" and "psychic phenomena".

The most common approach by scientists to "meaningful coincidence" has been to search for some kind of connection: There must be some kind of wave passing back and forth, or particle exchange. But the distinguishing feature of these phenomena is that they seem to exist whether or not there is any explanation for them.

The metaphysical assumption of separability led to a very puzzling question: How can physically separated objects, like the Earth and the moon, interact? In fact, Isaac Newton's theory of gravitation was initially attacked by critics because "action-at-a-distance" seemed to amount to reviving the idea of "occult properties" which were presumably being left behind with the Middle Ages. The psychological uneasiness of imagining seemingly separate things interacting was relieved by invention of the gravitational field. We have by now gone through generations of scientists trying to make us comfortable with action-at-a-distance by postulating electric fields, magnetic fields, electromagnetic fields, morphogenic fields, and so on. These field concepts are mathematical devices that link things, and they are very useful where they fit.

Almost all of present science is based, at least implicitly, on this ontological assumption of separateness, and an epistemological assumption that all knowledge is based on physical sense data—leading to this need to contrive "fields" to account for interactions between remote things.

TOWARD A COMPLEMENTARY SCIENCE

These assumptions of science are typically taken to be inviolate, to be an inherent and ineluctable part of the definition of science. But the contrary suspicion is growing stronger, namely, that it is precisely here that the resolution of some of the most fundamental puzzles in science may lie.

Thus we could imagine a different and complementary science, based on different assumptions—an *ontological assumption of oneness, wholeness, interconnectedness of everything, and an epistemological assumption that we contact reality in not*

one but two ways. One of these is through physical sense data—which form the basis of normal science. The other is through ourselves being part of the oneness—through a deep "inner knowing". This is obviously a very basic and controversial issue, namely, whether our encountering of reality is limited to being aware of, and giving meaning to, the messages from our physical senses (sometimes referred to as "objective"), or whether it includes a subjective aspect in an intuitive, aesthetic, spiritual, noetic and mystical sense. (It should not escape our notice that an intuitive and aesthetic factor already enters into normal science in various ways—for example, the aesthetic principle of "elegance"; the "principle of parsimony" in choosing between alternative explanations.)

The "Primordial Tradition"

If we were to take seriously the disclosure of an ontological and epistemological bias in Western science, it would lead to a very different attitude regarding what might be learned—and how it might be learned—from knowledge systems that start from a different perception of reality, such as Chinese medicine, Tibetan Buddhist psychology, or Native American interaction with nature.

The central finding of the study of comparative religion over the past half century or so has been that within any of the religious traditions there are typically various *exoteric* or public versions, and an "inner-circle", *esoteric* version. The latter tends to be more experiential and less sacerdotal, and usually involves some kind of meditative discipline or yoga. Although the exoteric versions may vary greatly from one another, and from one tradition to another, the esoteric versions are essentially the same. This "primordial tradition" or "perennial wisdom" is to be found in every religion and can be owned exclusively by none. "The Primordial Tradition is not merely an ancient system of belief and practice. . . . It is, rather, a whole set of archetypical realities waiting to be discovered, at the highest reaches of the human consciousness, by all people."[8]

The "perennial wisdom" tends to include convictions such as that Nature is directed from within by a higher intelligence or mind; that all minds in the universe are linked together by participation in one universal mind or source; that various mental or physical rituals can sometimes effect what they symbolize, or set the proper conditions in motion for the desired events or result to occur; that prayers, thoughts and mental projection might directly heal sick and diseased persons through the release of powerful, life-giving energies; that all individuals have a powerful, if hidden, motivation to discover and identify with a higher Self which is, in turn, in immediate connection to the universal mind. Since this "perennial wisdom" has been distilled from inquiry persisting over a far greater span of time than the duration of modern science, it can hardly be simply set aside as inconsequential.

Characteristics of a "Wholeness Science"

We have been led to the idea of a "wholeness science" complementing the very effective present science which is based on (a) an ontological assumption of separateness and (b) an epistemological assumption of physical sense data as the sole evidence on which the scientific picture of reality is to be based.

A proposed complementary science might, then, be built upon (a´) an *ontological assumption of oneness, wholeness*, interconnectedness of everything, and (b´) an *epistemological choice to include "all the evidence"*.

By "all the evidence" we mean to include all of the following:

1. *Those data admissible in the strict logical empiricism model—namely measurements of physical parameters.*

2. *Data depending on the connoisseurship of expert judges, such as those on which systematic (taxonomic) biology is based.*

3. *Data which are essentially self-reports of subjective experience*, obtained in an environment that promotes high levels of trust and candor, subjected to sophisticated skepticism because of our known capability for self-deception, and checked in other ways wherever possible.

4. *The subjective self-reports of trained "inner explorers" of various cultures.*

In none of these categories, of course, are data to be accepted without some sort of careful consensual validation.

(For further examination of a wholeness science, see the complete paper available from IONS.)[3]

We could imagine a science based on the assumption that we contact reality in two ways: First is through physical sense data, which form the basis of normal science. Second is through a deep "inner knowing" in an intuitive, aesthetic, spiritual, noetic and mystical sense.

IMPLICATIONS FOR SOCIETY

If science were to come to include a complementary body of knowledge based on the unitive or "wholeness" assumption, several important consequences can be postulated:

1. *It would tend to foster different attitudes toward nature.* We can imagine very different attitudes toward such issues as taking care of the environment; preserving species and habitat; avoiding irresponsible climate change, desertification, salination, etc.; raising animals for slaughtering; using animals in research, etc. This is not just a theoretical point; we have examples to look at. The worldview of the Native American Indian (and most other indigenous peoples as well) is just such a wholeness-based view, and the associated attitudes toward the Earth and our fellow creatures are there for anyone to observe. The Indians' relationship to their environment has proven to be sustainable over many centuries, which has not been true for most of the civilizations that have appeared throughout history.

2. *It would result in science's being more sympathetic to, and more amenable to, research relating to "meaningful coincidences"*. Survey research discloses that most people are aware of these "coincidences" in their lives; they say they definitely do not feel like random events. These include, for example, the "coincidence" of feeling that a distant loved one is in danger, and then receiving a confirming report. Other types are sometimes described as paranormal or religious phenomena, "hunches" or "miracles".

3. *It would tend to stimulate research in the entire spectrum of states of consciousness.* These include "religious experiences"; experiences of "mystical" states of

consciousness, of "other dimensions of reality". These experiences have been at the heart of all cultures, including our own. They have been among the main sources of the deepest value commitments. They cannot be ignored; yet modern science has denied their significance.

4. *It would tend to foster a worldview supportive of the highest values of all societies.* Such a worldview would contribute toward societal consensus with regard to central values, meanings, and purposes.

Resolving this issue of need for a "wholeness science" deserves to be a high-priority agenda for science. It should help achieve unity among the various sciences, and help resolve long-standing dichotomies and paradoxes of science (for example, mind versus matter; objective versus subjective; free will versus determinism). It could help science move toward paradigms that are rigorous and valid, and yet more in accord with the kind of wisdom we attain through life experience. It could clarify the relationship between science and values.

REFERENCES

[1] Robert A. Rubenstein, Charles D. Laughlin, Jr., and John McManus (1984), *Science as Cognitive Process: Toward an Empirical Philosophy of Science.* University of Pennsylvania Press.

[2] David Bohm and F. David Peat (1987), *Science, Order, and Creativity.* Bantam Books. Werner Heisenberg (1958), *Physics and Philosophy: The Revolution in Modern Science.* Harper & Row. Robert Jahn and Brenda Dunne (1987), *Margins of Reality: The Role of Consciousness in the Physical World.* Harcourt Brace Jovanovich. C.G. Jung and W. Pauli (1955), *The Interpretation and Nature of the Psyche.* trans. R.F.C. Hull and P. Silz. Pantheon. Richard F. Kitchener, ed. (1988), *The World View of Contemporary Physics: Does It Need a New Metaphysics?* State University of New York Press. Eugene Wigner (1967), "Explaining Consciousness," *Science,* 156, 798-9.

[3] Willis Harman (1990), "Reconciling Science and Metaphysics". Complete paper, #PRS1S001, available from IONS for $4.00 (member), or $4.50 (non-member).

[4] Michael Baigent and Richard Leigh (1989), *The Temple and the Lodge,* page 145. Arcade Publishing.

[5] Ian Stevenson (1987), *Children Who Remember Previous Lives.* The University Press of Virginia.

[6] John Beloff (1977), "Psi Phenomena: Causal Versus Acausal Interpretation." *Jour. Soc. Psychical Research* vol. 49, no. 773; Sept. 1977.

[7] F. David Peat (1987), *Synchronicity: The Bridge Between Matter and Mind.* Bantam.

[8] John Rossner (1989), *In Search of the Primordial Tradition.* Llewellyn Publications.

OUTGROWING THE CONFLICT BETWEEN SCIENCE AND RELIGION

Metaphysics (second meaning) is of course closely related to religion. The so-called "conflict between science and religion" is of long standing; it is time to outgrow it.

Science and religion will always be somewhat separate activities; there are important areas of science that have little to do with religion, and important activities in religion that have little to do with science. Nevertheless, there is an area of overlap, and *there the two should agree*. This common area includes the answers to questions basic to any culture: What kind of beings are we? What kind of a universe do we live in and how do we relate to it?

It appears that *two basic classes of phenomena* underlie much of the common ground between science and religion. These are:

1. The basic phenomenon of the sorts of *"meaningful coincidences"* that appear in people's lives that do not feel like random events.

2. The basic phenomenon of *states of consciousness*: of "religious experiences", of "mystical" states of consciousness, of "other dimensions of reality".

Science has so far had very little to say about either of these two areas; in fact, it tends to deny their existence or importance and is intrinsically unsuited to their exploration. This fact explains the limitations of present scientific research as its findings relate to the area of religion.

There is a third area also common to science and religion, namely:

3. *The origin of the universe and the evolution/creation of humankind.* Here the two have very different, and apparently incompatible, stories to tell. Yet as both science and religion become more mature their stories must converge.

On Meditation and the Western Mind

By Jack Kornfield

NOTE: *Jack Kornfield, psycholologist, author, and founder of the Insight Meditation Center in Massachusetts, was recently a guest of IONS' Meditation Research Program. Talking with a group of about fifteen psychologists and other researchers, Kornfield gave a general description of Buddhist maps of consciousness and posed specific questions that might be addressed through research on the insight meditation approaches, with which he is most familiar. He spoke also of plans for Insight Meditation West, a retreat center under development in California. Called Spirit Rock, this center will serve not only as a site for meditation teaching and practice but also as a place to integrate spiritual practice with life in community and society.*

Here are just a few of his very interesting comments and insights. The full text of his talk will be available through the Institute of Noetic Sciences Technical Reports Series.

Human Inside Rainforest Inside River: Amazonia. Sharon Skolnick

—STARTING ON THE BUDDHIST EIGHTFOLD PATH

The Eightfold Path encompasses several levels of training, the first of which involves the training of generosity. There are several different ways that generosity is trained: First, through reflection, especially through seeing all beings as if they were your mother or your father or other family members. You do this over and over until you get to the point at which you see even little bugs as relatives of yours. This totally changes your relationship to those beings if you do this kind of reflective, cognitive work in a repeated way.

Second, visualization. For example, you might visualize your heart as a fire, breathing in the sufferings of the world and breathing out compassion, picturing your arms as extending that compassion. Again, you do that visualization over and over until compassion becomes your response in situations, rather than the response of separate self.

Third, there is training in the practices of generosity and giving—of giving time, money, love, in a systematic way. There are three levels of giving and particular ways to practice each of them. Tentative giving is reluctant; you think, "Maybe I'm going to need this next year, I shouldn't give it away." Friendly giving is when you share what you have as if the recipient were a brother or a sister. Finally, kingly or queenly giving occurs when you see that the greatest joy in your life comes not from holding on to but from releasing things. Then you take the very best that you have and give it to someone else for the joy of it. And with certain practices, you can actually learn the enjoyment of letting go.

Another set of trainings has to do with virtue or morality—for example, right speech, right action, right livelihood. Again, these are first of all reflective practices. They also involve setting limits—that is, you learn not to harm through speech or action, and you look at the consequences of your behavior and see the energies of grasping or fear that motivate them. There are whole sets of practices for right speech alone; for instance, you might do a practice of not gossiping, which means not talking about someone you know either positively or negatively when they're not present. People who have done this practice have discovered that a good percentage of their talking is cut out and their lives become very silent; it's a very powerful awakening. Practices of right action—not to kill, not to injure, not to steal, not to take that which isn't given, not to abuse intoxicants or sexuality—then become transformed into positive disciplines. Instead of not stealing, you come to regard all things as common property and to care for them, for the Earth, and for what we share in common. Instead of not killing, you feel a reverence for every form of life. Instead of refraining from harming through sexuality, you might use sexuality to increase your sense of connection, intimacy and love in an appropriate way.

So there are whole sets of practices that develop an altruistic and a skillful relationship to the world, that quiet one and are considered the basis for meditation practice. To put it bluntly, it's very hard to do meditation after a day of killing and stealing. This is really important because in the West we think we can study meditation without realizing that meditation is built on a foundation of the consciousness that we bring to that moment.

Additional levels of training have to do with establishing calm and clarity and with the development of wisdom. As a whole these sets of practices constitute the Buddhist Eightfold Path and serve to bring mind and heart together.

—REALMS OF CONSCIOUSNESS

A major insight that the Buddha had was into the wheel of dependent origination. In the center of the wheel—as it is depicted in Buddhist iconography—are usually a cock, a pig and a snake, which represent greed, hatred and delusion. These are the forces that drive beings from one hour to another, from one day to another, from one birth to another.

Then the six realms within which beings are born are depicted. You can take them literally or metaphorically. There are the human realm, the heaven realm, the animal realm, and then three hell realms. The hell realms—which are archetypal or mythological or quite real, depending on your level of consciousness—include hot hells and cold hells, the realms of the hungry ghosts, and the realm of the jealous gods, the power realm. Each of these really represents a state of consciousness. The hungry ghosts are beings depicted with a tiny little mouth and an enormous belly, so that no matter how much they eat, they cannot be filled. You can encounter the hungry ghost realm by going to Las Vegas, if you want to find it in the human form. You could well encounter the realm of the jealous gods in Washington, DC, and various other places. You would encounter the animal realm, which is primarily a realm based on survival, in sub-Sahara Africa. To experience the hell realms, just go to some unfortunate place like Beirut, Lebanon, where aggression and pain are the main modes of experience. The human realm we know occasionally. And the heaven realms…I tried to teach a meditation retreat in Maui one year, but it was almost impossible. Halfway through a day of meditation, people would say, "Well, I have to go water my plants", or "It's such a good day to go to the beach." The pleasure was so great that it was very difficult to concentrate on meditation.

This raises the question, what are the optimal conditions for the awakening of human beings? That's the first question I'll raise; there are many more to come.

—MEDITATION RESEARCH

Let me shift the camera angle from the Buddha and ancient India to meditation research. Then we'll go on to meditation practices.

Meditation research for the most part has been enormously crude in this country. Early on, it focused a great deal on psychophysiological measurements. Most of it assumed that meditation was a single state, which is a fundamental error. There is no such thing as a meditative state. There are probably a hundred or a thousand different meditative states. You don't study the ocean by looking at a small part of San Francisco Bay. There are many states, they are induced in a variety of different ways, and they have different kinds of colors, flavors, levels and effects.

Also, meditation does not necessarily develop in a linear way, although I'm going to present some linear models. It has a more holographic and spiral nature to it. So what is perhaps most important, before we can do much more meditation research, is to undertake a basic mapping of the territory. *What are the dozen or hundred major meditative states? What are the main routes to those states? How do they relate to one another? What are the differences between state and trait learning? How does one achieve various states—through what objects or subjects or technologies— and what are their effects over the long term?*

—INITIAL EXPERIENCES ON A MEDITATION RETREAT

Let me describe a three-month vipassana retreat for you and the kinds of questions it might raise for someone interested in meditation research. A hundred people will come, take a vow of silence for three months—except for speaking to a teacher every couple of days for a ten to fifteen minute interview—and practice sustained meditation.

What happens when people do that? First there are all kinds of profound body openings and profound healings. If you sit for hour after hour and really pay attention in your body, then the body starts to open and the deepest kinds of body work happen without your doing anything but pay attention to the process. There is also an emotional opening that can take place, that can involve storms of pleasure, sorrow, loneliness, fear, joy or ecstasy that play through you like changes of weather, or it can be very centered.

Often people next experience what I call the layer of personal history. Many experience psychological regression. For example, people will come in and say, "Today I walked through the dining room and had a bite of food and suddenly I was one year old. I was back there with my spoon, banging on the table." So profound kinds of regression can occur in meditation. The key images and direct relations that underlie our sense of ourselves and other people will arise. Often people will experience pre-linguistic memories, where they'll feel themselves in the first months of life and know what their body felt like,

Photo: A. Raja Hornstein

what it was like to take their first step or their first bite of food. During this regressive period, there often arise the levels of conflict that we hold in body, emotion, and mind, trying to sort themselves out by bringing themselves naturally into attention.

After this, one comes to the level of access concentration, and a more profound series of insights and openings occur.

It would be interesting to look at the course of a retreat and do a much closer mapping of the processes that occur when the body opens in these ways. This would involve a really detailed listening to the accounts of people's experiences. There has been some writing about this in the West but there really isn't a very clear technology of how to work chakra by chakra with what arises, or a model that tells people what to expect.

A question this raises for research is: Can we trust that things want to unfold the right way? Do we actually have to direct it or do we just need to make the proper container or conditions for it?

Similarly, this raises questions about the death-rebirth process. Experiences of death and rebirth can be initiated through meditation, through holotropic breathing, through surrender in other contemplative practices, or through psychedelics, or through many other practices. Is this process, in some fashion, necessary for a new vision?

—LATER STAGES OF MEDITATION PRACTICE

After a time there arise several kinds of enlightenment experiences, spontaneously, almost by grace, if you will. One is an experience of cessation, in which everything simply stops. Seeing, knowing, hearing, thinking, the mind, the sense of self—all just stop. Afterwards you ask "Where was I?" There is a tremendous sense of the tentativeness of all created forms and consciousness.

One can also have what I would call an experience of void, of a positive void. Everything disappears but there is somehow a sense of pregnancy, an emptiness that is full of all potential. One can experience that to come into form is both painful and often driven by the forces of fear, greed and terror that create the sense of a separate self. In the most profound way you see the timeless and you see the forces that create suffering in form.

There are also enlightenments or awakenings that could be described as immanent rather than transcendent, experiences of the profound perfection of everything. These involve a timeless vision or realization within which there is no self, there is no other, there is nothing to do or to be done, there is no good and there is no bad.

These are extraordinary states of consciousness. *But the question that the Buddha was concerned with is, how do you change your life? Not just how do you have some interesting and profound altered state, but how do you actually change your life?*

The Buddhist map says that the first time you have a transcendental mystical experience of the deepest kind of nirvana, at that moment there are eradicated from the psyche three underlying tendencies. First, you've seen the void, you've seen how it all arises, you see the nature of life, and you also see that there is no separate self. The whole sense of self dissolves. Second, you realize that this "uncondition" doesn't arise because of performing any particular ritual; it simply is the true nature of things. Third, as belief in separateness of self is dissolved, one experiences the transcendence of individual consciousness.

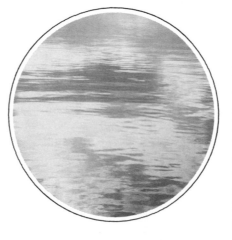

I've done an informal study by talking to as many people as I can who claim to have had different enlightenment experiences. There are three, four or five different kinds that appear to happen. Some people say that their lives are changed and others don't have much happen at all. I don't know why. *I would like to see an interview of all the various people who claim to have had a really profound enlightenment or mystical experience, and then see how their lives changed after.*

—MODELS OF TRANSFORMATION

At yet another level you attenuate greed and hatred. Then, according to this particular map, there is freeing from the last bits of pride or comparison of self with others; the last sense of ignorance or separation dissolves completely. *There are two very interesting models for how these tendencies are freed. This raises a profound question for psychologists who want to look at how human beings can transform themselves over time.*

According to one model, these experiences somehow uproot or do away with tendencies in the psyche to hold oneself as separate, to be fearful, to grasp, to interact from a limited sense of self.

A second model, which I think is equally interesting, is that rather than having an uprooting of those tendencies, there is a vision shift. People do not actually get rid of greed or hatred or fear, but their identity shifts so much that they can see themselves connected to all that is so that they can't really be greedy in practice. Hate might still arise, but it has so little to do with a new and expanded identity, a new sense of self, that there is no identification or impulse to act on it. This is a whole different vision about transformation over the long term.

Whether they've experienced a profound shift of identity, or an uprooting, many Westerners still have enormous difficulty after that. They don't know who they are, how to drive or how to get a job; their whole psychic world is shattered. Yet others seem to function quite well. *I'd like to see this studied.*

—PSYCHOLOGICAL ASPECTS

I think we need to inquire into the benefits of meditation practices in the long term. How do they affect our relationships to one another as human beings and to Earth itself? When I worked in the Asian monasteries there was very little attention to what might be called personal, or psychological, problems. In fact, upon returning from the United States, one of the great masters commented that he had seen a kind of suffering over here that he wasn't so familiar with—"they call it psychological suffering, whatever that is."

We find that when people come to meditation retreats, many of them need to work with parental issues, childhood trauma, alcoholism. We need to recognize, honor and see how to work with this. This has become part of our spiritual practice.

the positive feminine and the positive masculine?

Many Westerners have used spirituality to avoid the personal. I call them "skippers". I did it myself. You skip up to the higher levels and hope that if you have an enlightenment here and a mystical experience there, everything will be taken care of. This works until you get married, or take a job, or visit a parent. Half the people who want to enter this kind of spiritual practice can't even do it in the beginning. They're dealing with so much grief, so much unfinished business, so much fear. Part of the question for those of us interested in meditation is how can meditation serve those people really well. For I believe that it can.

Research on meditation would raise some profound questions for psychologists who want to study how human beings can transform over time.

So we need to look, as Westerners, at what will liberate or fulfill us, given the consciousness of our time and our culture. In Western culture we become much more conscious of ourselves as individuals than do people in Japan or India. There, to fulfill your destiny, your dharma, you become a shoemaker like your father or a housewife like your mother. That way you fit into that society. In our society, in order to fulfill our destiny, we need to become conscious of ourselves and individuate. That requires something different from meditation than what it seems to offer for people in the East.

Consider too the shift from the masculine to the feminine. Most Eastern spiritual practices developed in a warrior culture. The hero's journey is a dominant motif. That's how I practiced and, at first, taught. What I find now is that I need to change the language and the way I teach to a more feminine and relational mode. Most people need to start their spiritual practice with a deep ground of self-acceptance. Without loving kindness, self-acceptance and compassion, the experiences they have don't get integrated into their lives. *So the question is, how do we make that shift in spiritual life, in our meditation research, and, globally, from the negative masculine to*

For example, I've known people who were very skilled yogis. They had mastered the insight states, enlightenment, the jhanas, everything. Take, for example, an individual who had come from a very traumatic and painful background. Upon returning to this country, his father who had been in a mental hospital was dying, his relationship was breaking up, a lot of trauma was occurring. So he decided to turn to Reichian therapy, breathing, feeling his body as compatible with meditation. So in therapy, with the breathing, the therapist asked what he was feeling. "Well, over here there're tingling sensations, and over here there's heat shifting to cold." He could even describe the second cell to the left on his kidney or liver! The therapist asked again what the person was feeling. And the person had not a clue. He had developed an exquisite awareness of his body, but his emotions were completely untouched. Grief, rage, sorrow, all were untouched by the meditation.

Some people develop through the body while others have a lot of access to feelings but not to the physical body. Others have access to mind, to visions and mental processes. We need to understand the state-specific nature of what we can train in meditation.

Photo: A. Raja Hornstein

—RESEARCH AND INTEGRATION

In order to conduct research on meditation, first you have to at least posit that these things I've been talking about are possible. Second, to get your data, you have to be willing, in a "visionary" or anthropological way, to partially enter the worldview of the people you are studying. I think that's essential. But I don't think by doing so that you have to throw away the scientific method. Both Jack Engler and Dan Brown, for example, have shown research on meditation as a fruitful area to be legitimated in the scientific world. I would hope that Noetic Sciences would be doing more of this and would consider collaborating with Spirit Rock, given our mutual interests in meditation and consciousness research.

A second point. Because of the nature of our culture and language we tend to quantify things. But it's also important to remember the nonlinear nature of meditation—its spiral, holographic, interrelational qualities. So although the various meditative states are represented linearly in text, and by me in my talk today, in fact I don't teach this way very much any more. I tend to talk very little about goals, and much more about wholeness and integration.

I try to hold a dual vision. There is a place for linearity, for state studies, for mapping. I'm also wrestling with epistemological and visionary questions in order to discover a context in which to hold meditation that is wholer and more integrative and more useful for us as Westerners.

Business as Component of The Global Ecology

Willis W. Harman

This article is based on the recent book by Willis Harman and John Hormann entitled Creative Work: The Constructive Role of Business in a Transforming Society *(Knowledge Systems, Indianapolis; 1990).*

Hardly a week goes by without our hearing some new evidence of a major environmental disaster, ecological disruption, or man-made threat of long-term climate change. Almost always these have economic impact and result from economic activity. Frequently the blame is attributed to business. And almost always the response is to attempt to penalize the culprits, legislate environmental control, and repair the damage. However, what seems a reasonable enough response utterly fails to get at the heart of the matter.

We seem to find it difficult to think about these matters in whole-system terms; to recognize business and the economy as parts of the greater global ecological system, and to acknowledge that practically all of the remedies proposed are ineffectual attempts to patch up a system which will in the end require more fundamental change.

Fundamental change is not inherently more difficult or costly than patch-up, but we do have far more psychological resistance to considering it.

The Global Dilemmas in the Light of the Interconnectedness of Everything

One commonly hears, these days, the observation that "everything is connected to everything else." Although the truth of the statement is evident, discussion seldom progresses to the point where the implications for action are clear.

The Economy and the Environment. The familiar litany of environmental problems and man-made climate change needs no repeating here. No one can be unaware these days of the complex of global problems of environmental degradation, toxic chemical concentrations, species extinction, soil depletion, deforestation, desertification, "greenhouse effect" and the rest. The basic fact to be observed is the strong correlation between these and the characteristics of the world economy. Some of the environmental problems are strongly linked to industrial processes, or to the amount and kind of economic consumption; these are often tolerated because remedying them would reduce profits, entail economic costs, or have a negative impact on jobs. Other environmental problems result from the demands made on the environment by those in a state of chronic poverty. These latter include overgrazing, forest destruction for firewood, surface water contamination, soil erosion and removal of humus (dung) for fuel. They can only be ameliorated in the long term through doing something about the poverty.

A big part of the dilemma is that modern society guides (or at least defends) its major decisions mainly by economic values and economic logic. We are so used to this we fail to note that *there is no basic reason to assume that economic logic will lead to good social decisions, let alone decisions that will be sound in the whole-system sense.* To the contrary, economic logic is almost always applied toward the optimization of some aspect of a limited subsystem. It tends to downplay or omit those important qualities that are not quantifiable — "if you can't count it, it doesn't count."

Furthermore, economic logic discounts the future, which is a formalized way of saying that the well-being of future generations doesn't count either.

Economic logic is a particularly glaring misfit in the area of agriculture. The agricultural sector — including the production and distribution of food and other agricultural products — is the portion of the modern economy which is most out of consonance with the natural order. Agriculture cannot be understood and dealt with as an industry. The economy of industry is extractive; it takes, makes, uses, and discards. Agriculture, on the other hand, represents a replenishing economy, which takes, makes, uses, *and returns.* It involves the return to the source, not just of fertility, of so-called "wastes", but of care and affection. Otherwise, the soil is used exactly as a mineable fuel, and is destroyed in use. The old farming ethic involved passing the land on to future generations in an improved, not a depleted, state. The farmer, unlike the industrialist, is necessarily a nurturer, a preserver of the health of creatures.

When agriculture is treated as an industry like other industries, the economic incentives turn out to foster the wrong sorts of behavior. Furthermore, those who farm with concern for the health of the land and the long-term future tend to be put out of business by those who concentrate on production and return on investment over the short term.

With the present system of mass production of agricultural products and transportation to distant markets, when the energy costs of tractor fuels, fertilizers, transportation, processing, packaging, freezing, thawing, and the like, are counted in, the food on your table represents something like eight to twelve times as much fossil fuel energy as solar energy. Such a situation is clearly not viable in the long term.

Modern agriculture is extremely productive in terms of output per person-hour or output per acre of land. However, it is also extremely expensive in terms of loss of soil, in loss of farms and alienation of farmers, in soil and water pollution, in food pollution, in the decay of country towns and communities, and in the increasing vulnerability of the food supply system. The market is unable to assign a value to many factors vital to sound agriculture, such as topsoil, ecosystem, family, community. The excessive emphasis on productivity not only creates the effects just mentioned; it also inevitably causes over-production — which leads to low prices and economic ruin.

Employment and Economic Growth. The economic growth problem is usually posed: How can we get more of it? But the more penetrating system question is: How can we learn to get along without it?

The combination of increasing labor productivity, loss of some markets to overseas competition, the entry of new participants, especially women, into the workforce, and the psychology of investors and

workers expecting ever-increasing return, have all put pressure on the economy to grow and to create new jobs. The rate of increase of GNP has become the accepted measure of the health of the nation's economy. But that measure is highly correlated with the rate at which the economy consumes scarce resources, and the rate at which it creates environmental degradation. In other words, inadvertently *the economic incentives structure has come to favor resource depletion and spoliation of the environment.*

The pressure to create jobs no matter what consequences may ensue leads society to promote superfluous production and consumption; to see economic benefits in high "national security" expenditures; and to view approvingly the "speculation society" dominated by a large "financial industries" sector which generates jobs but contributes nothing in terms of basic goods or services, and rewards the lucky and the clever while discouraging honest toil. There is a tendency to accept the environmental and resource depletion consequences of these policies as unavoidable, as part of the price of "material progress."

The situation in the so-called "developing" countries is in general far worse. Forced out of their traditional village existence, hordes crowd into the already teeming urban environments seeking nonexistent jobs. Cities in the Third World bulge with displaced peasants, able only to scratch out the meanest of livings in the most ignoble occupations. In some of these countries underemployment is the condition of the great majority of the urban population. This result of economic forces is exacerbated in many areas by high birth rates and steadily increasing population.

In sum, the sociopolitical demand for jobs drives the economy in some ways that are ultimately detrimental to the planet, to the social integrity, and to the well-being of future generations.

The basic dilemma of the modern world is this. On the one hand, if a country does not continually increase labor productivity, the industry of that country tends to become noncompetitive in the international market. On the other hand, if productivity does increase, then by definition, to maintain the same number of jobs, the economic product must increase. Thus as various constraints — resource, environmental, political and social — tend to limit economic growth, chronic unemployment becomes an intrinsic characteristic of the future. In a few countries demographic trends are obscuring this unemployment dilemma for the short term, but the tendency is inexorable in the longer term.

The Misunderstanding of Development. There is perhaps no more misused word in the English language than "development." We speak of land development, and typically mean stripping the land of vegetation and paving it over with asphalt. We speak of human development, and typically mean destroying traditional community and conditioning people to survive in an urban environment. We speak of economic development, implying that it is equivalent with improvement of well-being, but typically mean increase of economic production and consumption — with concomitant pollution of the environment and squandering of resources. It is abundantly clear that the conventional concept of development does not lead to a long-term viable global, and in most cases does not produce shared well-being even in the medium term.

There is, indeed, a development dilemma of global proportions. The dilemma is that *it does not appear that the global system in anything like its present form is compatible with an ecologically sustainable global society or to a satisfactory resolution of the plight of the poorest countries.* Of the easily imaginable paths of global development, those that seem to be economically feasible do not look to be ecologically and socially plausible, and those that appear ecologically feasible and humanistically desirable do not seem economically and politically feasible.

For the two decades following World War II, development was more or less taken to be synonymous with economic development, that is, with "modernization," industrialization, and urbanization. One of the main goals of this development thrust was to alleviate hunger. The "Green Revolution", the development of high-yield grains that were to spell the end of hunger for

hundreds of millions, proved a mixed success. Yields did increase and more people were fed; but population continued to grow, and land ownership and political power remained concentrated in a very few hands. Massive application of artificial fertilizers and pesticides contributed to environmental problems. The net effect in many regions was that the opportunity for a family to grow its own food and sell produce from its own land actually diminished. The effect has been exacerbated where "cash crops" for export have displaced produced grown for local consumption.

Furthermore, political and cultural leaders in developing countries have come increasingly to see that the best development for them is not necessarily abandonment of their own cultural roots and adoption of the alien culture of Western industrial (consumer) society. There has been not only growing insistence on a different international economic order, but also on exploring alternative development paths.

On the one hand, if we imagine these difficulties to be somehow overcome and all the developing countries to be successful in following the examples of the industrialized and newly industrializing countries, it is clear that the planet would be hard-pressed to accommodate six or eight billion people living high-consumption lifestyles, and one could anticipate intense political battles over environmental and quality-of-life issues.

On the other hand, we may try to picture a future state where the high-consumption societies remain so, but the poorer countries remain low-consumption (i.e., poor), with low per-capita demand on resources and environment; it is hard to see how a global system with such a persisting disparity in income and wealth could avoid vicious "wars of redistribution," with terrorism as one of the main weapons.

There is no consensus on what constitutes a viable pattern of global development, but it is increasingly clear that present trends do not. In short, when the interconnectedness of everything is taken into account, it becomes clear that present economic, corporate, and social policies are, by and large, in consistent with viable long-term global development, and are being made without a picture of a satisfactory global future in mind.

It is essential to recognize the unresolvability of these dilemmas absent some sort of fundamental change in the world system. The required change is so fundamental, in fact, that it is almost impossible to imagine its being initiated and managed from the top. Throughout history, whenever the social system has undergone such basic change, it has come not from the top down, but through vast numbers of people changing their minds and demanding change. (On occasion when this happens, "leaders" rush out in front and may seem to have been leading the parade.)

The Whole-System View of Business

Business is part of a larger system and most constructively understood as such. In the broad view, *the world economy is part of the global ecology*. It is a component of the whole which, in terms of the whole, is bringing undesirable outcomes.

The Error of Separateness Thinking. When reality is wholeness, there is no greater error than separateness thinking. Imagine if the stomach were to get the idea that it could pursue its self-interest independent of the well-being of the whole body/mind/spirit. Justifying its appetites with the maxims "What's good for the stomach is good for the whole," and "The business of the stomach is growth of the stomach," it seeks to maximize its absorption of nutrients and minimize the fraction going to other parts of the body. It worries about such indicators as getting its "market share" of the food value, and "gross abdominal product." It sounds absurd, of course, because the stomach doesn't do anything of the sort. It concentrates on performing its function with regard to the whole system, and trusts that if it does that, the system will see to it that its nutrient, protection, and other needs are met.

In a whole-system view the various elements of global society, including corporations and other parts of the world economy, perform similarly. If they focus on performing their appropriate function in the overall system, they can trust that their various needs will be met.

The nature of the interconnected global dilemmas summarized above is such that there is no satisfactory solution short of whole-system change. Every part of the system must sense what is its particular contribution to that change, and do that, trusting that the system will then take care of its needs.

The Origins of Separateness Thinking. The fact that such a concept seems alien to us illustrates how deeply ingrained separateness thinking has become in modern society. We are not ordinarily taught about the scientific revolution in terms of its being the beginning of formalized separateness thinking. But the fundamental axiom of modern science has been that reality is made up of separate "fundamental particles" which, themselves or in various aggregations, interact with one another only through specifiable mechanisms such as gravitational or electromagnetic fields or — in quantum physics — particle exchanges. This is not an idea that would have made any sense to the medieval mind. However, it turned out to have tremendous power as a strategy for creating a science leading to powers of prediction and control.

It is only now, in retrospect, that we see it was but one of the possible choices of basic assumptions. (In fact, it is only with the development of quantum mechanics that the science of physics came to contradict its own initial assumption of the separateness of fundamental particles.) The concept of separateness — not only of fundamental particles from one another, but of observer from observed, of mind from matter, of man from nature — came to permeate the whole of modern society. Its other consequences, in terms of alienation and of the global dilemmas described above, are only now becoming clear.

The alternative ontological assumption — that of wholeness, oneness, everything connected to everything — has for several decades been gaining strength as a social force (manifesting as a new holistic emphasis in health, education, management training, bioregional systems thinking, the Gaia concept, eco-feminism, etc.) until it appears likely to take over. We have only begun to think about how different a scientific worldview would appear if science were to be restructured on the basis of the wholeness assumption. If the dominant worldview shifts, from the separate emphasis to the wholeness assumption, we can be sure that every institution in society will be affected, just as all institutions were affected by the shift, in 17th-century Western Europe, from the medieval to the modern view.

Self-Healing Forces in Society. In a more holistic view of our situation, we are immediately reminded that living organisms tend to be self-healing. The same can undoubtedly be said of societies even though the mechanisms are less studied. (The Gaia hypothesis, which has recently been attracting much favorable attention, suggests that the planet itself, as a living system, may be self-healing as well. Of course, there is no assurance that the healing process of the planet guarantees the continued existence of human civilization; humans will have to see to that themselves.)

Recognizing this capacity for self-healing, we see several things in a new light. The question is not so much how the problems arose, nor even how their effects can be ameliorated; the key question is: What went wrong with society's self-healing system such that it failed to handle the pathogenic challenges as they came along? What might be done to help the restoration of the societal self-healing processes?

Adopting the optimistic hypothesis that much of people's innovative activities these days can be interpreted as society-healing impulses, partially unconsciously-guided, we find it easy to recognize many indications of spontaneous creative response. These indications include a variety of social movements, as well as a host of innovative experiments in nonprofit organizations, intentional communities, alternative economies, alternative health-care programs, new forms of business entrepreneurship, citizen approaches to assisting new enterprise and community development in Third World countries, and many others.

There is much evidence to support the hypothesis that (a) whole-system change will be required for the major societal and global problems to become solvable; (b) at some deep intuitive level people seem to sense this, and as a result spontaneous social movements and experiments have arisen which, taken together, provide both a direction and a motive force for such whole-system change; and (c) as the dynamics of this process of social transformation are better understood, actions that foster constructive change can be supported to help minimize the kinds of social disruption and human misery that have so often in the past accompanied deep social change.

The Special Role of Business. It is of the greatest importance that business understand accurately the significance of these present indicators of fundamental change. In the first place, making good corporate decisions depends critically on accurate assessment of both the external and the internal environment. But also, and most importantly, business leadership is in a unique position from which to contribute constructively to peaceful transformation.

It is both typical and reasonable for the business executive to want to know: What should I do? By the very nature of the situation, the most creative response is not likely to be a specific action, but rather more like a different stance, a new way of viewing, a changed basis for choices.

If it is possible to give more concrete advice, perhaps it is something like the following:

(1) Come to understand the nature of the transformational forces present in the modern world so as to increase your organization's chances of survival through what is likely to be a chaotic transition period.

(2) Do what is necessary to prosper, in the sense of being strong and flourishing, because that strength will be needed to make an effective contribution to the evolution of the whole. One of the most important factors here is attracting and holding the most creative and competent people.

(3) Contribute, because only if everybody does are we likely to see a successful outcome following this very critical time. □

Be patient with all
that is unresolved in your heart
And try to love
the questions themselves
Do not seek
for the answers that
cannot be given
For you would not
be able to live them
And the point is to
live everything
Live the questions
now
And perhaps
without
knowing it

You will
live along
some day
into the answers.

—Rainer Maria Rilke

It is becoming increasingly clear that the human mind and physical universe do not exist independently. Something as yet indefinable connects them. This connective link — between mind and matter, intelligence and intuition — is what Noetic Sciences is all about.

— Edgar D. Mitchell

BOOKS FROM THE INSTITUTE OF NOETIC SCIENCES:

1980 - 1990

Health for the Whole Person
by Arthur Hastings and James Fadiman
Westview Press, 1980 (out of print)

Higher Creativity: Liberating the Unconscious for Breakthrough Insights
by Willis Harman and Howard Rheingold
Jeremy Tarcher, 1984
(paperback $8.95; members' price $7.85 order number BHC1E002)

Waking Up: Overcoming Obstacles to Human Potential
by Charles T. Tart
Shambhala, 1986
(paperback $14.95, members' price $13.15 BWU11001)

Paths to Peace: Exploring the Feasibility of Sustainable Peace
by Richard Smoke with Willis Harman
Westview Press, 1987
(paperback $11.95, members' price $10.50 BPP1G004)

Consciousness and Survival: An Interdisciplinary Inquiry Into the Possibility of Life Beyond Biological Death
edited by Bishop John S. Spong
Institute of Noetic Sciences, 1987 (out of print)

Global Mind Change: The Promise of the Last Years of the Twentieth Century
by Willis Harman
Knowledge Systems, Inc., 1988; Warner Books 1990
(hardback $16.95, members' price $10.50 BDM1G001
paperback $11.95, members' price $10.50 BGM1G001)

The Home Planet
by Kevin Kelley for the Association of Space Explorers
Addison-Wesley, 1988
(hardback $39.95, members' price $19.95 BHP1G002)

In the Footsteps of Gandhi: Conversations with Spiritual Social Activists
by Catherine Ingram
Parallax Press, 1989
(paperback $15.00, members' price $13.20 BIT1A001)

Drawing the Light from Within: Keys to Awaken Your Creative Power
by Judith Cornell
Prentice-Hall, 1990
(paperback $16.95, members' price $14.90 BDL1E001)

Creative Work: The Constructive Role of Business in a Transforming Society
by Willis Harman and John Hormann
Knowledge Systems, Inc., 1990
(paperback $12.95, members' price $11.90 BCW1G001)

Life's Finishing School: What Now, What Next
by Helen Green Ansley
Institute of Noetic Sciences, 1990
(paperback $7.50, members' price $6.60 BLF1B001)

PROGRAMS

HEALING OURSELVES — INNER MECHANISMS OF THE HEALING RESPONSE

A fundamental goal of the Institute has been to stimulate scientific understanding of the mind/body relationship and our capacity for health. The Institute's program, *Inner Mechanisms of the Healing Response*, has monitored the area of healing research for more than a decade, and has funded pioneering scientific research into the role of the mind in healing at major universities and hospitals in the US and Europe. The program supports proposals from selected researchers and targeted interdisciplinary working conferences on mechanisms of healing.

PROGRAM AREAS INCLUDE:

- the role of the mind and emotions in healing and survival
- spontaneous remission from cancer and other life-threatening diseases
- psychoneuroimmunology (PNI) — a relatively new field linking the mind, the brain and the immune system

- spiritual healing and its effects on health and well-being
- Bio-energetic or Energy Medicine — a leading-edge discipline which studies the body's electrical fields and circuits as they may relate to the healing system

CREATIVITY AND HUMAN POTENTIAL — EXCEPTIONAL ABILITIES

Emotional, intellectual and spiritual capacities of humans provide fertile ground for scientific inquiry and discovery. By studying people with outstanding and extraordinary capacities, we hope to learn more about the ways all of us can better realize our unique capacities — and, together, create a world that supports human fulfillment.

PROGRAM AREAS INCLUDE:

- extraordinary states of awareness, including meditation, peak experiences and altered mind/body perception
- conscious dying — an exploration of the role of the mind/body connection in the dying process: to what degree can we/do we will our own death?

- The Altruistic Spirit Program — study of the human capacity for unselfish love and creatively altruistic behavior. Our annual Temple Awards for Creative Altruism honor one or more people who exemplify the altruistic spirit — the irrepressible light of love in the heart of humanity.

NEW PATTERNS OF THINKING ABOUT THE WORLD AND HOW IT WORKS — EMERGING WORLDVIEWS IN SCIENCE AND SOCIETY

Another goal fundamental to the Institute is exploration of the ways in which belief systems and values affect our world. *Emerging Worldviews in Science and Society* studies the relationship between consciousness and global issues with the premise that a fundamental change of mind may be occurring worldwide. The program examines the phenomenon of changing paradigms in all levels of human society — in science, business, religion, education, politics and culture. Willis Harman's book, *Global Mind Change*, provides the framework for this Institute program.

PROGRAM AREAS INCLUDE:

- The Causality Project — an ambitious study of the changing foundations of science in physics, biology, the neurosciences, systems theory and other fields. The way the modern world defines reality has been shaped fundamentally by scientific theories which emphasize measurement of the physical world — thus, an emphasis on the material world. Through this program, respected scientists and philosophers of science have joined in a cooperative effort to address the ways in which the basic assumptions of 19th and 20th century science (reductionist/mechanistic) must now expand and deepen to include human consciousness for a more satisfactory understanding of scientific causality.

- The constructive role of business in a transforming society — seen by the Institute as a major key to fostering emerging worldviews. More and more business leaders are realizing their corporate mission is much greater than profits alone, and that it includes people development, environmental protection, and global citizenship. The Institute works with an international network of visionary executives and entrepreneurs to explore the role of intuitive leadership, creativity and the re-channeling of corporate resources to create a positive global future.

ABOUT THE INSTITUTE OF NOETIC SCIENCES . . .

AS A RESEARCH FOUNDATION . . .

We provide seed grants for scientific and scholarly research on:
1) mind-body relationships in health and healing;
2) exceptional human abilities, including altruism;
3) emerging worldviews in science, business and society.

Our goal is the contribution of knowledge which will expand understanding of human nature.

AS AN EDUCATIONAL ORGANIZATION . . .

We publish books; the quarterly *Noetic Sciences Review*, a journal covering people and ideas in the forefront of consciousness research; *Special Reports*, which cover these ideas in more depth; and a quarterly news *Bulletin*. We also have sponsored a national public television series, *Thinking Allowed*.

Our goal is to create a forum which contributes to contemporary dialogue, with a focus on questioning prevailing belief systems in science and society.

AS A MEMBERSHIP ORGANIZATION . . .

We hold a vision of a world in which expanded human consciousness leads to a deeper understanding of untapped human potentials. We are committed to individual and institutional action which contributes to this understanding, and to the integration and practical application of this knowledge in our rapidly changing global community. *Members receive the publications listed above.*

Members also receive discounts on carefully selected books, audiotapes and videotapes on the mind and consciousness through the Institute's mailorder service. Members also have opportunities to explore other cultures with like-minded companions through the Institute's Travel Program.

TO BECOME A MEMBER . . .

☐ **$35 Associate:** *Provides general support of the Institute and members receive the quarterly Institute publications.*

☐ **$60 Two Years**

☐ **$25 Student (fulltime) Membership**

☐ **$25 Senior (retired) Membership**

☐ **$100 Supporting Membership:** *Helps additionally to support the research budget.*

☐ **$250 Supporting Membership**

☐ **$500+ Sustaining Membership:** *Helps even more — and receives additional documents.*

☐ **$5,000 President's Circle:** *Full member benefits, plus individual conversations with President Willis Harman and other senior Institute staff members.*

☐ **$10** *additional for members outside United States ZIP codes to cover postage costs.*

☐ Enclosed is my tax-deductible contribution for the membership(s) checked.

☐ New   ☐ Extend/Renew

TO ORDER BOOKS . . .

I would like _____ copies of *Noetic Sciences Collection* at the members' price of $10 or the nonmembers' price of $12 plus handling and postage.*

I would also like to order these books from page 131 (Please include title and order number):

_____   (# copies)_____ at (price) $_____ = $_____

_____   (# copies)_____ at (price) $_____ = $_____

_____   (# copies)_____ at (price) $_____ = $_____

(Please use a separate sheet of paper for additional orders)

Subtotal $_____

* For book orders: • California residents please add 6% sales tax
• Handling and UPS charges: For orders up to $10 add $3; up to $20 add $4; up to $30 add $5; up to $40 add $6; up to $50 add $7; up to $70 add $8.

Plus tax (if applicable) and shipping $_____

Total $_____

— —

Name:_____

Street:_____

City/State/Province:_____

Country/ZIP Postal Code: _____

Telephone (   )_____

☐ Please charge my MasterCard ☐ Visa ☐
#_____

which expires_____

Signature:_____

Mail to: Institute of Noetic Sciences, PO Box 909, Sausalito, CA 94966-0909. Or FAX anytime, 415/ 331-5673.